MW00576285

ALSO BY FRANK BRUNI

The Beauty of Dusk:
On Vision Lost and Found

A Meatloaf in Every Oven:
Two Chatty Cooks, One Iconic Dish and Dozens
of Recipes—From Mom's to Mario Batali's

Where You Go Is Not Who You'll Be:
An Antidote to the College Admissions Mania

Born Round:
A Story of Family, Food, and
a Ferocious Appetite

Ambling into History:
The Unlikely Odyssey of George W. Bush

AVID

READER

PRESS

The Age

of

Grievance

Frank Bruni

Avid Reader Press

New York   London   Toronto   Sydney   New Delhi

AVID READER PRESS
An Imprint of Simon & Schuster, LLC
1230 Avenue of the Americas
New York, NY 10020

Copyright © 2024 by Frank Bruni

First Avid Reader Press hardcover edition April 2024

AVID READER PRESS and colophon are trademarks of Simon & Schuster, LLC

Simon & Schuster: Celebrating 100 Years of Publishing in 2024

For information about special discounts for bulk purchases, please contact Simon & Schuster Special Sales at 1-866-506-1949 or business@simonandschuster.com.

The Simon & Schuster Speakers Bureau can bring authors to your live event. For more information or to book an event contact the Simon & Schuster Speakers Bureau at 1-866-248-3049 or visit our website at www.simonspeakers.com.

Interior design by Ruth Lee-Mui

Manufactured in the United States of America

3 5 7 9 10 8 6 4 2

Library of Congress Cataloging-in-Publication Data

Names: Bruni, Frank, author.
Title: The age of grievance / Frank Bruni.
Identifiers: LCCN 2023057176 (print) | LCCN 2023057177 (ebook) |
ISBN 9781668016435 (hardcover) | ISBN 9781668016442 (paperback) |
ISBN 9781668016459 (ebook)
Subjects: LCSH: Political culture—United States. | Social justice—United States. |
Political parties—United States. | Political participation—United States.
Classification: LCC JA75.7 .B77 2024 (print) | LCC JA75.7 (ebook) |
DDC 306.20973—dc23/eng/20240109
LC record available at https://lccn.loc.gov/2023057176
LC ebook record available at https://lccn.loc.gov/2023057177

ISBN 978-1-6680-1643-5
ISBN 978-1-6680-1645-9 (ebook)

To the many generous and wise

teachers and editors in my life.

Anything I get right is a credit to you.

What I get wrong is entirely on me.

Contents

Author's Note

Some of the details and language in this book appeared previously in columns and newsletters that I wrote for the *New York Times*.

"Resentment used to be something that folks wanted to get rid of, now they water it and put it on a windowsill, like a favourite pot plant."

—Edward St. Aubyn, *Double Blind*

The Age *of* Grievance

One

Let Me Tell You How
I've Been Wronged

When I think about who we've become and where it leaves us, of the prism through which so many Americans insist on seeing the world and how it perverts their views, I flash back not to any of the biggest, strangest, and most menacing events and developments from the past few years—not to the bedlam in the halls and the blood on the floor of the US Capitol; not to Paul Pelosi, in his own home and in a pajama top and boxers, bracing for the blow from an assailant's hammer; not to a former president essentially crowing about his unprecedented indictments in four criminal cases, comprising ninety-one felonies, and treating them as a badge of honor—but to a brief and perfectly emblematic sequence of reports on Fox News in May 2022. The United States was then suffering a shortage of baby formula, and Fox had uncovered something scandalous. Something rotten.

A photo told the story. "Look at that," Sean Hannity instructed

1

his viewers as he put the image on the screen, his voice spiked with disdain. What it showed, he said, were "pallets and pallets of baby formula for illegal immigrants and their families." The Biden administration was supposedly rerouting this precious commodity to detention centers at the country's southern border and thereby depriving "hardworking American families" elsewhere. Hannity seethed—or at least performed a telegenic facsimile of seething. So did Representative Kat Cammack, a Florida Republican who had furnished Fox News with this visual prop and who told Hannity that it illustrated "how insane everything is right now" and "what a total dumpster fire the Biden administration truly is." "America Last— that is what the Biden administration is all about," Cammack said. The next morning, the hosts of the winsomely alliterative, deceptively friendly sounding *Fox & Friends* welcomed her on their show and echoed her disgust. The network's audience in turn took to social media to vent their fury.

But the photo told a fable. To anyone who cared to notice and decipher the labels on the boxes in those pallets, they identified the contents as powdered milk, not the formula in short supply. It was for children well beyond their first months of life. As Alex Koppelman explained in an article on the CNN website after Hannity's snit, "There is undoubtedly some formula being provided to babies in these centers at the border—you'd assume there would be, unless you expect the government to simply decide to starve babies in its care." But Hannity & Co. had contrived a scenario less nuanced and more politically charged than that. They'd detected a betrayal of law-abiding citizens. They'd uncovered an insidious plot. And they'd cynically and theatrically turned "the thinnest possible set of facts into days of outrage over Them getting something You deserve," Koppelman wrote.

He called it "an illuminating example" of how Fox News ginned up outrage. I'd call it a defining one—but not just of Fox's business model, which would lead in April 2023 to a $787.5 million payout to Dominion Voting Systems, the largest-ever publicly known amount for the settlement of a defamation lawsuit. Hannity's histrionics and his followers' freak-out distilled how an enormous, perilous share of Americans had come to regard and respond to a broad range of circumstances and to their places in an addled country and agitated world. When there was trouble, when there was disappointment, when dreams were unrealized, when goals were unmet, and sometimes even when things were going perfectly well but not exactly perfectly, they looked for insult and invariably found it, even if they had to invent it. They decided that they hadn't just been unlucky. They'd been wronged. And they dwelled on that raw deal, taking its measure and assigning a particular person or people responsibility for it. They were losing because someone else was winning or because some corrupt overlord had rigged everything against them. The blame game was America's most popular sport, and victimhood its most fashionable garb.

Around the same time that many Americans decided that the Biden administration was starving babies, they decided, too, that it was poisoning adults. J. D. Vance, a Republican running in Ohio for an open Senate seat, gave voice to this paranoia, suggesting as much in an interview with a right-wing news outlet (of sorts), the Gateway Pundit. He traced the drug-overdose deaths so prevalent in certain parts of the country—including the Appalachian tracts that he'd written about in his bestselling memoir, *Hillbilly Elegy*—to the illegal border crossings that the Biden administration was failing to prevent. "If you wanted to kill a bunch of MAGA voters in the middle of the heartland, how better than to target them and their kids with this deadly fentanyl," Vance said. He added that it "does look intentional. It's like Joe Biden wants to punish the people who didn't vote for him, and opening up the floodgates to the border is one way to do it."

It was a cockamamie analysis for many reasons, including these: illegal border crossings, seizures of fentanyl at the border, and deaths related to fentanyl in the United States had risen during Trump's presidency before they rose further still during Biden's, and the deaths that had gone up most since Biden's inauguration were among Black men, who, as a group, tended to vote for Democrats over Republicans by enormous margins. But Vance's imagining of a dastardly scheme worked the same emotional levers that almost every hour of programming on Fox News did. It exposed an outrage, identified the wounded parties, and validated their sense that there were forces—sometimes specific and nameable, other times shapeless but just as sinister—arrayed against them. It gave them and people around them permission to be angry, and anger had become the primary driver of much of American discourse and most of American politics.

It had particularly ugly contours and consequences on the political right. That was where conspiracy theories such as QAnon thrived and conspiracy theorists such as Marjorie Taylor Greene prospered. It was the staging ground for the fatal breaching of the US Capitol by the frenzied invaders who turned January 6, 2021, into a bloody grievance prom. And it was the truest home and most fertile territory for Donald Trump, who, like every president before him, personified key aspects of his era and served as a kind of tuning fork for its temper. He became a victor by playing the victim, and his most impassioned oratory, such as it was, focused not on the good that he could do for others but on the bad supposedly done to him—by the media, by snooty liberals, by devious and election-stealing Democrats, by the Republicans who initially resisted him (and then surrendered to him), by the FBI in general, by James Comey in particular, by the rest of "the deep state." The culprits were countless and their offenses infinite.

Not even Richard Nixon had made claims of persecution such a central part of his political identity, at least not until the final days. What an extraordinary and oxymoronic pose Trump struck, bemoaning his impotence amid proclamations of superpotency, demanding pity as he flew in his private jet to his gilded mansions with their fastidiously groomed golf courses. Preposterously but cunningly, he cast himself as both martyr and messiah, braving and transcending the condescension to which his supporters were also subjected and redeeming them in the process. He vowed to have the last laugh on all the people who'd ever laughed at him, and many Americans thrilled to that. It suited their spite. He was grudge made flesh, grievance become president.

But he had no monopoly on grievance, just as Fox News wasn't its sole marketplace. Before, during, and after Trump's presidency, grievance was everywhere you looked and in most if not many of the loudest voices you heard. The American soundtrack has become a cacophony of competing complaints. Some are righteous and others specious. Some are urgent and others frivolous. Those distinctions are too often lost on the complainers. How they feel is all that matters—it's their greatest truth—and they feel cheated. They feel disrespected. They're peeved unless they're outright furious. And that ire is neither confined to nor concentrated in any one race, any one region, any one political party, any one class, any one faith, any one gender, any one profession. It flares even where that makes the least sense. It burns at the very pinnacles of privilege.

The Supreme Court, for supreme example. It was once one of the most respected institutions in the United States, a panel of ostensibly principled individuals whose lifetime appointments, coolheaded demeanors, and measured forays into the public square suggested an ability to float above the temporal passions that buffet the rest of us. But over the past few decades and especially the past few years, its reputation has plummeted, and that terrible fall coincides with its transformation into a panel of transparently, almost unapologetically biased political actors who are nursing hurts, settling scores, and smarting from confirmation hearings that have devolved into grim carnivals of contempt. The justices occupy a singularly rarefied perch with trappings as august as trappings can be, and with extraordinary job security. But that's no match for the seductiveness of resentment and self-pity in an era overflowing with both.

"It's the greatest gathering of grievances we've ever seen on the high court," Maureen Dowd wrote in the *New York Times* in May 2023. "The woe-is-me bloc of conservative male justices is obsessed with who has wronged them." She noted how Justice Neil Gorsuch, the first of Trump's three appointments to the bench, had issued rulings concerning environmental issues that reflected and perhaps sought to complete or redeem the work of his mother, Anne Gorsuch Burford, a disgraced administrator of the Environmental Protection Agency under President Ronald Reagan. Justice Samuel Alito was developing a reputation for using his appearances at conferences and black-tie gatherings to deliver screeds against secularists, same-sex marriage, and such that made him sound less like a black-robed sage than like Rush Limbaugh back in the day. Alito wrote the opinion that overturned *Roe v. Wade*, and while he had to understand how regressive, repressive, and immediately threatening that would seem to tens of millions of American women, he subsequently whined to the *Wall Street Journal* about how nasty so many politicians, journalists, and others were being to him and the rest of the court's conservative majority. "We are being hammered daily, and I think quite unfairly in a lot of instances," he said. "And nobody, practically nobody, is defending us."

Those poor Supreme Court justices! At least they had rich friends. Justice Clarence Thomas was under intensifying scrutiny for receiving and failing to report lavish gifts from superrich conservatives with whom he romped and vacationed; the nonprofit investigative news organization ProPublica kept a running tally of the largesse it was methodically uncovering, and by August 2023 that included "at least 38 destination vacations, including a previously unreported voyage on a yacht around the Bahamas; 26 private jet flights, plus an additional eight by helicopter; a dozen VIP passes to professional and college sporting events, typically perched in the skybox; two stays at luxury resorts in Florida and Jamaica; and one standing invitation to an uber-exclusive golf club overlooking the Atlantic coast."

What might make him feel entitled to all that? Dowd theorized that Thomas was "still bitter over being outed as a porn-loving harasser of women who worked for him." She was referring to the part of his confirmation hearing decades earlier when Anita Hill recounted her experiences with him. How much did that bitterness drive him and his wife, Ginni Thomas, a brazen right-wing activist in her own regard who didn't seem to temper her activities one scintilla though they thickened the partisan stench around her husband? It's impossible not to wonder, given the extremeness of his rulings and her machinations in late 2020, when Trump was contesting the election results with his false claims of widespread voter fraud. In text messages to Mark Meadows, who was then Trump's chief of staff, she implored Trump to press on and get those results overturned. "Help This Great President stand firm, Mark!!!" she wrote in one of those messages, adding: "You are the leader, with him, who is standing for America's constitutional governance at the precipice. The majority knows Biden and the Left is attempting the greatest Heist of our History." She was up in arms. She was uppercase. And she vividly illustrated the hyperbole that takes hold among the aggrieved, no matter how twisted the narrative that delivers them to grievance.

Tucker Carlson, the media megastar, and Josh Hawley, the Republican senator, didn't let their enormous professional success and alpine positions of influence throw them off their identification of an ominous, intentional weakening of American men, who, as they told it, were being lured and lulled into a marginalizing flaccidity. Hawley spun that story in a 2023 book, *Manhood: The Masculine Virtues America Needs*, while Carlson explored it in "The End of Men," a *Tucker Carlson Originals* documentary for Fox Nation the previous year. Both manifestos of grievance rested, in their intellectually wobbly fashion, on a legitimate concern: more and more American men had slipped into sustained unemployment, more and more American boys were struggling in school, and the voguish phrase "toxic masculinity" had been thrown around casually and cruelly, sending all those men and all those boys the message that there was something intrinsically wrong with them.

But Carlson and Hawley encouraged those men and those boys not simply to feel pride and cultivate strength but also to feel pissed off and be cognizant of environmental factors that suppressed their testosterone, social changes that devalued their contributions, and evil Democrats who promoted an anything-goes world of blurred gender roles and contempt for traditional commandments. Both Carlson and Hawley constructed a #HeToo off-ramp to the #MeToo rush hour, assuring men that whatever their failings, it wasn't really their fault. In *Manhood*, Hawley maintained that corporations were deliberately creating "a nation of androgynous consumers," while godless, hedonistic secularists didn't care about virtue. "The Bible is right," he decreed. "The Epicurean liberals are wrong." And those liberals were conspiring against virility, according to Carlson's documentary, because they feared it and because they knew that with a full measure of brawn, brio, and brotherhood, "a few hundred men can conquer an entire empire," as the documentary's narrator intoned. "So that's why they want you to be fat, sick, depressed, and isolated." One interview subject, using "you" to refer to those oppressors, added: "You want them emasculated. You want them to create no threat to the ruling regime." How, then, to save civilization? Carlson prescribed testicle tanning as a testosterone boost—as one small, genital step in the manly direction. The documentary mingled grievance with gonads and gobbledygook.

Nuttiness like that has prompted many liberals to scoff at what they like to call a "grievance industrial complex" on the right, whose political warriors of course regard *them* as the overwrought ones—as "snowflakes," in the parlance of recent years. In the parlance of prior decades, conservatives themselves actually used "grievance industrial complex" to mock minority groups' claims of extensive harm and demands for elaborate protection and accommodation. It's a phrase with a rich and elastic history. And on both right and left, grievance seems to be its own burgeoning economy, its own default pitch. To make your argument, emphasize grievance. To build support, use the Sheetrock of grievance. To win sympathy and sympathizers, lead with grievance. To sell your wares as widely as possible, package them in grievance.

That's what Prince Harry and Meghan Markle did with their

escape-from-England media blitz, and the blowback they received spoke to how awkwardly their fixation on their hardships fit with their stations as a duke and a duchess who had not renounced their royal titles, who had resettled in a nearly $15 million estate in the coastal Eden of Montecito, California, and who were monetizing their outsize celebrity, a product of circumstance more than industry, to the apparent tune of hundreds of millions of dollars. Part of that revenue stream, a reportedly $20 million deal with Spotify, came to a premature and acrimonious end in June 2023—and Bill Simmons, a prominent sports commentator and top Spotify executive, publicly denounced the couple as "grifters"—after the amount of content that he and others had expected never materialized. Despite all of that, the couple edited their narrative around a central theme of how tough they'd had it, how terribly they'd been treated and at whose hands. They pitied themselves and pointed fingers.

They did some good, too—that can't be discounted. The racial element of the condescension and even contempt that the royal family and the British press exhibited toward Markle was obvious, odious, and excellent cause for her and Harry's disgust and sense of betrayal. By broadcasting that part of their story, the couple performed a public service. And for all Harry's vindictiveness, there was valor, captured beautifully by Caitlin Flanagan in a description in the *Atlantic* of his devotion to his wife: "When she was miserable, the way his own mother had been miserable, he didn't do what his grotesque father had done—cheat on her, treat her like a broodmare, ignore her suffering; he moved her and his family far away."

But the couple's beefs ranged far beyond and beneath their honor and immediate welfare, to dirty family laundry and to piffle such as the inadequate comfort of their royal cottage in England.

Their revenge tour (the Oprah interview, the Netflix series, Harry's memoir) lasted more than a year. Its goal seemed to be the biggest payday possible. And could they really have been so "shocked to discover institutional racism in the very institution that created the most enduring business model for it," as Alicia Montgomery asked in *Slate*? Chris Rock raised that question more bluntly in a Netflix stand-up comedy special, *Selective Outrage*, in early 2023, ridiculing Markle for "acting all dumb like she don't know nothing. Going on *Oprah*: 'I didn't know, I had no idea how racist they were.' It's the royal family! You didn't Google these motherfuckers? . . . They're the original racists! They invented colonialism!"

From Chris Rock it's a short hop to Will Smith, whose meltdown at the Academy Awards in 2022 was, insanely, about grievance. He revealed as much when, less than an hour after slapping Rock, he accepted his Oscar for Best Actor in a Leading Role and sought to justify that violence without yet apologizing for it. "To do what we do," he said, presumably referring to wealthy and pampered celebrities, "you gotta be able to take abuse. You gotta be able to have people talk crazy about you. In this business, you gotta be able to have people disrespecting you and you gotta smile and you gotta pretend like that's okay." Translation: He had acted out, yes, but only because he was so fed up with all that he'd been forced to endure. Only because he was so deeply aggrieved. Before you could denounce Smith, one of the richest and most influential actors and producers in Hollywood, as a perpetrator, you had to pity him as a victim.

How absurd. But how fitting. The entire Oscar ceremony was a grievance-palooza, devoted to the wrongs done to women, the wrongs done to Blacks, the wrongs done to gays and lesbians, the wrongs done to trans people. There was merit to all of that, but the pile-on smothered it. And the Oscars were just following statuette-season suit. At the Critics Choice Awards two weeks earlier, Jane Campion accepted her Best Director trophy, for *The Power of the Dog*, by emphasizing how tough she'd had it as a woman behind the camera. She spotted Venus and Serena Williams in the audience and felt compelled to say that she'd faced barriers even they hadn't, because their principal opponents on the tennis court were other women and Campion's rivals for movie-world jobs and accolades were men. *My grievance tops yours!*

That set off a predictable firestorm at Grievance Central, meaning Twitter, whose users were flamboyantly aggrieved on the Williams sisters' behalf. And when Smith accepted his Oscar—for playing their father, Richard Williams, in *King Richard*—he riffled through a list of Black women whom he was "called on" to protect from the indignities of the world. He was a knight in shining grievance. And a daisy chain of grievances was complete.

Two

A Good Word Spoiled

Not all grievances are created equal. I want to say that again. I want to be clear. And not all expressions of grievance raise identical concerns. Some don't raise any at all. There are wildly disproportionate outbursts, mildly disproportionate outbursts, and ones scaled defensibly and even commendably to their trigger. There is January 6, 2021, and there is everything else. Attempts by leaders on the right to minimize what happened that day and lump it together with protests on the left are as ludicrous as they are dangerous.

What's more, the fruits of the grievances on the left don't match the fruits of the grievances on the right, and for all the talk about how illiberal both camps have become, it's the right that currently poses the much greater threat to the country, both in terms of its disregard for democratic institutions—for democracy itself—and the behavior it provokes, sanctions, and sometimes even glorifies. The foiled plot to kidnap and possibly assassinate a prominent elected official, Michigan governor Gretchen Whitmer, was hatched by right-wing terrorists. It's Marjorie Taylor Greene, an enormously popular right-wing lawmaker, who's infamous for statements such as one in a speech at a gala for the New York Young Republican Club in December 2022, when she made light of January 6 by saying, "I will tell you something. If Steve Bannon and I had organized that, we would have won. Not to mention, it would've been armed."

It's Ron DeSantis, the Republican governor of Florida, who lashed out at the federal bureaucracy and indulged the darkest fantasies about the dimensions and depravity of the "deep state" by saying that if elected president, he'd "start slitting throats on Day One." It's Kari Lake, the failed Republican candidate for governor of Arizona in 2022, who seemed to be emulating Greene (what a thought) when she reacted to Trump's federal indictment for treating classified documents like a personal stamp collection in June 2023 by saying: "If you want to get to President Trump, you are going to have to go through me, and you are going to have to go through 75 million Americans just like me. And I'm going to tell you, most of us are card-carrying members of the NRA."

It's Trump himself whose response to the far-ranging, grave legal predicament that he brought upon himself went beyond any sort of rebellion and resistance that a Democrat of comparable stature in modern times had called for. He waged an unfettered verbal assault on the American government and issued an unqualified vow to demolish certain American institutions. As the indictments rolled in, as the civil trials in which he was a defendant commenced, and as his fury pinballed from one courtroom and judge to another, his language grew ever darker, ever more dangerous. He labeled the Department of Justice, the FBI, and other byways of the federal bureaucracy in general and the Biden administration in particular "a sick nest of people that needs to be cleaned out immediately," "fanatics,"

"fascists," and "sinister forces" who were engaged in "vicious persecution." No, no, make that "demented persecution." He called Leti-
tia James, New York's attorney general, a "monster" and, on the first
day of his civil trial on the fraud charges that she'd brought against
him, publicly stated that people "ought to go after this attorney general." That chilling directive belonged to a lengthening sequence of
violent musings, including his insinuation that General Mark Milley,
the chairman of the Joint Chiefs of Staff during Trump's presidency,
should be executed for treason and his recommendation, during a
speech to California Republicans, that shoplifters be shot as they left
stores. His remarks increasingly amounted to sputtering thesauruses
of thuggery with which he seemed to be pledging bloody payback. As
Andrew Coyne, a columnist for the *Globe and Mail* of Toronto, wrote:
"This is not the reaction of a normal person. It is not even the reaction of a mob boss. It is the reaction of a Batman villain."

And that was *before* Trump used the occasion of a Veterans Day
speech in New Hampshire in November 2023 to say that if he won
the presidency anew in 2024, he would "root out" what he referred
to as "radical left thugs that live like vermin within the confines of
our country." Challenged about the echoes of Nazism and fascism in
that pledge, a Trump campaign spokesman defended it, exulting that
the "sad, miserable existence" of its critics "will be crushed when
President Trump returns to the White House." The tenor of that
vow matched the totalitarian fantasies of Trump, his advisers, and
his allies, who envisioned and made plans for a federal workforce
meticulously stocked with Trump loyalists and an army of federal
prosecutors intensely focused on Trump's enemies.

What's more, there's no left-wing analogue to Fox News, no
media enterprise of commensurate reach that consciously pursued
a commercial strategy of lying to its viewers, as Fox did about one

of the most consequential matters of all: who won a presidential election in the most powerful country on earth. That's what led to the settlement with Dominion, a maker of voting machines and the butt of hour upon hour of Fox programming that aired baseless claims—claims that Fox's hosts and executives knew to be laughable: that those machines were rigged to switch votes from Trump to Biden.

But it's also true that on both sides of the political divide, there's a quickness to grievance, a tendency among many people to identify themselves and interpret events in terms of past, current, and looming hurts. There's a psychological and emotional impulse—a way of approaching and assessing the world—that transcends partisan affiliation. It's not so much bipartisan as it is pan-partisan or suprapartisan, and it's getting worse. It exiles nuance. It rejects the kind of triage that a checks-and-balances government, which can deal with only so much so quickly, must do, even as it lengthens the odds of that government being able to do anything at all. It places personal over public interest. It turbocharges conflict.

That was one of the saddest revelations of the coronavirus pandemic, which posed a threat so universal and dire that it should have put the usual animosities on ice. At the start, I naively thought—or, more accurately, hoped—that it would. As we confronted a previously unthinkable shutdown of life as we knew it and fumbled our way through remote work, contactless grocery shopping, virtual family get-togethers, and the whole surreal rest of it, I wondered whether the suspension of normalcy would include an abnormal (but welcome!) discovery of the kind of solidarity that the country had experienced for a brief period after the terrorist attacks of September 11, 2001, when President George W. Bush suddenly had an approval rating north of 85 percent. (The intensely pitched debates about national security versus civil liberties and about the wisdom of invading Iraq came later.)

But much had changed in the nearly two decades between the shattering of the World Trade Center and the shuttering of all of New York City, and by 2020, national solidarity was a political yeti. Battle lines were quickly drawn. Rival camps promptly emerged: people who wanted to err on the side of epidemiological caution and those who felt that individual preference took precedence over any government edict, no matter how well intentioned, especially given how fledgling and fluid our understanding of the pandemic was; people who gave experts the benefit of the doubt and those who rebelled against what they saw as facile groupthink; people who instinctively admired Dr. Anthony Fauci and people who reflexively abhorred him; masking evangelists, some of whom muttered the wish that the virus would winnow the ranks of the reckless, and masking apostates, for whom all the shutting down and covering up was rank liberal opportunism.

At one point in that first year of the pandemic, long before the nation's top health officials said that it was safe not to cover our faces outdoors, I was accosted at a gas station on the Merritt Parkway in Connecticut for wearing a mask. I'd put one on as I got out of my car to fill the tank because another motorist or two might pull up at any moment and there wasn't much space between the pumps. To be masked made sense. It was the considerate thing to do. But as I absent-mindedly pumped fuel, I heard a man shouting. *Screaming* is more like it. A few seconds passed before I began to register his words and realized, with a quickening pulse, that they were directed at me and that he was walking in my direction.

"Take off your fucking mask!" he demanded. I looked away, but he kept at it, planting himself about ten feet from me. His hands curled halfway into fists. His chest was thrust forward. He fired off a fusillade of insults, calling me an "idiot," a "moron," a "dope." I started trembling, stopped pumping, and retreated inside the station, just to still my heart and take a breath. From that perch of relative safety by the gum and candy bars, I could see him walk back to an enormous pickup truck decorated with MAGA regalia. He stood beside it, glancing around. He looked to be in his midtwenties, and he was slight in build, not a pound over 150. Still, he terrified me.

He and his truck hadn't budged when, five minutes later, I felt I had to liberate the pump I'd used and be on my way. So I hurried to my car. The haranguing resumed: "Do you do everything you're told?!? *You're* the problem! *You're* why we're no longer free!" I felt like a character in a horror movie, racing to get the engine to turn over and the car in gear before the monster could reach me. I drove away as fast as I safely could. I spent the next thirty minutes staring into my rearview mirror.

I spent much longer than that feeling spooked, in part because I couldn't dismiss what had happened as some freak occurrence. The volume and vocabulary of it—sure, that was extreme. But friends and acquaintances were routinely telling me about tense pandemic-related encounters of their own. The news was lousy with stories of hostile confrontations between the masked and the unmasked, the vaccinated and the unvaccinated.

That sparring and sniping mirrored what was happening among politicians, who took their disputes to intensely spiteful lengths. In congressional hearings, Republicans treated Fauci, an octogenarian who had spent an honorable lifetime in public service, like some bespectacled Beelzebub. They projected Trump's megalomania onto him. And they threatened nothing less than a government shutdown in response to President Biden's vaccine-and-testing mandate for large employers, which was in line with the dominant scientific thinking at the time.

Their protest filtered down to states under Republican control. As Catherine Rampell explained in a November 2021 column in the *Washington Post*, "At least four states—Florida, Iowa, Kansas and Tennessee—have recently extended benefits to workers who are fired or quit over their employers' vaccine requirements. For context, workers who are fired for cause or who quit voluntarily are usually not eligible to receive unemployment benefits. With limited exceptions, only those laid off through no fault of their own have been able to receive such aid." The headline on her column: "Red states are now paying people not to get vaccinated."

The political squabbling was suffused with grievance. It wasn't any composed disagreement over policy, any rational discussion of competing values in circumstances where difficult choices had to be made. Many people on each side felt genuinely threatened by those on the other. To the man at the gas station, I wasn't just some dumb, timid liberal; I endangered his very existence, and he was being held back by, and forced to persevere through, the compliant likes of me.

Trump characteristically introduced yet more bad feeling into the mix, blessing many Americans' desires to attribute their troubles to foreigners in general and the Chinese in particular. He spoke of the "China virus." He referred to "Kung flu." And in short and sadly predictable order, there were high-profile incidents of violence against Asian Americans and reports of a rise in such hate crimes. Grievance had casualties, and they mounted.

While my fascination with grievance mostly reflects its prominence in public affairs, I have private reasons, too. In late 2017, I experienced one of those bizarre medical episodes that can happen at any point but are increasingly common as we age. Overnight, I was diminished. I woke one morning—I was fifty-two—with blurred vision, and that set me on a dark odyssey of extensive testing and "investigative" treatments, of doctor-administered injections in my right eye and self-administered shots in my left and right thighs, of theories and uncertainty and fear.

I'd had, essentially, a rare stroke of the optic nerve behind my right eye, and that nerve, briefly deprived of adequate blood flow, had been irrevocably damaged. It put a dappled fog over everything it took in. I had to adjust to seeing clearly with my left eye alone. My brain had to train itself to edit out the pointless efforts of my right eye, which warped and smudged what I saw. I was now a slower reader, a more typo-prone writer. And I had a sword dangling above me: Doctors said there was about a 20 percent chance that the optic nerve behind my left eye would frazzle in a similar fashion, also without warning. I might go blind.

I wanted to feel sorry for myself. I *did* feel sorry for myself. But I soon realized what a danger and dead end that was. To focus and dwell on the obstacles that had been dumped in front of me, the extra effort I had to make, and the terrible luck of it all was attractive, understandable, warranted—and wholly unconstructive. It didn't improve the situation one whit. I kept reminding myself of that, and whenever my mood sank and my resentment surfaced, I reminded myself harder. Measuring misfortune is no strategy for living.

Yet many Americans—some with great reason, some with none—organize their politics and construct their identities around such assessments. That became more obvious to me through the prism of my affliction. So did the downsides of it. The analogy wasn't neat and clean: The optimal ratios of rage and resignation are a trickier calculation in the arena of politics than in the realm of illness.

But the seductiveness and peril of victimhood exist in both, and I was more attuned to that than before.

After I wrote several columns for the *Times* about what had happened to me and what I was learning from it, I got emails from various advocacy groups for people with vision-related disabilities. They were looking for publicity and thought that I might be more inclined than another journalist to provide it. Or they wanted a spokesperson or board member and wondered whether I was the right person. Or they invited me to address members of their group. All of that made sense. Much of it was a lovely compliment. But I was troubled by how some groups made their pitches. They cast the affliction to which they were dedicated or the kind of work that they did in terms of how much less attention and funding it got than other afflictions and other kinds of work. How overlooked it was. They were either genuinely fixated on being shortchanged or felt that taking that tack was the most fruitful bid for sympathy and support. They might have described the enormous, heartrending challenges for the people they served or the strong possibility of developing better treatments and finding cures if they could garner more financial support. But their read of our culture—or their channeling of it—pointed them toward claims of deprivation and neglect.

I later wrote and did many interviews to promote a memoir about what I'd lost, what I'd gained, and how I'd worked to forge a relatively upbeat attitude about it all. The response to that was also telling. While many people contacted me to say they'd found hope and inspiration in the book, more than a few chided me for my supposed cruelty. They pointed out that resilience and optimism weren't universally attainable and anyone who hadn't found a path there—who wasn't blessed with the right constitution or resources—might feel belittled or shamed by my message. One man sent me a blistering email after hearing an interview I did with Terry Gross on NPR's *Fresh Air*.

He said that it was "extremely false, hurtful, and damaging" for me to tell Gross that I'd realized that "if I let myself give in to terror, if I let myself sink into depression, unless I'm willing to live in that state forevermore, I'm going to have to at some point pull myself out of it, and the deeper I let the hole get, the harder it's going to be to climb out of it."

"Mr. Bruni, depression is *not something one allows themselves to sink into*," he wrote. (The italics are his, not mine.) "Would you ever state that you decided not to let yourself 'sink into cancer' or 'sink into AIDS' or, better yet, 'sink into a stroke in your optic nerve'? I think not." He added that comments like mine "do further damage to people like me whose lives have been destroyed by depression" and that I was "not courageous" for resisting depression. "You are just lucky. Sending this message to bolster your own character is damaging to me and many others."

He made an almost excellent point. I say "almost" because while he was of course right about serious, clinical depression and the unacceptable tendency among some people to attribute a failure of will to those who suffer from it, I hadn't been talking about depression with a capital *D*, and there were ways other than his to hear what I'd said. Some of those ways were helpful—and were, indeed, helping people, to judge by other emails I received. Didn't those people matter, too? Also, I hadn't—not in my book, not to Terry Gross—said that I was courageous nor boasted about my character, which, trust me, is a mixed bag. But because my story and my take were rosier than his, they apparently didn't have the same validity. I was less aggrieved. I had less standing.

• • •

I'm treating grievance as a dirty word, and it isn't. Or wasn't. Or needn't be. Grievance has been the precursor of justice, the prelude to enlightenment. The United States is a nation born of grievance, in the revolt of royal subjects unwilling to accept a bad deal, and we're hardly the only democracy brought into being by rightly aggrieved people recognizing and refusing to accept inequality and exploitation. In the last words of the First Amendment, Congress is prohibited from making any law that would abridge people's right "to petition the Government for a redress of grievances." Across the nearly 250 years of our existence as a country, grievance has been the engine of morally urgent change, the principal force in propelling us—in a staggered, messy, and incomplete fashion—toward the "more perfect union" we so frequently invoke. Our legal system, admired and emulated around the world, honors grievance. With intricately choreographed processes and an extensive, expensive infrastructure, it grants people an opportunity for their complaints against their government, employers, service providers, or neighbors to be heard, judged, and potentially resolved in some manner.

So, grievance is good. But what happens when all sorts of grievances—the greater ones, the lesser ones, the authentic, the invented—are jumbled together? When grievances become all-encompassing lenses, all-purpose reflexes, default settings? When people take their grievances to extreme and even violent lengths that they didn't before?

And when they have powerful new megaphones for those grievances? The internet and social media, which I'll revisit later in this book, were the great promise of connectedness that became a great curse of disconnectedness. "Previously, a lot of people who were resentful about what was happening would sit in the corners of dark bars, muttering in their beer, or in their parents' basement complaining" is how Steve Phillips, a civil rights lawyer and newspaper columnist, put it to me. Now they have Facebook, X (previously called Twitter), YouTube. They have not merely voices but *viral* voices, and they have something else, too, something crucial, a permission structure for using those voices however they wish. They have the example of Trump. He reached and stood astride the political summit saying whatever the hell he wanted, no matter how nasty, no matter how dangerous, so why should they speak any other way? Phillips noted how rare it was for Americans to look up and see someone "with this much credibility and celebrity" giving validation to "some of the darkest sentiments that people had."

But Americans aren't the only ones in a strange new place. Over recent years, upsized and outsize grievances have challenged and transformed various nations on various continents in various ways. In India, Prime Minister Narendra Modi has dipped into the same populist, nationalist bag of tricks that Trump loves to rummage through, for much the same reason: Grievance simplifies and clarifies everything, providing a ready explanation for lingering frustrations, painful humiliations, unmet goals. Modi and his political allies have trained the Hindu majority's attention on the Muslim minority, blaming India's Muslims for episodes of disorder and an array of disappointments. Muslim political activists have been arrested, Muslim journalists have been detained, and there are barriers for Muslim immigrants that don't exist for immigrants of other faiths. Small wonder that India's Muslims are disproportionately the victims of violence. "Hindu mob attacks have become so common in recent years that India's Supreme Court warned that they could become the 'new normal,'" Lindsay Maizland wrote in a 2022 report for the Council on Foreign Relations.

The kind of grievance-amplified partisanship behind the

January 6, 2021, storming of the Capitol in Washington, DC, led to the January 9, 2023, storming of government buildings in Brasilia, the capital of Brazil, where the enraged supporters of the former president, Jair Bolsonaro, smashed windows, lit fire to carpeting, and destroyed furniture and artwork. More than a thousand of them were arrested. Bolsonaro, like Trump in late 2020, had rejected the integrity of an election that declared him the loser and his political nemesis, Lula da Silva, the winner. And Bolsonaro's loyalists, like Trump's, turned rage into rampage.

Brexit was an act of grievance—the culmination of many of the anxieties and much of the nostalgia at play in the United States and other Western democracies as well. The argument for it and appeal of it included the girding of the United Kingdom's borders against so many newcomers with different languages and customs and skin colors; the rejection of globalization and of governance by distant and detached elites; the protection of native workers and native manufacturing; the restoration of local control; the exaltation of local traditions. One of Brexit's loudest champions, Boris Johnson, was a maestro of grievance, which he deployed in the service of his country's withdrawal from the European Union and which he clung to in the aftermath of that: when his turbulent three-year stint as prime minister came to a mortifying end in 2022, he gave a boastful exit speech that skimmed over his flamboyant personal failures and suggested that he was the victim of a sort of mob mentality that none of his allies had the spine to resist. "The herd instinct is powerful and when the herd moves, it moves," he said. Taking the measure of his legacy in an article in the *Atlantic*, Tom Nichols wrote: "Johnson . . . is one of the wealthy populists who gained power by supercharging a sense of resentment among ordinary people. This is the great danger to democracy in the 21st century, and it is the work of men and women who have no sense of decency or duty."

But the United States may well be the most fascinating laboratory for grievance, given our unmatched diversity, given our extreme income inequality, given our polluted media ecosystem, given the promises of unfettered social mobility that have been made by our leaders and encoded in our national mythology, given how robustly grievance grows when such promises are broken. We're an instructive example. And, these worrying days, a cautionary tale.

Just look at all the political violence—the domestic terrorism, to use an equally apt and aptly sinister phrase. It predated and postdated the January 6 insurrection. In October 2018, a madman fatally shot eleven Jewish people inside the Tree of Life synagogue in the Squirrel Hill neighborhood of Pittsburgh; it was "the deadliest attack on Jews on American soil—a jolt back to other times in history, in other places, when violence was part of the rhythm of Jewish life," as Emma Green wrote in the *Atlantic*. In August 2019, a twenty-one-year-old whose online presence suggested white nationalist convictions and anti-immigrant fixations entered a Walmart in El Paso that he'd seemingly chosen for its popularity with Latinos and fatally shot twenty-three people while injuring another twenty-two. In May 2022, an eighteen-year-old who'd written a manifesto decrying what he saw as a "white genocide" in the United States opened fire in a Buffalo supermarket and killed ten Black people. In January 2023, a Republican candidate for state office in New Mexico who'd called himself a "MAGA king" was arrested for the attempted murders of local Democratic officials in four separate shootings.

That's just a macabre smattering of examples, leaving out many other politically or ideologically motivated attacks or arrests of people plotting along those lines; the ugly (and, in the case of a Jewish man in Thousand Oaks, CA, deadly) confrontations and altercations between pro-Israeli and pro-Palestinian demonstrators after the Oct. 7, 2023, bloodbath in Israel; and other frightening indicators: Between 2016 and 2021, according to the Carnegie Endowment for International Peace, the number of threats against members of Congress investigated by the Capitol Police rose more than tenfold, to 9,600 from 902. That laid part of the groundwork for a six-part series, "The Danger Within," in the Opinion section of the *New York Times* in late 2022 that began with an editorial by Alex Kingsbury titled, "America Can Have Democracy or Political Violence. Not Both." It informed a sprawling, ambitious April 2023 cover story in the *Atlantic*, "The New Anarchy," by Adrienne LaFrance, who wrote that the United States was entering "a new phase of domestic terror, one characterized by radicalized individuals with shape-shifting ideologies willing to kill their political enemies," and who asked: "How can America survive a period of mass delusion, deep division, and political violence without seeing the permanent dissolution of the ties that bind us?"

That's a question raised by nonpolitical violence as well. "Hundreds of Miles Apart, Separate Shootings Follow Wrong Turns" was the headline on an April 2023 article in the *Times* about two such incidents. In one, a sixty-five-year-old man in upstate New York fatally shot a twenty-year-old woman when, according to initial police reports, she and her friends drove up his driveway, mistaking it for the one they'd meant to turn into. In the other, an eighty-four-year-old man in a suburb of Kansas City, Missouri, shot and injured a sixteen-year-old boy who rang his doorbell, also by mistake. The victim in the latter case was Black, while the shooter was white, and both cases reverberated across the country because they suggested a larger defensiveness, suspiciousness, and twitchiness among people who were less and less inclined to give one another the benefit of the doubt.

That twitchiness travels into all corners of American life. To road rage we've added air rage and so many assaults on flight attendants that federal lawmakers in 2022 introduced and in 2023 reintroduced the Protection from Abusive Passengers Act, which would put the worst of those passengers on a no-fly list. We've added restaurant rage and retail rage, with a growing number of news reports and viral videos of customers gone berserk. "In stores, parks, schools, restaurants, arenas, subway cars, congressional hearings—pretty much anyplace where human beings rub elbows—the banal frictions of everyday life explode into spittle-flecked shouting matches, and worse," Bruce Handy wrote in *Air Mail* in June 2023. "With anger now the defining emotion of our own times, and in splenetic tribute to the previous century's Roaring 20s, I suggest we dub the current decade the Raging 20s."

Deadly, or just unruly, confrontations have been occurring on so many occasions, in so many places, and in so many ways that we can no longer credibly do what we long preferred to and characterize all or most of them as spasms of mental illness without greater significance. The perpetrators are indeed broken, lost people. But many of them have been goaded into action—have been pulled across the line between deranged media posts and injurious or lethal behavior—by the metastasized grievances all around them.

Grievance sets our culture wars in motion. It escalates them. Behind the arguments over what history should be taught and which books children should be allowed to read are rival interpretations of who is being cheated and muscled out of the public square, and the stridency of those interpretations turns what could be calm discussions into vicious battles and leads, too often, to the puritanical banning of books. One group of parents and their allies believe that the world is being inverted in a way that vilifies and diminishes their own children; they point to some progressive schools' "antiracist" teaching, which tells white students that they're the inherently racist, undeserving beneficiaries of white supremacy, and those parents understandably question the wisdom—and kindness—of filling young children with such shame and guilt. They question, too, the reduction of the world to racial categories and the suggestion that no lens reveals the world as clearly and comprehensively as the prism of race. The other group of parents and *their* allies focus on generations of brutal discrimination and bitter injustice that demand acknowledgment and, they believe, atonement. "Woke" versus "unwoke" simplifies what's going on, turning it into jargon and casting it as a reflexive partisan struggle. That's not quite right. It's a contest of deeply felt grievances during a time when the aggrieved have lost—or lost interest in—the ability to see beyond their slights to a common good in which they don't get all that they want. Grown-ups are supposed to be able to compromise like that. But ours is an era of mass immaturity.

In such an era, a puerile former president in unprecedented legal jeopardy counted on his talents for modeling grievances and for stoking them to save him. He assessed the psychological and political currents of his country and determined that if he stuck with the shtick that the system was corrupt, that everyone who targeted him was an unscrupulous political hack, that he was a martyr and his torture a symbol of the contempt to which his supporters were also subjected, he might survive and prevail. On the wings of grievance, he sought to fly above the sordid messes he made.

In such an era, the House of Representatives kept devolving into chaos. Representative Kevin McCarthy needed four days and fifteen rounds of voting in early 2023 to ascend to the speakership of the US House of Representatives, making the process the longest and most acrimonious in 164 years. And then, to keep the superlatives rolling, a small but unappeasable cadre of fellow Republicans engineered his ouster after fewer than nine months in the job, the shortest stint since a House speaker died of tuberculosis in 1876. The "motion to vacate" that was filed by Representative Matt Gaetz, a Florida Republican, and that triggered a House-wide vote on McCarthy's fate, was, like Trump's indictments, unprecedented. Ditto for the removal of McCarthy by that vote, which commenced a surreal three-week period during which the House remained leaderless and the nation's business on hold while various candidates to succeed him rose up one moment only to be taken down the next. And that mess—coupled with an impeachment inquiry into President Biden and the recurring threats of the government's shutting down or defaulting on its debt—reflected a new and nihilistic breed of lawmaker intent on being mad and insistent on being heard, no matter how loudly they had to bellow or how little of coherence they had to say. They had no impulse to compromise, zero interest in solving problems. They were performers in a shrill theater of the absurd, and they thrilled to the spectacle of their own tantrums.

In such an era, two of the world's richest tech entrepreneurs, Elon Musk and Mark Zuckerberg, spent weeks in apparently serious negotiations about the terms for a public "cage match" in which they would channel their robust contempt for each other into an actual physical brawl: punches, kicks, body slams, headlocks. Zuckerberg ultimately nixed the idea in August 2023, saying that Musk clearly had cold feet. "Elon won't confirm a date, then says he needs surgery, and now asks to do a practice round in my backyard instead," he wrote in a post on Threads, the social media platform that his company, Meta, created to compete with Musk's X (formerly Twitter). On X, Musk wrote: "Zuck is a chicken."

In such an era, self-serving public figures cheapened their experiences as minorities by significantly exaggerating those challenges or invoking them in spurious ways, as if they were gambits in a child's board game, to be deployed without regard for anything but the possible advantage in doing so. New York City mayor Eric Adams repeatedly accused critics or opponents of treating him as if he were Kunta Kinte, a slave in the landmark 1970s novel and television miniseries *Roots*. Senator Robert Menendez, a New Jersey Democrat, responded to the bribery and corruption charges against him by denouncing "how quickly some are rushing to judge a Latino" and claiming that his accusers "cannot accept that a first-generation Latino American from humble beginnings could rise to be a US senator." Hasan Minhaj, a comedian and writer whose Netflix series *Patriot Act* won an Emmy, fabricated anecdotes about his persecution as a Muslim man and an Asian American—tales at the core of his persona. When an article by Clare Malone in the *New Yorker* in September 2023 exposed those fictions, he defended them, calling them "emotional truths" whose ornately embroidered details didn't matter and dismissing Malone as "a white woman with a keyboard." He was speaking for victims, giving voice to the aggrieved, and facts paled in importance beside that.

In such an era, a gay, Black actor named Jussie Smollett staged and then reported a hate crime in Chicago in January 2019, during which two supposedly homophobic, racist assailants yelled "This is MAGA country!" as they put a noose around his neck. Smollett, who had a supporting role in the hit show *Empire*, gambled that those details would so powerfully confirm so many Americans' beliefs about their own vulnerability and victimization that they'd proclaim their solidarity with him—and raise his public profile—without questioning the oddities in his story. Kamala Harris, then a US senator gearing up for a presidential campaign, called it "a modern-day lynching." A jury decided otherwise, finding Smollett guilty of felony disorderly conduct for lying to the police, and a Chicago judge sentenced him to five months in jail, decrying the "national pity party" that he had orchestrated for himself "for one reason: You wanted to make yourself more famous."

In such an era, some histrionically disenchanted young Americans were so intent on novel expressions of their inchoate (and often incoherent) upset that they disregarded how indecent the vessels for it could be, and on TikTok in the aftermath of that October 2023 slaughter of more than 1,000 people in Israel, they circulated and celebrated one of Osama bin Laden's decades-old screeds against the United States. The barbaric details and horrific dimensions of what happened in Israel did little to prevent it from being claimed and reframed by campus groups, by members of Black Lives Matter, by President Biden's right-wing critics, by various activists and pundits whose grievances took precedence over a period of mourning or constructive acknowledgement of complicated, tragic crosscurrents.

Colleges had by then established themselves as fertile ground for grievances of all kinds, and more than a few college students cared more about those grievances—or the grievances of the people in whose interests they claimed to be acting—than about free speech and spirited discourse, so they shouted down or ran off speakers whose words offended them. Students' grievances mandated long discussions about "microaggressions" that missed the humor and the tell of that neologism's prefix, which admitted to both a search for fault and a conflation of the picayune and the profound. Those grievances warped language itself: to render it immaculately inoffensive in a society itching for offense, a bulging glossary of words had to be sacrificed, no matter the farce of the overreach. Such recommendations or edicts traveled beyond campuses—to, for example, the Equity Language Guide of the Sierra Club, which "seeks to cleanse language of any trace of privilege, hierarchy, bias, or exclusion," as George Packer explained in the *Atlantic* in April 2023.

"In its zeal, the Sierra Club has clear-cut a whole national park of words," Packer wrote. "*Urban, vibrant, hardworking*, and *brown bag* all crash to earth for subtle racism. *Y'all* supplants the patriarchal *you guys*, and *elevate voices* replaces *empower*, which used to be uplifting but is now condescending. *The poor* is classist; *battle* and *minefield* disrespect veterans; *depressing* appropriates a disability; *migrant*—no explanation, it just has to go." Packer noted that such equity language guides had popped up at a range of universities and institutions, including the American Cancer Society, the American Medical Association, the National Recreation and Park Association, and the Columbia University School of Professional Studies. The pace of their proliferation almost made me worry that metaphor would soon die on the altar of grievance.

Unless democracy perished first. I think and certainly hope that I'm being a tad dramatic, but our divisions have grown so wide and our grievances so florid that over recent years, the prospect of the unraveling and disintegration of the United States has become a topic of regular discussion by rational scholars. It has migrated from fiction to nonfiction, with such titles as *How Democracies Die* (Steven Levitsky and Daniel Ziblatt, 2018), *Twilight of Democracy* (Anne Applebaum, 2020), *Divided We Fall* (David French, 2020), *Last Best Hope* (George Packer, 2021), *Our Own Worst Enemy* (Tom Nichols, 2021), *How Civil Wars Start* (Barbara F. Walter, 2022), and *The Next Civil War* (Stephen Marche, 2022) dedicated at least in part to the questions of how much damage we've done to ourselves, how frightened we should be, or how we might save ourselves. I'll summarize the answers: a lot of damage, plenty scared, and first and foremost by recognizing that we may very well be on borrowed time.

Almost no cultural event, no bit of news, no topic of national conversation is roped off from grievance, by which I mean a complaint or concern that should or could be a modest point of dispute, negotiable with businesslike diction and businesslike decorum, but is blown up wildly out of proportion. I mean a profoundly important cause being undermined and cheapened by its self-pitying, other-demonizing, simplistic expression and execution. I mean an animosity that's reflexive, not considered. I mean a drama with needlessly dire proclamations, with corrosively epic dimensions.

There was a time when I wouldn't have thought it possible for the same gauzy, misty, feel-good Super Bowl advertisements to elicit howls of protest from both the left and the right, but in the age of grievance, two "He Gets Us" commercials did precisely that after they were shown during the February 12, 2023, game. Part of an ambitious campaign run by a nonprofit group with ties to conservative religious organizations that want to spread the word of Jesus (the "He" in that three-word phrase), both ads were black-and-white montages set to music; one showed Americans in violent confrontation with one another, then flashed the sentence "Jesus loved the people we hate," while the other presented children of different races embracing each other as examples of how we adults might behave.

Although, as AJ Willingham wrote on the CNN website, "He Gets Us" ads in aggregate portray "the pivotal figure of Christianity as an immigrant, a refugee, a radical, an activist for women's rights and a bulwark against racial injustice and political corruption," Representative Alexandria Ocasio-Cortez was aggrieved, and she tweeted: "Something tells me Jesus would *not* spend millions of dollars on Super Bowl ads to make fascism look benign." *Fascism?* Trying to figure out how the congresswoman had made the leap from images of Black and white children hugging to the *F* word, Tish Harrison Warren observed in the *Times* that the "He Gets Us" campaign's wealthy evangelical donors "had also donated to conservative causes like religious liberty and anti-abortion efforts." "While white evangelicalism certainly deserves a lot of critique," Warren wrote, "it is hyperbolic to the point of dishonesty to equate it to fascism." Regardless, more than twenty-five thousand people retweeted Ocasio-Cortez's nuance-free protest. More than 200,000 Twitter users "liked" it.

But where the congresswoman detected fascism, Charlie Kirk, a mega MAGA radio host and the founder of a Trump-supporting youth group, Turning Point USA, divined a marketing group of "woke tricksters" who had duped the campaign's organizers and hijacked their proselytizing effort by replacing biblical verities with social-justice imagery. Kirk's tweet decried "one of the worst services to Christianity in the modern era." "So sad!" it concluded, with a Trumpian flourish. I concur—also with an exclamation point!— but not about the mood and imagery of the "He Gets Us" ads. I'm heartsick over the pervasive impulse and ability to see malice and conspiracy behind every bush, burning or otherwise.

"The partisan reactions to the 'He Gets Us' ads are unsurprising," John Inazu, a professor in the law school at Washington University in St. Louis, wrote in his Substack newsletter, *Some Assembly Required*. "What I found more surprising in this case was the degree of mental gymnastics required to watch these ads and conclude that they are either 'right-wing' or 'an unbiblical Jesus.'" Ah, but such gymnastics are the preferred sport of the aggrieved. And they perform it with all the limberness, agility, and razzmatazz that lofted Simone Biles to Olympic gold.

Look—it's Marjorie Taylor Greene on the uneven parallel bars. In early April 2023, Jack Teixeira, a twenty-one-year-old member of the Massachusetts Air National Guard, was charged with leaking classified information about US surveillance of Russia that was vital to our assistance to Ukraine. To the best of anyone's knowledge at the time, he hadn't done that as some high-minded protest of US involvement in the fighting between Russia and Ukraine. He was more postadolescent punk than principled dissident. But through her cracked goggles of grievance, Greene espied a nefarious motive and context for Teixeira's arrest. "Teixeira is white, male, christian and antiwar," she tweeted, capitalizing on her professed faith without properly capitalizing it. "That makes him an enemy to the Biden regime." *Regime?* "Ask yourself who is the real enemy?" she added. "A young low level national guardsmen? Or the administration that is waging war in Ukraine?"

President Biden of course wasn't waging war in Ukraine. That's what Vladimir Putin was doing. And Teixeira's gender, color, and religion had nothing to do with his looming prosecution, nor were they relevant to a legitimate, necessary debate about the degree, nature, costs, and long-term usefulness of Americans' aid to Ukrainians. But they had everything to do with how an alarming fraction of Americans engage with politics today—by foraging for and, in a pinch, fictionalizing the abuse of whatever group of people they identify with. Their predetermined sense of grievance is the prism through which all is passed and all is parsed.

It distorted the reaction to Russian authorities' politically motivated imprisonment of the basketball star Brittney Griner after charging her with bringing two hashish oil vape cartridges into the country in February 2022. Ridiculously, outrageously, those authorities claimed that she was a drug smuggler and sentenced her to nine years in a penal colony. I was aware of all those developments in great detail and in real time, as was just about everyone I knew, because the American media coverage of Griner's unjust and terrifying fate was intense and sustained. Her wife appeared on prominent news shows. The Biden administration released statements protesting what was happening to her and promising to do everything that it could to secure her release. And it *did* secure her release in December 2022, by agreeing to a prisoner swap and freeing a convicted Russian arms dealer—a real, dangerous criminal, unlike Griner.

But that didn't prevent or stanch commentary on the left about supposed American indifference to Griner because she's a woman, Black, and lesbian. "America Hates Black Female Athletes" was the headline of an article in HuffPost in July 2022. Its author wrote that Griner was "in this position for a number of reasons: She's a Black woman and a lesbian, thus occupying two of the lowest rungs on America's social ladder. I know, I said the quiet part out loud." No, the author said the politically voguish part in circumstances to which it didn't apply. Griner's celebrity held greater sway than anything else about her, so that she got *more* attention than the usual American political prisoner. Many Americans only learned of another American that the Russians were holding, Paul Whelan, a white former marine who'd been convicted of what US Secretary of State Antony J. Blinken called "sham espionage charges," when he was mentioned in an auxiliary fashion in news reports about her. Whelan had been arrested by the Russians in late 2018. He remained in Russia, in a grim penal colony eight hours from Moscow, serving a sixteen-year sentence, long after Griner's return to the United States.

Grievance can turn the innocuous into the noxious, and it ignores good intentions. Those were lessons that First Lady Jill Biden kept learning. Although she didn't go looking for trouble, it found her regardless. A few Hispanic groups and commentators slammed her in 2021 for mangling the pronunciation of the rallying cry "sí se puede"—never mind that the flub came during an appearance and remarks on Cesar Chavez Day that signaled her solidarity with Hispanic farmworkers and union members. She was slammed anew in 2022 when she said that the Latino community was "as unique as the breakfast tacos here in San Antonio"—never mind that she was lending her presence and voice to a conference of the largest non-profit advocacy group for Latinos in the United States and that San Antonio, Texas, indeed prides itself on those tacos.

And then, in 2023, after attending and watching the NCAA women's basketball championship game between Louisiana State University and the University of Iowa, she overexcitedly suggested that perhaps not only LSU, who won, but also Iowa, who lost, should be invited to the White House, given how well they both played. That broke with tradition and prompted accusations that Biden was disrespecting LSU and indulging Iowa because LSU's star player, Angel Reese, and most of her teammates are Black, while Iowa's star player, Caitlin Clark, and most of her teammates are white. "The coincidence of first lady Biden inviting a majority white runner-up team signifies white privilege," a university professor wrote in an essay on the website the Conversation that was republished in the *Des Moines Register*. "I believe the racial dynamics at play reflect the double standard that is applied to Black people and white people in the U.S. In other words, Black people have the burden of doing more to get the same access and opportunity as their white counterparts."

A spokeswoman for Biden—who, incidentally, had been turned away from the LSU locker room *before* the game because the team's players were upset that her husband hadn't picked them to advance far in the tournament—said that the first lady had intended no offense and had been caught up in the exhilaration of what was the most watched college women's basketball game ever, a stride toward female athletes being treated on a par with male athletes. Reese publicly rejected that quasi apology. On the podcast *Paper Route*, she said that Iowa could have the Bidens; perhaps LSU players would visit the Obamas instead. (LSU did ultimately go to the White House, sans Iowa.) *The Daily Show* hashed through the whole mess in a segment that pondered whether it revealed more about racism or about sexism, because of course there had to be *some* ism in the mix. In the age of grievance, there always is.

If pressed, I can read or theorize something at least adjacent to racism in what happened: Perhaps the first lady was sorrier for Iowa and more eager to include the team than she would have been for LSU, had it lost, because she has a stronger subconscious affinity for white people and because white people are supposed to be society's winners. Or: Biden's failure to pause, wonder about the appropriateness of including Iowa at the White House, and realize that LSU's Black players might feel slighted by a joint invitation demonstrated racial insensitivity. I suppose I can find sexism, too: Biden assumed that young women, unlike young men, wouldn't mind sharing the spotlight because they're less ruthlessly competitive, more touchy-feely in the end. But I have to *want* to find that racism. I have to go looking for that sexism. An ism or a phobia has to be my presumptive and preferred interpretation.

For too many Americans, racism, *reverse* racism, sexism, classism, homophobia, transphobia, xenophobia, and the rest of it are indeed the go-to explanations, the fail-safe calls. They're invoked when they must be, as a matter of moral urgency. But they're also invoked to make a splash, to make a buck, to gain entry to a conversation, or to get the final word. That's not a new phenomenon. But it's a pronounced and dangerous one.

Three

Grievance Now versus Grievance Then

I suspect that we Homo sapiens began pointing fingers and appointing scapegoats shortly after we stood upright, if not sooner. We're an ingenious species with a talent for anger and with potent tribal instincts; our wars—both the epic and the everyday ones—reflect that. And just as nations the world over have been born of grievance, they've been undone by it, century after century. Each country is to some extent a grievance stress test: Can its binding ideals, its commonly accepted narratives, or sheer repression keep the disillusionments at bay, the divisions under wraps? That's a challenge complicated by the demagogues and revolutionaries who sow and reap grievance and by the less flamboyant political operators who nonetheless till it to varying degrees. The purveyors of grievance in the United States today haven't invented anything new. They're just adept at and shameless about purveying it.

Most of the battle lines aren't new, either, and one period of time that keeps roaring back in my memory is the early 1990s, when, all at once, journalists and public intellectuals started sounding alarms about college curricula that cast the past and present in the terms of oppressors versus oppressed; about the left's quickness to see and call out racism and sexism in every nook and rivulet of society; about a constructive regard for multiculturalism degenerating into a destructive obsession with putting every culture into an inviolable jewel box; about the vogue of victimhood; about an insistence that we all think and speak in a narrowly circumscribed and supposedly more enlightened manner. Sound familiar? That demand wasn't called "wokeness" then, and the phrase "cancel culture" hadn't yet been popularized, perhaps because cancel culture's greatest colosseum and cudgel—social media—hadn't yet been born. But the arguments and the angst were much the same.

In an article in the *Times* in October 1990 headlined "The Rising Hegemony of the Politically Correct," Richard Bernstein defined political correctness as "a sort of unofficial ideology of the university" with "roots in 1960's radicalism." It promoted "the view that Western society has for centuries been dominated by what is often called 'the white male power structure' or 'patriarchal hegemony.' A related belief is that everybody but white heterosexual males has suffered some form of repression and been denied a cultural voice." Bernstein went on to observe that "the cluster of politically correct ideas includes a powerful environmentalism and, in foreign policy, support for Palestinian self-determination."

Two months later, *Newsweek* magazine, which then had a robust circulation and significant influence, ran a cover story about political correctness, "Thought Police," that asked: "Is this the New Enlightenment—or the New McCarthyism?" A month after that, the cover of *New York* magazine asked the question: "Are You Politically

Correct?" The accompanying story, sprawling over nine lavishly illustrated pages, had a tone of menace. It described and decried a new group of "demagogic and fanatical" fundamentalists that included "multiculturalists, feminists, radical homosexuals, Marxists" and was defined by the belief "that Western culture and American society are thoroughly and hopelessly racist, sexist and oppressive." Camille Paglia told the story's author, John Taylor: "It's fascism of the left."

That perspective occupied a brimming subgenre of general nonfiction, beginning in some ways with the shockingly big commercial success in 1987 of *The Closing of the American Mind*, by the philosopher Allan Bloom. Bloom, who had taught at several of the country's leading universities, portrayed higher education, its administrators, and its consumers as increasingly faddish, entranced with popular culture and drawn to a lazy moral relativism. To treat that ailment, he prescribed a return to the "great books" of Western thought—to Plato, Machiavelli, and the like. And he sparked an animated and sometimes acrimonious national conversation about whether the country was losing essential moorings. Different authors assessed the situation with different degrees of subtlety, and their unease overlapped with growing worries that many Americans were rejecting personal responsibility in favor of explanations and lamentations that pinned their frustrations and failures on dynamics beyond their control.

Culture of Complaint was the title of a prominent 1993 book by the well-known art critic Robert Hughes. It expanded on a cover story, "The Fraying of America," that he'd written for *Time* magazine, and it asserted that multiculturalism, which he regarded as a just and positive force under the right circumstances, was pulling the United States in a negative direction by encouraging people to see themselves in terms of whichever marginalized category they could claim affiliation with and the attendant damage they'd suffered. Summarizing his argument in a television interview with Charlie Rose after the book's release, Hughes said that the United States was coming apart "because people increasingly define themselves only in relation to their rights and not to civic duties. That's number one. But secondly, you have this kind of corrosive culture of victimology that's seeping over the land. Everybody wants to be identified with some kind of 'out' group or as a victim." It explained whatever was wrong in their lives. And whatever was right? That, then, was the product of improbable, extraordinary perseverance.

A Nation of Victims: The Decay of the American Character, by Charlie Sykes, appeared a year earlier. It noted how frequently and loosely people were spotting and claiming racism, sexism, and other isms, and how readily they were pathologizing undesirable behavior as mental illness. He cited a school district employee who sued after he was fired for repeated tardiness; the employee said that "chronic lateness syndrome," not some character lapse, was the culprit. Other writers such as Wendy Kaminer, the author of the 1992 book *I'm Dysfunctional, You're Dysfunctional*, and David Rieff, the author of a 1991 cover story for *Harper's* magazine titled "Victims, All?," took aim at trendy therapeutic notions, championed by the "recovery movement," that unideal childhoods and unrecognized, subtle forms of abuse were the roots of all woes.

Mark Muro quoted both of them, along with like-minded naysayers, in a 1992 article for the *Boston Globe* that was syndicated in many other newspapers as well. Muro wrote: "These dissidents ridicule recovery guru John Bradshaw's claim that 96 percent of Americans come from 'dysfunctional' families. They reject the movement's all-comers-welcome definition of 'abuse,' which equates 'inadequate nurturance' with real rape and actual battery. And they regret the movement's apparent readiness to blame failings on others, namely one's parents."

Kaminer told Muro: "Basically, reveling in how Mommy ignored you in order to discover self-esteem makes little sense for most people." Rieff: "What this nation needs is a little stoicism. Look, life is hard; you do not escape its rigors; much of it involves struggle, and pain, and 'abuse,' and I say thank goodness for that."

That's harsh, but I was old enough in 1992—twenty-eight, to be exact—and attuned enough to the zeitgeist that I can look back and understand where Rieff and Kaminer were coming from, what they were pushing back against, and why they might feel the need to be a tad provocative in doing so. They were responding to some of the forces that the political theorist Wendy Brown wrote about in her 1995 book *States of Injury: Power and Freedom in Late Modernity*, which wondered at the degree to which people, including those in marginalized groups, dwelled on the wounds they carried and the protection they felt they needed.

Rieff and Kaminer were responding as well to the prevalence and extravagance of media testimonials from—and strenuously poignant magazine articles about—prominent people who suddenly wanted to bare their private pain, tell their secrets, advertise their hardships, and exult in their ultimate triumph. The popular VH1 series *Behind the Music*, which debuted in 1997, was the apotheosis of this trend: Behind the music of most of the successful performers whose careers it chronicled was a dark past or period of hardship that put the lie to the glamorous images they projected. Sure, they were dancing and strutting across some of the biggest stages in the world. But they were also wounded.

• • •

Those celebrity confessionals never went away, though they shed some of their excess, jettisoned some of their cant, and descended less often into unintended caricature. They're humdrum staples now. And the contention that the Western world's institutions disproportionately reflected and venerated the contributions of white men—and that change was in order—endured, for one reason above all others: it was (and is) simple fact. Fair-minded, sensible people couldn't dispute it. They could argue over *how much* change, over whether those who had benefited from unfair advantages owed those who hadn't some kind of recompense, and over whether that debt could fairly be saddled on privilege's descendants, many of whom had no direct hand in any wrongdoing. But sometime after the mid-1990s, the temperature of all of this feverish soul-bearing seemed to decrease for a while.

That changed with Trump. Actually, it changed before Trump. In retrospect, you can see the seedlings of him in Sarah Palin, whose proud lack of erudition and contempt for the expert class foreshadowed his declaration, "I love the poorly educated!" You can see the makings of MAGA in the Tea Party. And you can see that what seemed to many of us to be heady markers of long-awaited and hard-fought progress—the election of the country's first Black president, Barack Obama, in 2008; the Supreme Court's 2015 ruling that legalized same-sex marriage nationwide—were provocations to other Americans, who were feeling more and more disoriented, more and more displaced, and were less likely to raise a white flag than to dust off a Confederate one.

Trump took full and flamboyant advantage of that impulse. He not only validated their convictions that they'd been neglected, condescended to, and maligned, but also blessed whatever meanness they mustered. He goaded them to shout insults at the journalists at his rallies. He exhorted them to "knock the crap out of" protesters, saying he'd pay any legal bills that ensued. He even tweeted erroneously that four progressive Democratic congresswomen who were vocal critics of his "originally came from countries whose governments are a complete and total catastrophe" and should "go back and help fix the totally broken and crime infested places from which they came." Supporters at one of his rallies subsequently chanted "send her back" about one of those congresswomen, Representative Ilhan Omar, and Trump was just fine with that. "These are people that love our country," he said, defending those supporters. "I want them to keep loving our country."

The fury of MAGA mobs was met with fury from those on the other side of an increasingly wide partisan divide. They couldn't believe the ugliness they were witnessing and viewed it as a rallying cry. Chronologically speaking, there wasn't a neat and clean cause and effect between Trump's ascent and a new, funhouse-mirror version of the "political correctness" of the early 1990s—you could chicken-and-egg the situation until the cows came home—but their concurrence was more than sheer coincidence. Each found motivation and justification in the other. They intertwined. Cultural progressives saw Trump as confirmation of their worst fears about American society—he was white privilege on steroids, the patriarchy on minoxidil, part robber baron, part sexual predator—and as cause to call out that society for its full range of transgressions. He then pointed to their excesses and asked: Is this really the America you want?

Excesses like the ones spotlighted in a stunt that three disgruntled scholars played in 2018. Zack Beauchamp described it in an article published by *Vox* on October 15 of that year:

An argument for men self-penetrating with dildos to reduce transphobia. An ethnography of men who attend "breastau-rants" like Hooters. Research on rape culture among the dogs at Portland dog parks.

These are all real articles, published in real, scholarly jour-nals, written by a group of three people—magazine editor Helen Pluckrose, mathematician James Lindsay, and philosopher Peter Boghossian. But if they sound to you like parodies of a certain style of academic research, you're right. Pluckrose, Lindsay, and Boghossian wrote and published the articles as part of a year-long hoax campaign targeting fields like gender studies.

Pluckrose et al. wrote 20 papers and submitted them, under false names, to a variety of journals. By the time they ended the experiment in early October, seven out of the 20 had been ac-cepted for publication.

The one about dogs found a home in the journal *Gender, Place and Culture*. It was titled "Human Reaction to Rape Culture and Queer Performativity at Urban Dog Parks in Portland, Oregon" and supposedly mined ten thousand hours of close observation of ca-nine carnality. Sample sentences: "Do dogs suffer oppression based upon (perceived) gender?" "Because of my own situatedness as a human, rather than as a dog, I recognize my limitations in being able to determine when an incidence of dog humping qualifies as rape."

Upon the hoax's revelation, Pluckrose, Lindsay, and Boghos-sian explained that they wanted to expose an absurd ardor for what they termed "grievance studies" in higher education. "Something has gone wrong in the university—especially in certain fields within the humanities," they wrote in an article in the online journal *Areo*, adding that too many scholars cared less for objective, verifiable truth than for "attending to social grievances."

Did their success in publishing faux research prove this? Maybe. Sort of. It wasn't representative of most scholarship—and didn't succeed in breaching journals of such traditional disciplines as sociology and political science. And from the vantage point of my position on the faculty at Duke University, where a large majority of my fellow professors and my students are somewhat or significantly left of center, I can say that I've never run into scholarship this fatuous. But the fact that the dog-park "study" had a legitimate hearing anywhere was troubling and meaningful. It signaled a strong tendency in higher education, in many political circles, and in much of the news media to prioritize certain prisms and filters, and to treat conclusions that adhere to and buttress a liberal worldview with less skepticism than conclusions that don't.

"Grievance studies" mocked the left's exhausting inventory of bigotries and its indiscriminate panic over every one of them, but the right spins yarns—like Big Tech and Big Government sneaking microchips into vaccines—that make the study of dog rape look quaint. Trump-era Republicans' exuberant bid for the crown of Most Aggrieved isn't the only difference between the culture of complaint in the 1990s and the grievance extravaganza today. But it's a prominent and obvious one.

Sykes does even more cultural commentary than he used to—regular contributions to the *Bulwark*, frequent appearances on MSNBC—and he told me that back when he wrote *A Nation of Victims*, the phenomenon that he was describing was "confined to the precincts of academia, largely" and was most conspicuous among liberals. At that time, he said, he couldn't have imagined "that political conservatives would enthusiastically adopt the culture of victimization as well, because this seemed to me a kind of dividing line—that you had the world of personal responsibility, stiff upper lip, and traditional values versus this new culture of victimization." That world of personal responsibility was the one that Republicans extolled. "Well, that's been turned on its head now," Sykes marveled. "Every line that you're hearing from the MAGA right is 'we are endangered,' 'we are being discriminated against,' 'Great Replacement Theory.'"

Did the right take a cue from the left? Possibly. "People saw the effectiveness of it," Sykes told me. "Look, victim politics is convenient. It's a useful cudgel. It's a shortcut from having to make a detailed policy argument." As a result, "it seeped out into the general public," he theorized. "It became part of the language of our politics." That dividing line, he conceded, was always porous. He noted that in his book's discussion of "people who were playing the victim card, one of the first people I mentioned was Clarence Thomas." During Thomas's confirmation hearing in the Senate, "he claimed that he was the victim of a high-tech lynching, and my point was that you could immunize yourself against responsibility—you could assert some kind of moral authority or superiority—by claiming this, and so people who were backed into a corner would claim being a victim." Weirdly, Sykes remembered, "one of the first calls I got after that book came out was from Clarence Thomas. He called to say how much he liked it! And I was of course tempted to say, 'Do you know that you're in it?'" He conceded that Thomas probably hadn't read more than a few pages, if that—and had a vision of himself as someone who was looking askance at, and not a member of, this nation of victims.

But Republicans' embrace of victimhood in the Trump era was more than mimicry. There were precedents for it. They'd been primed for it. Go back to Pat Buchanan's insurgent campaign against President George H. W. Bush for the Republican presidential nomination in 1992, not so coincidentally when the left was parsing oppression in its infinite forms, and you hear the gathering strains of the reciprocal response so thunderous on the MAGA right today. Buchanan spoke famously and presciently of a culture war—actually, he used the phrase "*cultural* war" in his remarks at the Republican National Convention that year—and warned that radical feminists, homosexuals, and other secularists were coming for good Christians like him. Go back further still, to the 1960s, when Barry Goldwater and Richard Nixon validated many white Americans' fears that emboldened minorities were putting them and their way of life on the defensive.

Those fears lingered, alternately waxing and waning and then assuming a whole new shape when Obama came along and made history. He took office in 2009, and later that same year came the Tea Party, whose adherents tended to be "Republican, white, male, married and older than 45," according to a 2010 analysis by the *Times*, which added that "while most Republicans say they are 'dissatisfied' with Washington, Tea Party supporters are more likely to classify themselves as 'angry.'" Their foreground complaint was economic, and the motivations they cited were the $700 billion federal bailout for failing banks and corporations and what they saw as runaway federal spending in general. But the *Times* analysis, based on a *Times*/CBS News poll, also showed that they were "more likely than the general public, and Republicans, to say that too much has been made of the problems facing Black people." In an assessment of the Tea Party in the *New Republic* the following year, Jonathan Chait referred to those findings and other observations about the Tea Party's evolution to conclude that it was "demonstrably true that Tea Party sympathizers hold distinctly reactionary views on racial issues." In 2012, Obama handily won a second term. That seemed to indicate that such views had limited traction. Four years later, Donald Trump succeeded him. That suggested the opposite.

What a riddle Barack Obama represented and still represents, one that will never be definitively solved. I don't mean the man himself. I mean his reception—what he says about his country. Among many liberals, including many Black activists, it became popular to downgrade or outright dismiss the significance of his election and reelection as barometers of racial progress. But that's absurd: he wasn't *so* uniquely talented, so adept at distracting people from matters of race, or running in such remarkably advantageous circumstances that his Blackness was eliminated from the equation. It was front and center, and it didn't doom him, as it surely would have in presidential contests past. For some voters, including many people I know, it helped him: they cared about the symbolism of his possible victory; they felt that his perspective, forged by membership in a horrendously treated group, was immensely valuable; and they deemed his achievements all the more remarkable for the obstacles he'd faced. For other voters, his Blackness wasn't his first, second, or even third most relevant attribute. While those dynamics didn't herald an end to racism, they did support the possibility that the country had moved—and was moving—in a better direction.

Yet there was blowback. That, too, is undeniable. Many Americans struggled to digest Obama's political success, and some of them surely found Trump so appealing because he'd long acted and spoken in racially coded or flatly racist ways, including his demands that Obama provide a long-form birth certificate and then that Obama share his college transcript from Columbia and his law school transcript from Harvard (to establish that his time in those Ivy League institutions amounted to more than mere tokenism). Trump didn't just repudiate Obama. He gleefully tormented him.

Which raises the question: Did Trump's triumph in 2016—when he got many million fewer votes than Hillary Clinton but bested her in that dubiously democratic arena called the Electoral College—reflect the flowering of florid racism? A column by Thomas Edsall in the *Times* many years later, in early 2023, promised to reveal "The Unsettling Truth About Trump's First Great Victory," meaning over Clinton, and the opening paragraphs summarized the findings of three well-regarded books by serious academics that charted a connection between many white voters' fixation on their status in a changing America and support for Trump. So that, then, was the truth? Trump rode to victory on Americans' racism?

Not so fast. Edsall's column pivoted to talk about a *newer* book that showed that those fixated white voters—who scored high on a measure of racial resentment—were much smaller in number and less consequential to the 2016 election's outcome than less resentful white voters. "The bulk of support for Trump came from more moderate whites," Sean Westwood, a political scientist at Dartmouth College, explained to Edsall, analyzing the competing books and all the accumulated data and scholarship. "Trump managed to pull in support from racists, but he was able to pull in much more support from economically disadvantaged whites." Daniel Hopkins, a political scientist at the University of Pennsylvania, added: "It's critical to avoid the idea that there is a single skeleton key that can explain all the varied undercurrents that led to Trump's 2016 victory." Edsall's unsettling truth was that the truth was complicated.

But take racism per se out of the picture and you still had an intensifying outcry from those "economically disadvantaged whites," especially in exurbs and rural areas, who felt that their struggles and the woes of their communities, in which factories had shut down and overdose deaths had skyrocketed, were being ignored— and were being ignored in part because of Democrats' attention to cities and minorities. As politicians on the right appealed to this group, they played on that feeling, lambasting such schools of thought and such initiatives as affirmative action, "amnesty" for immigrants who'd entered the country illegally, critical race theory, and DEI (diversity, equity, and inclusion). They turned these into dirty words, phrases, and initials, sending the message or validating the idea that white people were now the objects of discrimination and neglect.

But that wasn't the only form that Republicans' embrace of victimhood took. Once they decided they were victims, they saw their abusers *everywhere.* Kevin McCarthy's creation in early 2023 of a new Judiciary Committee panel called the Select Subcommittee on the Weaponization of the Federal Government distilled Republicans' new posture of extreme aggrievement. The panel's, um, philosophical underpinnings were sketched by Representative Ryan Zinke, a Montana Republican, when he spoke in support of it in the House in mid-January 2023. "Despite the 'deep state's' repeated attempts to stop me, I stand before you as a duly elected member of the United States Congress and tell you that a deep state exists and is perhaps the strongest covert weapon the left has against the American people," Zinke proclaimed, adding that "the deep state runs secret messaging campaigns" and is trying "to wipe out the American cowboy." But for someone on some vaguely defined federal hit list, a target for cancellation by the big bad government itself, Zinke had enjoyed enormous success: After serving in office in Montana, he was first elected to the US House in 2014, left Congress in early 2017 to become President Trump's secretary of the interior, and was then elected to the House anew in 2022. Clearly those deep-state secret-messaging campaigns weren't doing their job.

Ah, the weaponization subcommittee, the mewling and implacable child of "the bottomless sense of grievance that sends a shape-shifting narrative of victimization coursing through the right-wing mediasphere and political funding complex," as Chris Lehmann described it in *The Nation*. "The committee will probe the phantom mobilization of 87,000 I.R.S. agents to harangue middle-class and working-class citizens—even though the last Congress's budget hike for the chronically understaffed and underfunded agency stipulated that it was aimed chiefly at high-income tax evaders," Lehmann wrote, as he provided various examples of the subcommittee's selective and nefarious revisions of events. Also on its agenda: claims that the Justice Department under President Biden and US Attorney General Merrick Garland was treating parents who opposed the teaching of critical race theory in schools as domestic terrorists and had mistreated the January 6 rioters by exaggerating their transgressions. In the telling of the weaponization subcommittee, there were all sorts of Americans just like Zinke's endangered cowboy, people who dared not to think, speak, and live as liberals demanded. Due to all of that, they were targeted for extinction.

Part of what's so striking about the current state of political play and what distinguishes it from the early 1990s is the directness and fierceness of the competition between Republicans and Democrats, conservatives and liberals, people on the right and people on the left, for the Grievance Bowl's Lombardi Trophy. To the victims go the spoils. Their senses of persecution overlap even as their realities diverge, and there's a point-by-point, tit-for-tat, yin-yang quality to the battles between the most fervent and immoderate camps on each side, whether the front is trans rights, voting rights, immigration reform, or affirmative action. What the left sees in the right and what the right sees in the left are almost the same: a bullying force intent on imposing its out-of-touch, out-of-whack values on unbelievers and on crushing them if they persist in their heresy. What the left feels and what the right feels are identical: oppressed. There's a perverse mirror-image tidiness to it, a nasty reciprocity, even a strange symbiosis.

Take the issue of DEI, which encourages greater consideration—specifically when it comes to hiring and promotion—of people from different racial backgrounds (and, to a lesser extent, of women and of people with different religions, sexual orientations, and gender identities). In many companies and government agencies over recent years, DEI became an omnipresent shorthand, an ineluctable admonishment, a mantra. But in an offensively domineering or insultingly performative way? People on the right and people on the left often looked at the same developments and came to diametrically opposite conclusions while feeling comparable degrees of disgust.

That was clear in a flurry of attention in late 2022 and early 2023 paid to DEI initiatives in higher education in particular. That expanded significantly following George Floyd's murder by Minneapolis police officers in May 2020, as colleges across the country devoted much more money and many more people to DEI efforts. Membership in the National Association of Diversity Officers in Higher Education increased by 60 percent from 2020 to 2022, according to a report in *Inside Higher Ed*. A former economics professor estimated that the University of Michigan alone would spend $18 million on salaries and benefits for its DEI staff in 2023.

That figure spread fleetly through conservative circles and

publications, intensifying Republican politicians' denunciations of DEI and resolves to eradicate it. Those denunciations were more than posturing, while those resolves were paired with action, enough of it that *The Chronicle of Higher Education*, on its website, maintained a tracker of what it dubbed "anti-D.E.I. legislation" at the state level, meaning measures that sought, for the most part, to prohibit or strictly diminish DEI offices and staff or to ban the consideration of race and ethnicity in hiring and admissions decisions; by the fall of 2023, the tracker counted forty states where such legislation had been introduced, seven where it had received final legislative approval but awaited a governor's signature, and another seven that had enacted anti-DEI laws. Florida governor Ron DeSantis and other prominent Republicans cast DEI as an affirmative action boondoggle that leeched money and opportunity from all those people it didn't favor, turning *them* into the new underprivileged. Watching and listening to the critics of DEI, I discerned a firm conviction that they were the marks of some woke scam. I sensed genuine offense.

And watching and listening to the promoters and defenders of DEI, I sensed as much or more of that. They contended that DEI efforts were paltry in the context of the centuries of discrimination that had created the need for them and were also halfhearted, token remedies. Yes, there were more bodies and dollars being thrown at DEI, but that had created a Potemkin infrastructure, inhabited by people who weren't being given much power, weren't getting much support, and weren't shown much appreciation. In late 2022, the Princeton University newspaper reported that three people who'd been hired by Princeton to do DEI work had resigned recently, reflecting their frustration. Just like the estimated $18 million that Michigan was spending, this detail circulated fast and far, generating widespread notice.

In an interview with the *Daily Princetonian*, one of the three former Princeton employees, Jordan Turner, who had served as the first-ever associate director of athletics for diversity, equity, and inclusion, said: "I am a Black queer non-binary person who came to Princeton to create a more just and equitable playing field for all." But, Turner added, the Princeton officials who'd invited him wanted only "a symbol of progress but not the driver for progress itself.... It was made clear that approaching conflict and potential harm in ways that center the experiences of women, trans people, queer people, and other current and historically marginalized people were not welcomed." His take wasn't unusual. I spotted similar comments from DEI workers embittered rather than encouraged by the roles they'd received—and suspicious of the people who created and filled those jobs.

DEI promoters' and opponents' dueling claims of grievance reflected and were sharpened by what arched over that contest and so many related ones during this chapter of American life: dueling definitions of freedom. Each side wrapped itself in the idea of freedom, in the language of freedom, in the very word, claiming that its agenda was nothing more and nothing less than "freedom," which didn't merely justify but compelled what it was doing, making its actions profoundly American and intrinsically righteous. The conflict's special sharpness and starkness made consensus, compromise, and conciliation all the more elusive.

As Conor Friedersdorf wrote in the *Atlantic* in April 2023, DeSantis "has long presented himself as a principled champion of 'freedom.' In Congress, he was a founding member of the Freedom Caucus. He refers to himself as 'governor of the free state of Florida.' And while laying the groundwork for a possible presidential run, he is promoting a book on his approach that he titled *The Courage to*

Be Free." He and many like-minded conservatives laid out that approach as a freedom agenda. As they told it, they forbade certain classroom talk (about LGBTQ+ people and issues, about systemic racism), banned certain books (ditto), and punished certain actors (the College Board and the Disney corporation, in DeSantis's case) not in violation of free speech or contradiction of free markets but in the urgent, vital service of freedom from a liberal elite's attempts to indoctrinate all Americans into one officially sanctioned school of thinking, one permissible manner of living, and from those elites' determination to cancel all dissent. They weren't engaged in government overreach; they were *responding to* and fighting back against government overreach. They were restoring liberty.

But whose liberty? That's the hell of government and lawmaking, and that's the question that has driven Republicans and Democrats so far apart. Many Democrats, long aligning themselves with marginalized groups, see no freedom for Black people unless the reference to their skin color is capitalized like that, unless institutions are compelled to account and answer for the percentages of minorities in their ranks, unless there are financial reparations along the lines of a California task force's recommendation, greeted coolly by Governor Gavin Newsom, of up to $1.2 million per person. Anything short of those measures denies Black people's horrific treatment in the past, minimizes the aftereffects of that, ignores the racism of the present, and thus effectively discriminates against them, leaving them very much unfree. Many Democrats likewise see no freedom for trans people unless the bigotry against them is confronted and eradicated in public schools early on, unless the word "women" gives ground in certain contexts to "pregnant people" (because a trans man might still have a uterus and vagina) and "menstruators" (ditto), and unless trans women are allowed to participate in women's athletic events, where some of them may enjoy significant advantages. All of that is necessary if they're to be as free—from fear, from violence—as the other Americans around them.

When you believe that freedom itself is on the line, in a country that identifies itself as "the land of the free," how do you peaceably resolve your disagreements or humbly retreat from them? Often, you don't. You can't—they're too important for any accommodation or surrender. So you fight harder. And you come to see the people you're fighting against not as compatriots with a contrary point of view but as combatants to be vanquished.

One of the more disturbing hallmarks of our era—a grievance amplifier, a grievance multiplier—is the large and growing percentage of Republicans who regard Democrats as dangerous and detestable and the large and growing percentage of Democrats who return the favor. "Over the past few decades, American politics has become like a bitter sports rivalry, in which the parties hang together mainly out of sheer hatred of the other team, rather than a shared sense of purpose," Alan Abramowitz, a professor of political science at Emory University, and Steven Webster, a graduate student there, wrote in *Politico* in October 2017, during Trump's first year in office. "Republicans might not love the president, but they absolutely loathe his Democratic adversaries. And it's also true of Democrats, who might be consumed by their internal feuds over foreign policy and the proper role of government were it not for Trump."

Abramowitz and Webster were writing about "negative partisanship," a phrase that appeared in the headline of their article and would become not just a fixture of political analysis over the years after the article appeared but the subject of such dark fascination— of such legitimately acute concern—that pollsters and pundits were forever seeking new ways to measure and frame it. They often started with findings by the Stanford University political scientist Shanto Iyengar and several of his colleagues that from 1960 to 2010, the percentage of Republican parents who said they'd be displeased if one of their children married a Democrat rose to 49 percent from a mere 5, while the percentage of Democratic parents cold to the idea of a Republican in-law rose to 33 from 4. That's a profound change, indicative of how much our politics had degenerated by 2010. They have deteriorated much, much further in the decade and a half since.

A poll conducted in 2020 by the Survey Center on American Life, which is affiliated with the right-leaning American Enterprise Institute, found that 64 percent of Democrats deemed Republican policies to be a "serious threat" to the country, while 75 percent of Republicans had that view of Democratic policies. A poll conducted by the Pew Research Center in 2022 determined that 72 percent of Republicans considered Democrats "immoral," which was a jump of twenty-five percentage points since 2016, while 63 percent of Democrats felt that way about Republicans, a jump of twenty-eight percentage points. The percentages of people in each party who judged those in the other party to be "dishonest" tracked the "immoral" findings almost exactly and revealed a similarly stark erosion of respect for voters on the other side of the political divide over the previous six years. Also in 2022, YouGov polling for CBS News showed that when Americans in each party were asked whether they viewed those in the other as their political opposition or as their enemies, about half of Republicans and half of Democrats chose the latter.

I could go on and on in this vein, marshaling data from the past five years about the shocking percentages of Americans who are as freaked out by their political rivals as they are by hostile foreign nations or who think that blue states or red states should secede from the country, leaving those right-wing yahoos or left-wing fruitcakes to fend for themselves, but these statistics all begin in the same place, end in the same place, and tell the same damning story: Most Americans don't simply feel frustrated by those who disagree with them politically. They feel diminished, besieged, and imperiled by them.

That contempt explains the contemporary rarity of ticket splitting—most Americans vote only for Republicans or only for Democrats—and the dwindling number of states in play in a contemporary presidential contest. We're down to a dozen at best. "We became more consistent in the party we vote for not because we came to like our party more—indeed, we've come to like the parties we vote for *less*—but because we came to dislike the opposing party more," the *Times* columnist and podcast host Ezra Klein noted in his 2020 book, *Why We're Polarized.* "Even as hope and change sputter, fear and loathing proceed."

And that contempt drives voters' demands, candidates' promises, lawmakers' actions, and all of our most intense cultural and political disagreements, creating a feedback loop of fury and teasing out or supersizing any and all possible grievances. "The most effective politicians thrill their supporters," Klein wrote. "But they do so in the context of the threat their opponents pose. And as politicians become less well-known and capable on the stump, they rely more and more heavily on activating fear of the other side. The lesson is known by politicians the world over. You don't just need support. You need anger."

"That's why fundraising emails often border on the apocalyptic," he continued. "It's why Trump is always fighting with the media. It's why presidential candidates find it hard to keep their supporters engaged when they win the White House—the terror of losing an election is more viscerally motivating than the compromises of daily governance." Abramowitz and Webster put it this way: "In today's environment, rather than seeking to inspire voters around a cohesive and forward-looking vision, politicians need only incite fear and anger toward the opposing party to win and maintain power. Until that fundamental incentive goes away, expect politics to get even uglier."

Shortly after the Supreme Court struck down *Roe v. Wade* in 2022, I had a long, off-the-record chat with a prominent Democratic politician who is known and esteemed for his tempered approach, his avoidance of inflammatory language, and his ability to work across the aisle. Substantively, he was troubled by and worried about the ruling—very much so. But in terms of the approaching midterm elections? He was excited. His eyes gleamed as he described the silver lining he spotted. Republican voters in the Trump era were always in a lather, he told me, and that boosted their turnout. Now Democrats had a way to get *their* voters as or even more agitated. "Angry voters are voters who show up," he said, almost joyously. He was right, of course, but he didn't finish the thought, didn't acknowledge or address some of its implications, specifically this: Is the ire so useful on Election Day appeasable and manageable in the weeks and months afterward? Or does it become a kind of toxin coursing uncontrollably through the body politic?

James Kimmel Jr., a lecturer in psychiatry at the Yale University School of Medicine and the founder and codirector of the Yale Collaborative for Motive Control Studies, sees it as a kind of drug. "I've been researching the way grievances affect the brain," he wrote in *Politico* in 2020, "and it turns out that your brain on grievance looks a lot like your brain on drugs. In fact, brain imaging studies show that harboring a grievance (a perceived wrong or injustice, real or imagined) activates the same neural reward circuitry as narcotics."

He added that what your brain wants to do with that grievance—how it both extends the high and brings it to its most satisfying conclusion—is retaliate. "To be clear," he wrote, "the retaliation doesn't need to be physically violent—an unkind word, or tweet, can also be very gratifying." So can making sure a political opponent is quashed. Your brain on grievance is a gift to the party and the candidate you support.

While that's not a new phenomenon, Kimmel told me in a subsequent interview that Trump's ascent and behavior had a catalytic effect on it. Trump modeled what Kimmel calls "revenge addiction," and there's evidence that addiction can spread from one person to another, becoming a "social contagion," he said. "Imagine the scenario where we elected somebody who's not only an opioid addict but is enjoying that and encouraging people to become opioid addicts with him, and you get a daily dose of that kind of teaching and leading people toward that behavior from the highest pulpit that the country has. We have no examples in human memory of anybody like that with that kind of power. He's like a grievance drug kingpin."

And he was visibly benefiting from his revenge addiction. It was a core part of his identity, arguably the foundation of it, and there he was, at the pinnacle of politics, the spectacularly vengeful leader of the free world. "He has enjoyed some of his success by *being* viciously retaliatory," Kimmel told me. Both those who'd voted for him and those who'd voted against him undoubtedly noticed that. Other politicians sure did.

Trump, obviously, didn't introduce vengeance to American politics. Well before him, it produced some of our most overblown political scandals and longest-running political melodramas: Just ask Bill and Hillary Clinton, whose careers were defined by their opponents' unflagging attempts to catch them in wrongdoing and shame them, and by their own self-destructive girding for and defensiveness about that. But we've entered a fresh and frightening epoch of vindictiveness in American politics. And in this case, there's no clean symmetry: The right is more committed to retaliation than the left. Anyone who tries to refute that by pointing to Trump's two impeachments and his postpresidential legal travails isn't being honest about the scope and severity of his transgressions. The investigations into him may be punitive, and there's enormous spite in them, but there's just as much justice. A leader can't incite violence, try to steal a presidential election, routinely flout the rule of law, and then call any harsh treatment of him petty political payback.

That's an accurate description, though, of DeSantis's attempt to strip Disney of a special tax-exempt status in Florida that reflected all the jobs it created, all the tourists it attracted, all the infrastructure it maintained, all the money it not only brought to but also *saved* the state. Disney's sin? Its chief executive officer in the winter of 2022, Bob Chapek, publicly opposed a controversial education measure that DeSantis was championing to much conservative fanfare nationally and that he indeed succeeded in signing into law. Nicknamed the "Don't Say Gay" bill by its detractors, it prohibited schoolteachers from any discussion of sexual orientation or gender identity among young schoolchildren, and it was worded in a sloppy, vague way that left the door open to more sweeping, stringent banishments of those topics.

DeSantis so convinced himself that Disney embodied all of the "woke" ideology that he and his supporters detested—and was so confident of the political points he'd score by torturing the corporation accordingly—that he didn't fully develop his plan or look far enough down the road. Disney outmaneuvered him, finding a fine-print ploy to retain control over its special district, and it filed a free-speech lawsuit that, in the long run, had an excellent chance of succeeding. DeSantis ended up looking hasty, clueless, and weak, all because he was intent on vengeance and certain of its currency.

His rise was a case study in a new mainstreaming of grievance politics. In the past, long-shot political challengers such as Buchanan had wallowed in and promoted grievances as a way of being a nuisance, drawing attention, and guaranteeing themselves at least some fringe support, but DeSantis was no desperate insurgent: In November 2022, he won reelection to a second term as governor of Florida, the nation's third most populous state, by more than nineteen percentage points, the largest margin in nearly forty years. In late 2022 and early 2023, the GOP establishment and pundits of all stripes regarded him as the only Republican with a chance of beating Trump for the party's 2024 presidential nomination. But like Trump, he was all about grievances. He was fixated on revenge.

If Trump was grudge made flesh, DeSantis was grudge made strategy, and his embrace and weaponization of grievance was exponentially more telling because it was infinitely more deliberate. Trump's route to the White House had been the haphazard zigzag of someone responding viscerally to various stimuli and then sloppily repeating the behaviors that yielded the greatest immediate reward. DeSantis, in contrast, studied the moment, fashioned a plan, and then executed it. More than two decades after George W. Bush made his bid for the presidency with the slogans that he was "a compassionate conservative" and "a uniter, not a divider," DeSantis essentially said: "I have neither compassion nor mercy for our liberal adversaries. It's us versus them."

The Florida governor gambled on the sunset of the political wisdom that voters tend to prefer forward thinking and good cheer over dire prognostications, and that they favor candidates who are more hopeful and optimistic over their rivals. And he proceeded to shape his political identity and construct his agenda around enemies lists and acts of retribution. He pledged to eradicate this, to exile that, to thwart one band of foes and thwack another. There was a paucity of pro, an overabundance of anti.

Disney had plenty of company as a target of his ire. To humiliate and harass liberals for not figuring out how to prevent so many people from illegally crossing the border between Mexico and the United States, DeSantis in September 2022 sent two planeloads of migrants from Texas to Martha's Vineyard, a favorite vacation spot for former president Barack Obama and many other high-flying Democrats. In June 2023 he repeated the stunt, sending another two planeloads of migrants from New Mexico to Sacramento, the capital of California, whose governor, Gavin Newsom, had made anti-DeSantis and anti-Florida commercials and public statements a big part of his national profile. To sate the antipathy that opponents of abortion rights felt toward supporters of them, he suspended and publicly shamed a Tampa-area prosecutor who had made his own commitment to legal, safe abortions clear—and then, the following year, DeSantis signed into law a ban on most abortions after just six weeks of pregnancy. To feed the fury that many Americans, especially those on the political right, felt about the changing, incomplete, and sometimes inaccurate information that they'd received about Covid vaccines, he exhorted Florida's Supreme Court to convene a grand jury to look into precisely what vaccine makers had said and how they might be held accountable for any errors.

He advocated or enacted measures to rein in teachers on matters beyond LGBTQ+ issues, to ban any consideration of ESG (environmental, social, and governance) factors in decisions about how and where to invest Florida funds, to edit the College Board's advanced placement exams, to muzzle the media. He traced every fault line in America's culture wars, then peacocked and planted a marker along it, an effort striking in its comprehensiveness and, even more so, its relentless negativity. He played not to voters' aspirations but to their anger, an approach epitomized by the signature promise that united his deeds and diatribes: instead of describing Florida as a lush nursery for big dreams, he labeled it a graveyard for bad ideas, saying that the Sunshine State was "where woke goes to die."

In early 2023, as most of the country's journalists completed their pivot from the 2022 midterms to the 2024 presidential race, they seemed to realize en masse that what DeSantis and several other Republicans trying to wrest the party mantle from Trump were saying and doing was a sea change—that Trump's "American carnage"–caliber darkness and divisiveness weren't proprietary to him or passing phenomena. Within a span of just two days in mid-March 2023, two of the *Washington Post*'s most prominent and astute political writers published articles focusing on precisely that. Dan Balz marveled that "DeSantis's message is confrontational, framed as a conflict that demands to be won outright. Talk of national unity, the currency of many successful presidential candidates, is fleeting to nonexistent. He revels in the country's left-right divisions rather than offering a path out of them." And Ashley Parker noted that "much of the rhetoric from declared and potential Republican candidates so far is remarkable for its dystopian tone" and for its description of a country with "warring camps of saviors vs. villains." She recalled that the previous month, in the official Republican response to President Biden's State of the Union address, Arkansas governor

Sarah Huckabee Sanders said: "The dividing line in America is no longer between right or left; the choice is between normal or crazy." And Trump, in a speech in early March at the Conservative Political Action Conference, told the audience: "I am your warrior. I am your justice. And for those who have been wronged and betrayed: I am your retribution."

DeSantis seemed determined not to cede that turf to Trump, to "own the libs" in the manner that Trump relished, but to do it with more than trash talk, trashed norms, and name-calling—to do it with punitive strokes. That's what lured him into that ultimately self-defeating and mortifying dance with Disney, which, as the conservative writer Charles C. W. Cooke noted in *National Review*, was gratuitous and performative: the corporation's stance against his cherished education law neither threatened nor ultimately managed to block its implementation. DeSantis got his way. "There is no need for the Republican Party of Florida to salt the earth here," Cooke wrote. "It has prevailed in every particular." "So why salt the earth?" asked Charlie Sykes in a commentary of his own in the *Bulwark*. "Because this is the politics of revenge and punishment."

Revenge and punishment: Trump, who lavished his political energy on those as on nothing else, threatened to take them to cataclysmic extremes following his arraignment in a federal court in Miami in June 2023 on thirty-seven counts of wrongdoing for mishandling—or, really, frolicking with—all those classified documents. He said that if he won the 2024 election and got another term as president, "I will appoint a real special prosecutor to go after the most corrupt president in the history of the United States of America, Joe Biden, and the entire Biden crime family. I will totally obliterate the Deep State." From any lips other than Trump's, that statement—made in a speech to supporters at his Bedminster,

New Jersey, golf club—would have been stunning, and it was chilling regardless, because that vow, that "real prosecutor" reference, and that "obliterate" all added up to a new vision of the Justice Department under a second, restored Trump administration as a clique of presidential sycophants and a vessel for presidential vendettas. Trump separately said that he and his supporters were engaged in "the final battle" against Democrats, for whom he repurposed an archaic political slur. "Either the Communists win and destroy America," he said, "or we destroy the Communists." That hyperbole and hyperventilation seemingly inspired Charlie Kirk, the MAGA radio host I previously mentioned, who told his listeners in July 2023 that Biden "should honestly be put in prison and/or given the death penalty for his crimes against America." Meanwhile, another right-wing radio host, Stew Peters, publicly suggested that Anthony Fauci and Hunter Biden deserved to be executed.

Revenge and punishment: they explain why and how Republicans turned on other Republicans in early 2021, as various state and county Republican parties formally censured Republican members of the House who backed Trump's second impeachment and Republican senators who voted for his conviction for his part in the January 6 rioting. This retribution came from a party that had long accused *liberals* of enforcing a stringent orthodoxy and brooking no dissent, a party that denounces "cancel culture" while readily practicing its own version of it. But then Republicans' vindictive itch superseded anything so quaint as intellectual or ideological honesty.

Revenge and punishment: they fired J. D. Vance's imagination as he ran in 2022 for an open seat representing Ohio in the US Senate, pledging to strike back at all those awful East Coast elitists and glossing over his diploma from one of their shrines, Yale Law School, a credential that played a major, validating role in the Appalachia-to-Ivy arc of his bestselling memoir, *Hillbilly Elegy*. James Pogue captured Vance's resentment-drenched campaign in an article in *Vanity Fair*, dwelling on Vance's stated desire to see the leadership class in the United States ripped out and replaced, even if that required the quasi-dictatorial overreach of a would-be autocrat like Trump. Pogue plucked out some priceless remarks Vance made when he did a podcast interview with the head of a conservative men's rights group. "I tend to think that we should seize the institutions of the left and turn them against the left," Vance said on the podcast. "We need like a de-Baathification program, a de-woke-ification program." Vance also flashed forward to a possible Trump victory in 2024. "I think that what Trump should do, if I was giving him one piece of advice: Fire every single midlevel bureaucrat, every civil servant in the administrative state, replace them with our people," he said. If that sounded extreme, well, so was the contempt for and subjugation of real Middle American folks like him. "If we're going to push back against it," he said, "we're going to have to get pretty wild, and pretty far out there, and go in directions that a lot of conservatives right now are uncomfortable with." Vance went on to win that Senate race, against a deft and potent Democratic opponent, by almost seven percentage points. Barring an unusual turn of events, he will be a US senator at least through 2027.

Revenge and punishment: they prompted Republicans in the Tennessee House of Representatives in early 2023 to take the extraordinary and self-defeating step of expelling two Black Democrats who, after a school shooting in Nashville left three children and four adults (including the assailant) dead, used bullhorns in the House chamber to demand new restrictions on firearms. Those bullhorns violated House rules, but Republicans could simply have voted to censure the Democrats. Or to fine them. Or to serve them with a stern letter of reprimand. Expulsion did the opposite of silencing them, instead turning them into martyrs and political superstars, their names and faces recognizable to many more Americans than would have been aware of them otherwise. It went beyond any previous penalty for rules violations in the House.

Republican governors around the country followed DeSantis's lead, courting those constituents most consumed by enmity and nurturing their spite. In Texas in late 2021, Governor Greg Abbott signed legislation that effectively encouraged citizens to turn against one another and existed at the misbegotten nexus of vigilantism, bounty hunting, and weapons-grade partisanship. It enabled anyone who knew or suspected that a Texan had helped a pregnant person get an abortion to file a civil lawsuit against that abettor—maybe, in the spirit of the draconian law, I should say accomplice—and potentially collect a reward of at least ten thousand dollars. There was no one-lawsuit limit. It set up the theoretical possibility of abortion snitching as a whole new line of work.

And a whole new kind of surveillance state loomed. In Virginia, Governor Glenn Youngkin established and publicized an email address— basically, a digital tip line—where parents could report any untoward activity or instruction that they became aware of in their children's schools. It was a cheap shot in ideological cahoots and political tandem with DeSantis's attention-seeking stunts. While Youngkin's supposed goal was to guard against the teaching of "critical race theory" or anything that smacked of white guilt, no such parameters were placed on the alarms that parents could raise. Youngkin and his Republican allies were fashioning a tool easily used for pure harassment and partisan recrimination. Maybe that was part of the point. Maybe that tool was meant largely, even primarily, to indulge the antipathy that consumed so many voters.

Meanwhile, in West Virginia, the Republican secretary of state,

Mac Warner, emulated Trump's fearmongering about illegal voting and announced a "See Something, TEXT Something" program that created a phone number to which the state's residents could send text messages about suspicions that someone was voting illegally or otherwise engaged in voter fraud. When I learned of that, I was disgusted: voter fraud is an invented panic. I was impressed: Warner had nonetheless found a clever way to clamber aboard that bandwagon. But I was above all baffled: How do you spot illegal voting? Do you use binoculars, as with bird-watching? "Look, sweetheart, there's an American goldfinch—and *there's* a Honduran migrant with a stack of fraudulent ballots in his backpack!" When politicians start sating grievances, they stop serving logic.

Four

The Lost Shimmer of
the City on the Hill

It had been clear for years that China was rising and rising—erecting skyscrapers at a rate that the United States didn't come close to, building rail lines and airports that put ours to shame, purchasing the favor of poor countries paradoxically rich in resources, filling the world with its wares—when, in April 2014, I happened upon a bit of news that I'd on some level been expecting for a while. CNBC, citing a "new study from the world's leading statistical agencies," reported that China's rapidly growing economy would rank first in the world, surpassing the United States', by as soon as the end of the year. Our century-plus reign as the world's wealthiest nation was over or about to be. What a run we had!

But the study, which used debatable methodology and turned out to be wrong, interested me less than something else I learned when I began poking around the internet to put it in some sort of context. I discovered that most Americans thought that China already *had* become our economic superior. And they'd thought that—erroneously—for several years. In 2011, Gallup polled Americans on the question of whether the United States, China, the European Union, Japan, Russia, or India was the leading economic power in the world. More than 50 percent answered China, while fewer than 35 percent said the United States. Those numbers held when Gallup did the same polling the next year and the next and in 2014, when the split of Americans choosing China versus those choosing the United States was 52 percent to 31 percent. That's a whopping differential, especially considering its wrongness.

China's economy still lags behind ours. Yet, according to Gallup, Americans have clung to the opposite belief—with an interesting exception. In 2020, when China was perceived and pilloried as the cradle of the coronavirus pandemic, 50 percent of Americans saw our economy as the mightier of the two nations', versus 39 percent who thought China's was, a margin of eleven percentage points. That rediscovered swagger was short-lived. In 2021, 50 percent gave the crown back to China, while only 37 percent chose the United States.

A fundamental misperception of global affairs by Americans isn't surprising. Too many if not most of us feel little tug to look or think beyond our shores. But this particular misperception startled and fascinated me: We'd traditionally been such a confident, even cocky, nation, enamored of our military might (and often too quick to use it), showy with our foreign aid, schooled in stories—true ones—about how desperately foreigners wanted to make new lives here and what extraordinary risks they took to do so. We saw ourselves as peerless, and we spoke a distinctively American vocabulary of infinite possibility, boundless optimism, and better tomorrows.

"American dream." "American exceptionalism." "Land of opportunity." "Endless frontier." "Manifest destiny." Those were the pretty phrases that I grew up with, words that appeared not in only in political ads but also in history lessons and elevated analyses of the American psyche. We welcomed newcomers, or at least didn't tightly seal our borders, because we weren't as worried as other countries might be about having enough to go around. We were always making more. We were always making better. We were inventors, expanders, explorers. Putting the first man on the moon wasn't just a matter of bragging rights—though it was indeed that, and we bragged plenty about it. It was also an act of self-definition, an affirmation of American identity. We stretched the parameters of the navigable universe the way we stretched the parameters of everything else.

That perspective, obviously, was a romanticized one, achieved through a selective reading of the past. It discounted the experiences of many Black Americans. It minimized the degree to which they and other minorities were shut out from all this inventing, all this expanding, all this exploring. It mingled self-congratulatory fiction with fact. And it probably imprinted itself more strongly on me than on some of my peers because of my particular family history. My father's parents were uneducated immigrants who found in the United States what they left southern Italy for: more material comfort, greater economic stability, and a more expansive future for their children, including my father, who got a scholarship to an Ivy League school, went on to earn an MBA, and became a senior partner in one of the country's biggest accounting firms. He put a heated in-ground pool in the backyard. He put me and my three siblings in private schools. He put our mother in a mink. And he pinched himself all the while.

It was nonetheless true that the idea of the United States as an unrivaled engine of social mobility and generator of wealth held sway with many Americans, who expected their children to do better than they'd done and their children's children to do even better. That was the mythology, anyway. "Notably among nations, the United States has long been shaped by the promise, if not always the reality, of forward motion, of rising greatness, and of the expansion of knowledge, of wealth, and of happiness," Jon Meacham wrote in his 2018 book *The Soul of America*, noting that Thomas Jefferson "spoke of the animating American conviction that tomorrow can be better than today." Sure, we hit lows, but we climbed out of them. We suffered doubts, but we snapped back. The tumult of the late 1960s, Nixon's degradation of the presidency and the gas lines, international humiliation, and stagflation of Jimmy Carter's presidency gave way, in 1980, to the election of Ronald Reagan, who declared that it was "morning in America" and found an abundance of voters eager to welcome that dawn, to reconnect with an optimism that seemed more credibly and fundamentally American than deviations from it.

I don't detect that optimism around me anymore, not when I take the emotional temperature of my fellow Americans, not when I examine what they tell pollsters, not when I analyze the nature of their political engagement, not when I look at the entertainment they consume. I see a crisis of confidence. I see retrenchment. I see manifestations of, and metaphors for, our lost bravado that are so on the nose they could be a playwright's invention. Take our fitful and beleaguered attempt to get *back* to the moon in the late summer and fall of 2022. Although Neil Armstrong, an American, had made that "giant leap for mankind" more than a half century earlier, in 1969, NASA struggled to send an *unmanned* spacecraft moonward. That vessel, the Orion, rolled out to its launchpad at the Kennedy Space Center in Florida on August 17, 2022, but only after a series of delays caused by problems discovered during preflight tests. People then gathered on August 29 to watch Orion rocket into space, but NASA canceled the launch at the last minute due to a faulty engine temperature reading. On September 3, the launch was canceled yet again; this time, the culprit was a leak during fueling. Not until November 16 would Orion take off. It was as if we just couldn't defy gravity the way we used to.

The aggrieved mindset of so many Americans is a kind of perfect storm, fed by various weather patterns. The ascendance of social media, the breakdown of traditional media, increased income inequality, the continued diversification of a country more heterogeneous than others, a manner of individualism often indistinguishable from narcissism: all are climate changers, all the more so in combination. But perhaps none figures as prominently in our distemper as many Americans' suspicion or outright conclusion that our best days are behind us, that growth and improvement are no longer a given, and that our problems are multiplying faster than we can find solutions for them. It's a seismic shift in our national identity, a violent rupture of our national psyche. It's a whole new American pessimism.

Well, maybe not entirely new. In *Democracy in America*, published in 1835, Alexis de Tocqueville noted a perpetually unsatisfied yearning in Americans, who, he wrote, "are forever brooding over advantages they do not possess." He found Americans unusually attuned to their misfortunes, and that made (and still makes) sense: With big promises come big disappointments. Boundless dreams are bound to be unattainable. The titanically influential developmental psychologist Erik Erikson observed that American adolescents in search of their identities got contradictory and conflicting signals from their country, which blended the "open roads of immigration and jealous islands of tradition, outgoing internationalism and defiant isolationism, boisterous competition and self-effacing cooperation," as he wrote in his 1950 book *Childhood and Society*.

Even in periods of American history that we associate with prosperity and tranquility, like the 1950s, there were rumblings and disenchantment: *Rebel Without a Cause, The Man in the Gray Flannel Suit*. And the late 1960s and early 1970s were an oxymoronic braid of surgent hope for necessary change and certainty that the whole American enterprise was corrupt. There were headstrong and heady demands for dignity, for equality, for justice. There were also cities on fire and assassinations.

But the overarching story—the general trend line—of the United States in the second half of the twentieth century was progress. Possibility. Western Europe moved along a similar path; the European Union, an answer to the enmities and atrocities that racked the continent during the first half of the twentieth century, expanded and took ever deeper root. And that informed the political scientist Francis Fukuyama's contemplation of "The End of History?", as he titled his widely influential and vigorously debated essay in 1989 about the fizzling of the Soviet Union, the fading of the Cold War, the expansion of prosperity, and the triumph of liberal democracy as a model form of government. In the 1990s, the American economy roared.

Then, in 2001, the Twin Towers fell. In 2008, the global economy nearly collapsed. By 2012, I noticed that our "shining city on a hill," to use one of Reagan's favorite terms for the United States, was enveloped in a fog that wouldn't lift. I heard statements, witnessed behaviors, and saw statistics that spoke to that. In June of that year, Jeb Bush visited Manhattan, had breakfast with several dozen journalists, including me, and mused about the country's diminished position and fortunes. Perhaps because his political life was then on pause—he'd finished his two terms as Florida governor and his 2016 presidential campaign was still years away—he allowed himself a bluntness that he might not have otherwise. "We're in very difficult times right now, very different times than we've been," he said, and while that was already more downbeat than mainstream politicians' usual prognostications, his following words were even starker and darker: "We're in decline." He added that "that distinguishes us" from Americans at previous moments in our country's history.

I perked up. I paid greater and greater heed to evidence that supported his appraisal, which mirrored my own. I was struck by how tempered and tentative President Obama seemed by the second year of his second term, when he often mulled the smallness, not the largeness, of his place in history, telling David Remnick, the editor of the *New Yorker*, that each president is just "part of a long-running story. We just try to get our paragraph right." "Mr. President," my *Times* colleague Maureen Dowd wrote in response to that, "I am just trying to get my paragraph right. You need to think bigger." Of course, when Obama *had* thought bigger, he'd bucked up against an American political system that was polarized and paralyzed—that had turned "hope and change" into tweak and tinker. Obama's longtime adviser David Axelrod told the *Times*'s Michael Shear: "I think to pretend that 'It's morning in America' is a misreading of the times."

That was in 2014, when I registered and explored the revelation that so many Americans thought China was wealthier than we were. Around the same time, I also noticed a long memo by the prominent Democratic political strategist Doug Sosnik in *Politico*. He observed that for ten years running, the percentage of Americans who believed that the United States was on the wrong track had exceeded the percentage who thought it was on the right track, according to polling by NBC News and the *Wall Street Journal*. "At the core of Americans' anger and alienation is the belief that the American dream is no longer attainable," Sosnik wrote. "For the first time in our country's history, there is more social mobility in Europe than in the United States."

Also in 2014, my *Times* colleague Nick Kristof wrote about America's rank on a new "social progress index" that included 132 countries. It placed us thirty-ninth in basic education, thirty-fourth in access to water and sanitation—access to water and sanitation!—and sixteenth overall, just two spots above Slovenia, a country probably unfamiliar to many Americans. (Melania Trump would soon change that.) The headline on Nick's column was a dig at American arrogance, often unwarranted and now on its way to extinction: "We're Not No. 1! We're Not No. 1!"

But 2014 was a patch of clover next to the scorched earth of 2016, which was apparently the first of what, in the Western world, would become a succession of years that each established a new nadir of doom and gloom—until the next year proved even gloomier. "Thanks to global warming, 2016 was the hottest year on record," Andrew Potter, an associate professor at the Max Bell School of Public Policy at McGill University, wrote in his 2021 book, *On Decline: Stagnation, Nostalgia, and Why Every Year Is the Worst One Ever.* "Hurricanes ravaged the Gulf, while the Zika virus emerged as a global threat, especially to pregnant women. There were terrorist attacks in Brussels, Nice, and at a nightclub in Orlando. In June, Britain shocked the world by voting to leave the EU, something that would have stood as the most notable political story of the year if it hadn't been eclipsed in November by the election of Donald Trump as president of the United States." And so, Potter added, "The pattern seemed to be set:

A stable international order collapsing amid renewed Great Power machinations, populist retrenchment, and decay amongst the established democracies fueled by fake news and Russian manipulation, terror attacks abroad and mass shootings at home, and the constant menace of a looming environmental catastrophe." Potter's run-on litany underscored the West's pile-on of woe.

Potter expanded on his thinking in an interview with the Canadian journalist Nahlah Ayed during a September 2021 episode of the CBC Radio show that she hosted, *Ideas*. She asked him, "What, exactly, is in decline?"

"Broadly speaking, civilization," he answered. "What I'm arguing is that the whole trajectory of modernity, of economic growth, of liberal democracy—the general idea that things are getting better all around—has probably peaked and is quite possibly in terminal decline."

She pressed him on his definition of "decline."

"It's not the apocalypse, right?" he said, in what qualified, in context, as good cheer. "This isn't a Hollywood thriller where there are comets crashing or anything like that. What I'm arguing is that civilization—what we call civilization—advances through the process of us figuring out how to resolve increasingly larger and more complicated collective-action problems, the various problems that kept us for centuries or millennia in something close to subsistence-level living." But, he explained, we had seemingly hit "the limits of our ability" on that front and were in the early stages of "a retreat into more localistic identity politics or tribalistic forms of social organization that are, in many ways, more fearful of others and less tolerant and less trustful."

This interview took place after the January 6 insurrectionists stormed the US Capitol but *before* Vladimir Putin started launching missiles toward Kyiv and Russian troops began slaughtering Ukrainian civilians; *before* the Omicron variant showed us how stubborn and wily the coronavirus pandemic was and how unpredictable future plagues might be; *before* the trucker convoys in Canada and the United States amplified the unappeasable anger that so many people felt about pandemic restrictions and their painful economic effects; *before* that mass shooting in Buffalo in May 2022 that left ten people dead and then, about two weeks later, a mass shooting in Uvalde, Texas, that claimed another twenty-one lives, most of them young children. So, nine months after Potter's first conversation with Ayed, she invited him back on the show. There was ample reason—pressing need, really—for a decline-and-stagnation update.

The temperature in Pakistan, he noted, had just crested 120 degrees Fahrenheit. "They're in a twelve-hundred-year climate drought in the southern United States," he said. Then, apparently reading from his book, he added: "The bill for our exploitative approach to the natural world is finally coming due." And that wasn't just about heat in Pakistan and fires in California and floods elsewhere. "To that, we can add a growing antibiotic resistance crisis," he said. "Even more frightening, nature itself: the buzzing, blooming plenitude we take for granted seems to be emptying out. Insects are disappearing, as are animals. The oceans are full of plastic."

He said it was as if we'd long ago "stumbled onto a buffet and ate up all the food, and after a few hundred years looked around and went, 'Hey, where did all the food go?' I think that's where we are right now."

You can take issue with the extreme selectiveness of Potter's focus. What of our continued and profoundly meaningful scientific advances? What of the more inclusive nature of many institutions around the globe? Historically speaking and by the numbers alone, we're living in an epoch of less poverty, less hunger, less abject want than our forebears did. There are fewer wars and fewer mass casualties, the violence and despair in places as diverse as Ukraine, Haiti, Israel, and Gaza notwithstanding. And in the next chapter, I'll come back to that—to the question of whether our liberation from direr, more epic tribulations has given birth to a pettiness and selfishness that pollute our social interactions and our politics in a manner as ultimately destructive as grander cataclysms and catastrophes are.

But I don't think there's any quibble with Potter's assertion that many of his fellow Canadians, many Americans over their border, and many denizens of countries to the south, west, and east of us harbor a feeling that the feast might be over and a day of smaller portions may be upon us. The beef that younger generations had with us Boomers was that we'd exploited our turn at the carving station. Now came the divvying-up of gristle and burnt ends.

In 2021, Pew Research surveyed nearly nineteen thousand adults in seventeen relatively affluent countries about their confidence in the future. Sixty-eight percent of the respondents in the United States said that they thought their children would not do as well financially as they had, an increase of six percentage points from Pew's findings two years earlier. Just 32 percent of Americans said that their children would be more prosperous. But that made the United States only the sixth most negative of the nations surveyed, tied with Canada. People in Japan, France, Italy, Spain, and Belgium expressed even less confidence about how their children would fare financially.

"The coronavirus has made parents pessimistic about their children's future" was the first sentence of a report on Pew's findings on CNBC.com. Actually, no. The pandemic had simply made them *more* pessimistic. They were already remarkably downbeat in 2019, at least according to Pew's own previous measurements on that particular question. Pew had summarized those earlier, 2019 findings in an article on its website that noted that "majorities of Americans foresee a country with a burgeoning national debt, a wider gap between rich and poor and a workforce threatened by automation."

"Majorities predict that the economy will be weaker, health care will be less affordable, the condition of the environment will be worse and older Americans will have a harder time making ends meet than they do now," the article continued. Its headline spotlighted the same *D* word to which Potter was drawn: "Looking to the Future, Public Sees an America in Decline on Many Fronts."

And Pew wasn't alone in surveying Americans and finding that most parents in the country that had so often claimed to epitomize social mobility and lidless opportunity didn't expect their children to earn more and live in greater economic comfort than they had. In September 2013, the "Heartland Monitor Poll" that the *National Journal* conducted annually in conjunction with Allstate showed that only 20 percent of Americans expected children in the country to have more opportunities than their parents had benefited from, while 45 percent expected them to have fewer. (Other Americans were in the middle or undecided.) The following year, in a *Wall Street Journal*/NBC News poll that asked Americans whether they were confident that their children's generation would be better off, 76 percent of the respondents said that they weren't.

By the early 2020s, American pessimism was so bountiful and such a given that cultural observers did vaguely comic riffs about it. "More young people are opting not to have kids not only because they can't afford them but also because they assume they'll have only a scorched or sodden wasteland to grow up in," the cartoonist and essayist Tim Kreider wrote in the *Times* in July 2022. "An increasingly popular retirement plan is figuring civilization will collapse before you have to worry about it." That article was titled "It's Time to Stop Living the American Scam." It resonated deeply and widely, which is to say it went viral.

In March 2023, the *Times* published another, more expansive essay, this one by Jessica Grose, about the specific and special disillusionments that American millennials were feeling. It went even *more* viral. "Is This It?" was the headline, while the subhead explained: "Millennials are hitting middle age—and it doesn't look like what we were promised." Grose ticked off "cascading crises" since 2001 that had contradicted millennials' previous understanding of their world and undercut their ability to navigate it with the success that some preceding generations achieved. "Our childhoods," she wrote, "were marked by an unusually high level of prosperity in the United States and the expectation that such stability would continue." It didn't, and the millennials whom she interviewed for her essay "said they felt they couldn't be having a midlife crisis because there was no bourgeois numbness to rebel against. Rather than longing for adventure and release, they craved a sense of safety and calmness, which they felt they had never known."

Their craving was at least partly rational. Saddled with much higher college debt than their parents had accrued, landing their first jobs in the shadow of the worst recession since the Dust Bowl, living in childhood bedrooms into their twenties as housing costs skyrocketed and the traditional markers of adulthood and independence receded into life's horizon, millennials could be forgiven for a sense of generational ennui. A major 2016 study by the Harvard economist Raj Chetty, the Stanford sociologist David Grusky, and several other prominent scholars found that social mobility had decreased markedly for millennial Americans, meaning those born between the early 1980s and the late 1990s. The study's authors explained that they were measuring mobility "by comparing children's household incomes at age 30 (adjusted for inflation using the Consumer Price Index) with their parents' household incomes at age 30." And they found that while 90 percent of children born in 1940 had exceeded their parents' earnings, only 50 percent born in the 1980s had. "These findings are unaffected by using alternative price indices to adjust for inflation, accounting for taxes and transfers, measuring incomes at later ages, and adjusting for changes in household size," they wrote. They titled the study "The Fading American Dream."

More current data complicates that picture, showing that over recent years, millennials have enjoyed a strong job market that has enabled them, belatedly, to build wealth at levels close to that of their Gen X parents. Millennials who graduated from college have fared especially well. And the picture has been brightening even for those without college degrees: after decades of stasis, working-class wages began to rise in the years just before and following the Covid pandemic. Regardless, the narrative of a generation scarred by hardship has persisted, driven in part by the fact that expectations for the timing of major life milestones—marriage, home ownership, offspring—haven't shifted all that much since World War II, even as the economy and changing social mores have pushed those milestones deeper into life.

That hardship narrative is driven, too, by the fact that catching up to previous generations isn't the same as outpacing and outachieving them, which is what the idea of America demands. "This country's identity does not depend on having merely a good standard of living or a better one than many decades ago," my *Times* colleague

David Leonhardt wrote in his 2023 book, *Ours Was the Shining Future: The Story of the American Dream*. "It depends on progress in our time." Economically and in other ways, he concluded, that progress had stalled—hence the *Was* instead of *Is* before the *Shining Future* in the book's title. "The United States is suffering through its worst period of stagnation in living standards since the Great Depression," Leonhardt determined. "I refer to it as the Great American Stagnation."

Millennials are hardly the only ones whose tether to good old-fashioned (and partly apocryphal) American optimism is conspicuously looser. The adolescent mental-health crisis in the early 2020s suggested a measure of hopelessness about the future among teenagers. In a haunting essay in the *Times* in October 2022, the clinical psychologist Jamieson Webster probed that feeling, writing that these teenagers were touching "an open wound in this society: What happens when we realize the escalator—so crucial to the American dream—didn't go anywhere (and maybe never really worked, at least not for many?)"

At least several times a year beginning in 1979, the Gallup organization has polled Americans on the question of whether they are generally satisfied or dissatisfied with "the way things are going in the United States." It has tracked and graphed those answers across the decades. And what's most instantly striking and remarkable about those results is that up until 2004, the share of Americans who professed satisfaction routinely crested 50 percent and even 60 percent. But since January 2004, it has never again reached or exceeded 50 percent. It has almost consistently been below 40 percent, and it has quite often been below 30 or even 20 percent. In early January 2021—when the Capitol was stormed—it plunged to 11 percent.

That's what I mean by the stubborn fog around our shining city, whose glimmer gets harder and harder to remember. Within our stubborn fog, the American suicide rate increased each year from 2000 through 2018, and while it toggled slightly downward in 2019 and again in 2020, it rose anew in 2021 and, according to provisional data, rose again in 2022. Within our stubborn fog, American life expectancy isn't climbing the way it once did. It dropped in recent years. "Even before the pandemic, life expectancy in the U.S. declined for consecutive years in 2015 and 2016, largely because of the opioid epidemic and drug overdoses," Derek Thompson noted in an article in the *Atlantic* in September 2022. Under the headline "America Is a Rich Death Trap," he cited recent research that shows that, in comparison with Europeans, "American babies are more likely to die before they turn 5; American teens are more likely to die before they turn 20; and American adults are more likely to die before they turn 65." The United States "has more guns and gun violence than any other rich country," he wrote. Also, more drug-overdose deaths and an unusually high death rate from road accidents. He concluded: "Despite our extraordinary wealth, innovation, and panoply of glittering appliances, Americans overall suffer from something like a lifelong death premium."

For the subgroup of white working-class Americans between the ages of forty-five and fifty-four, life expectancy hasn't simply dropped in some recent years but has generally been dropping *since* 2000, making them "one of the only demographics in the world that has seen its life expectancy fall," as Jeff Bloodworth wrote in the *Free Press* in March 2023. He was referring to research in the 2020 book *Deaths of Despair and the Future of Capitalism*, by the Princeton economists Anne Case and Angus Deaton, and he correctly noted: "These deaths are mostly suicides. Some are officially blamed on alcoholism and addiction, but that's just suicide in slow motion." Bloodworth added that just as "the working class is succumbing to our increasingly digitized, globalized, automated, post-industrial era, the working stiffs—the assembly-line workers, welders, mechanics, miners and their kin, the people who once made up the working class—are tacitly acknowledging that they have no role anymore."

Within our stubborn fog, "a coalition of intellectual catastrophists on the American right" has been working feverishly—and with considerable success—to convince Republican officeholders, political strategists, and judges "that the country is on the verge of collapse," Damon Linker wrote in the *New York Times* in late 2023. "Some catastrophists take it a step further and suggest that officials might contemplate overthrowing liberal democracy in favor of revolutionary regime change or even imposing a right-wing dictatorship on the country." The catastrophists are numerous enough that Linker provided a taxonomy of them: The ones who dream of a theocracy of sorts, the monarchy-curious types, the self-styled he-men yearning for a more primitive past. Their fantasies differ, but not their assessment of America as a nation in terrible trouble.

Within our stubborn fog, a kind of nihilism spreads, a "rot at the very soul of our nation," as Mike Allen wrote in his *Axios* newsletter on the morning of March 28, 2023. Under the headline "We're Not OK," he summarized the results of a *Wall Street Journal*/NORC poll of more than a thousand American adults early that month. It not only confirmed the oft-chronicled collapse of faith in American institutions but also showed an abandonment of tradition and traditional values. Only 38 percent of respondents said that patriotism was very important, in contrast to 70 percent of respondents from a similar *Journal*/NBC survey a quarter century earlier, in 1998. Over that time frame, the percentage of respondents who deemed religion very important dropped to 39 percent from 62 percent, while the percentage who deemed community involvement very important dropped to 27 percent from 47 percent.

Did these various trends and statistics inform Americans' waxing pessimism, or did they reflect it? Impossible to say. Either way, they affirmed it. So did all the zombies.

Over the past few decades, I have read countless words on what the popularity and ubiquity of the Kardashians have to say about America—how they capture its commercialism, its greed, its veneers, its injectables. But the walking dead are a much better barometer. Every era gets the monsters it deserves—Frankenstein as a metaphor for the uncertainties of industrialization and scientific progress, Godzilla after the world went nuclear, Hannibal Lecter for the foodie set. (I'm kidding, *mostly,* about that last example.) Our era has pustular, purulent humanoids who roam postapocalyptic hellscapes and are so desperate to survive that they've jettisoned altruism and etiquette in favor of a brunch of your innards. And we have a grillion of them, all with plenty of work across all forms of entertainment, from streaming to gaming. If popular culture is one of an era's most telling mirrors, we seem to see ourselves as zombies—deprived of free will, manipulated by social structures and systems that we can't control, desperate, merciless, grotesque, and effectively dead.

Zombie movies are so numerous that if you ask Wikipedia for a list of them, the alphabetized results—a disproportionate share of which are from the past two decades—take up dozens of screens and require such extensive scrolling that you need a bowl of buttered popcorn just for that. Meanwhile, there have been so many zombies on cable networks and streaming services that the website

Rotten Tomatoes has a special Tomatometer just for "Best Zombie TV Shows." It opened my eyes to an ornate oeuvre beyond such conspicuously zombie-forward touchstones as HBO's *The Last of Us*, to zombies where I hadn't even realized there *were* zombies: Every time that Netflix had suggested I watch *Santa Clarita Diet*, starring Drew Barrymore and Timothy Olyphant, I took a look at the image of the two comely stars in the Southern California sunshine and assumed that the comedy was about cardio and paleo in the cradle of all fads. Only when I spotted it high (number seven!) on the Tomatometer for zombies did I read up on it and realize that the "diet" in question was human flesh, craved by Barrymore's character after some freaky metamorphosis. The shows on the cable network AMC that received the most acclaim may have been *Breaking Bad* and *Mad Men*, but neither was nearly as popular—or as crucial to the network's fortunes— as *The Walking Dead*, which premiered in October 2010 and not only became AMC's biggest hit but also "remade AMC into a *Walking Dead* delivery system," as Ben Lindbergh wrote in *The Ringer*, with spin-offs including *The Walking Dead: World Beyond*, *Fear the Walking Dead*, *Tales of the Walking Dead*, and *The Walking Dead: Dead City*.

Almost always, the zombies are harbingers, emblems, or by-products of a world-threatening or world-destroying event. They're apocalyptic emissaries, the ravenous and furious flotsam from a world used up, worn out, poisoned, plundered. In that sense they're mascots for modern pessimism. And they belong to a broader, bloated genre of dystopian television, film, and fiction. For the past few decades, cineplexes and streaming services have been awash in visions of societies in ruins, be the cause climate change (*The Day After Tomorrow*, *Snowpiercer*, *After Earth*), general environmental degradation (the various *Mad Max* installments, *Wall-E*, *The Happening*, *The Road*), or some vaguely sketched political dysfunction, usually having to do with tyrannical haves and powerless have-nots. It's the same with bookstores, and while portraits of dystopias both plausible and fantastical have long captured the imaginations of directors and writers, their recent ubiquity may be unrivaled (especially when you factor in the zombies).

"We're saturated with dystopia," Nicholas Junkerman, an English professor at Skidmore College, told Charley Locke for a 2017 article in *Wired*, adding that when he was sketching out a course on dystopian and utopian narratives, the former far outnumbered the latter. For an article in the *Washington Post* in 2019, Calvert Jones and Celia Paris searched news sources in the LexisNexis database for mentions of "dystopia" or "dystopian" across the decades. They found only five in 1985. But, they added, "that number increased dramatically every five years—and by last year, it had shot up to 25,078." They concluded that "Americans are more interested in dystopian fiction than ever, particularly in totalitarian-dystopian fiction."

They're drawn to worlds like the candy-colored but blood-soaked colosseum in *Squid Game*, a dystopian nightmare of the most lugubrious order—and the most watched series that Netflix has ever presented, its 1.65 billion hours of views putting it 300 million hours ahead of the peak season of *Stranger Things*. *Squid Game*'s unrivaled reach is all the more remarkable for several factors: it's a Korean-language production, so most of its audience had to choose between dubbed and subtitled versions; it commanded special favor among viewers under thirty, who weren't thought to be keen on such formats; and its extreme grimness and brutality make other dystopian visions look cheery. *The Hunger Games*, with its own life-and-death contests, is a sylvan romp next to this labyrinth of horrors.

The plot, for those who didn't, um, treat themselves: A group of 456 people are so irredeemably in debt that they agree to be transported to an island and imprisoned in a bizarre arena where they compete in adult iterations of children's games whose losers are slaughtered, most often with a bullet to the head. Aware of the stakes and knowing that only one person can reach the winner's circle—i.e., *survive*—they elect to continue "playing," because they've been promised a future-changing amount of prize money and their existences before and beyond the arena, in a society with an almost unfathomable divide between rich and poor, were just as dehumanizing and held even less promise. In the first episode, in a scene that calls to mind a school shooting, the contestants play a game of red light, green light, and the ones who fail to stop or stand still quickly and fully enough are gunned down. As the bodies crumple to the ground, an unidentified mastermind watching the massacre from a nearby aerie cues up music and pours a cocktail to savor along with the spectacle. God is an assassin, tipsy and merciless in his gilded lair.

Squid Game became more than a hit; it became a cultural phenomenon. It debuted in mid-September 2021. By mid-October, the hashtag #SquidGame had been viewed on TikTok more than 22.8 billion times. By Halloween, costumes based on *Squid Game* were all the rage. There were *Squid Game* pop-up stores. There were recipes inspired by *Squid Game*. All of that paid homage to a nine-episode extravaganza of haplessness and death whose second episode begins with the boxed corpses of hundreds of gunned-down contestants being loaded into incinerators. One of the bodies twitches; its fingers crawl out of a gap between the lid and the rest of the box. So the lid is stapled shut. Into the fire the body goes.

I repeat: This is the most watched show in Netflix history, beloved in particular by young viewers. Maybe that means little, given how phenoms tend to build on themselves, reaching a point where everybody is watching because everybody else is watching. But maybe it means a whole lot. Maybe it factors into and reflects all our seething, all our sniping.

"For America to work, you have to have optimism," Jean Twenge told me. Twenge is a professor of psychology at San Diego State University who, across seven highly regarded books, has explored changes in Americans from one generation to the next, including a waxing narcissism, an intensifying sense of entitlement, and the addling, isolating effects of smartphones and other modern technology. It's not a sunny area of research, but it's an essential one. And it has revealed to her a faltering faith in the American experiment, a pronounced drift from the idea that this country is a charmed and virtuous one.

"That shows up in lots of survey data as a really pervasive negativity, especially among Gen Z but among Millennials, too," she said. The Millennial and Gen Z generations, in that order, cover people who were born between 1981 and 2012 and, in 2024, would be anywhere from twelve to forty-three. She noted that majorities of Americans in both of those groups say they disagree with the statement that the United States is a fundamentally fair society where everyone has a chance to get ahead. But that finding, she said, doesn't intrigue and unsettle her as much as a related but separate one. She told me that when contemporary Americans were asked whether they believe that the founders of the United States are better described as heroes or as villains, "hardly any Boomers said 'villains.'" (Boomers are people born between 1946 and 1964—the so-called Baby Boom.) "*Forty percent* of Gen Z said 'villains,' which is just stunning."

"What are the social consequences of that view?" she asked.

Whether it's more or less correct than a conventionally patriotic take, she said, "it explains a lot about our politics right now—the pessimism, the negativity." I observed that it's antithetical to the mythology of the country—to the words on the Statue of Liberty, to President George H. W. Bush's "thousand points of light," to President Barack Obama's presentation of himself as living proof of the American dream. "That's absolutely true," she said. "That's what we're struggling with right now. For capitalism to work, there has to be the idea that you can pull yourself up by your bootstraps. And for democracy to work, you have to trust that the government will have the people's interests at heart."

I've been working as a journalist for nearly four decades, and for nearly four decades, I've listened to American politicians talk about growth, growth, growth. I've heard them say it at the national level, at the state level, at the city level. We'll grow our way out of fiscal crunches. We'll get the money to attend to certain social ills by, well, expanding productivity and attracting investment and using that investment wisely. We shouldn't and needn't quibble too nastily over how to slice the pie because we can instead make the pie bigger— that's what we Americans do.

The politicians didn't always use that exact metaphor or language, but they used that line of thinking, and there are obvious reasons. It's not popular to say, "Sorry, there'll be less for you over here because we need more for them over there." And saying that, they presume, is no way to cultivate amity and comity.

So what happens to amity—and comity—when politicians can't sell that thinking anymore? When few people believe it? Do those people get more possessive of and pettier about whatever share of the aggregate wealth they possess? Do they see themselves not in collaboration but in competition with the people around them, so that when they determine they're not "winning"—which Trump promised them they'd return to and tire of once they put him in charge—they feel anxious, angry, aggrieved?

Benjamin Friedman, a professor of political economy at Harvard University, wrote a 2005 book, *The Moral Consequences of Economic Growth*, that addressed that question. He cast his gaze backward at a few centuries of American and European history to argue that economic stagnation and pessimism are welcome mats for repression, for authoritarianism, for all manner of closed thinking and ungenerous impulses. We're mean when we're lean. And when we're fat and happy? Friedman observed that robustly growing, optimistic societies are more likely to expand rights to more people and show a stronger commitment to democracy. The book had critics, who argued that events didn't graft quite as neatly onto Friedman's thesis as he suggested. But Friedman furnished plenty of evidence for his conclusions, and there was—and is—a human logic and emotional wisdom to them as well.

In *How Civil Wars Start*, which extracts lessons from hundreds of such conflicts in the past to sound alarms about the future, the political scientist Barbara F. Walter gave several of her early chapters titles that chart the conditions that tilt a country in the direction of violence and dissolution. "When Hope Dies" was one of them. "Citizens can absorb a lot of pain," she wrote in that chapter. "They will accept years of discrimination and poverty and remain quiet, enduring the ache of slow decline. What they can't take is the loss of hope. It's when a group looks into the future and sees nothing but additional pain that they start to see violence as their only path to progress."

Jon Meacham vented similar concerns in *The Soul of America*: "Extremism, racism, nativism, and isolationism, driven by fear of the unknown, tend to spike in periods of economic and social stress—a period like our own." Trump was midway through his presidency when Meacham made that assessment, and he noted that "the alienated are being mobilized afresh by changing demography, by broadening conceptions of identity, and by an economy that prizes Information Age brains over manufacturing brawn."

Andrew Potter, the author of *On Decline*, pondered the implications of a grinding national pessimism in a 2021 op-ed in the *Globe and Mail* of Toronto. "Economic growth doesn't just give us more stuff, it tends to make us better people," he wrote. "When everyone believes that things are getting better—that the pie is getting bigger for everyone and will continue to do so—they become more open to newcomers and more sanguine about diversity. But when growth slows or stalls, the opposite happens. People look at the shrinking pie, look askance at their neighbors, and become more closed-minded and suspicious. This leads to reactionary politics, which are greatly exacerbated by the highly toxic hothouse nature of the internet, especially social media."

Doug Sosnik, the political strategist who wrote in 2014 about many Americans' creeping sense that "the American dream is no longer attainable," told me that the deepening of that feeling has delivered the country to an even darker place a decade later. "It has further ripped apart the idea that we're all in this together," he said, making us less patient, less civil, less kind. And the problem, he explained, isn't just the dread that the pie is finite or contracting. It's people's unprecedentedly acute understanding of how large, medium-sized, or small their slices are—and, more to the point, precisely how those slices differ from others' shares. "You have a society of haves and have-nots" in a manner more pronounced and immediate than in the past, he said. Then he sketched it out for me.

Five

I Love Me, I Hate You, and We Are So Many Rungs Apart

The Joneses and the Johnsons are traveling separately from the metropolitan area where they both happen to live to Orlando, Florida, to go to Disney World. They're leaving from the same airport, on the same flight. The Joneses zip from the curb to the departure gate, because they've paid the premium to vault beyond the minor pampering of TSA precheck to the hassle-free Arcadia of Clear. The Johnsons, without the budget for either, spend thirty-five minutes on the security line. The Joneses are in first class, and they're invited onto the plane a good fifteen minutes before the Johnsons are, and they find plenty of overhead space for their carry-ons. By the time the Johnsons board—after the people in the extra-legroom section behind first class, after the frequent fliers who get dibs next—that space is gone. They must check their bags, which means extra time in the Orlando airport as they idle at the luggage carousel.

The speed and smoothness of the Joneses' experience doesn't end there. Their check-in at their hotel is instantaneous: they've graduated, by dint of their many work and play trips, to an honors category of guests who use a different, special stretch of the counter. When the Johnsons reach their lesser lodging, they stand on yet another slow, long line. And so it goes at Disney World as well. The Joneses shelled out for Genie+ Lightning Lane privileges that allow them to cut ahead of others on many rides. The Johnsons wait and wait, legs cramping, backs knotting, tempers fraying. They had to strategize which rides they'd do in which order, because they may not be able to fit in all the ones that interest them. But perhaps the worst part is that they keep getting glimpses of and brushing up against the Joneses and families like the Joneses, whose no-fuss glide through every stretch of their vacation—through every hour of life—is a kind of taunt. The plane, the hotel, and the amusement park aren't even the half of it.

There have always been big gaps between how the rich, how the middle class, and how the less fortunate live. Inequality is nothing new. But its present iteration is distinctive, and it's distinctive in a manner that encourages grievance. The United States has become an "envy engine," to borrow a phrase from Tom Nichols's *Our Own Worst Enemy*, as never before, thanks not only to the grossly uneven distribution of our wealth but also to the arc and immensity of it. Additionally, cultural developments—social media, in particular—give us more acute, immediate glimpses of how life is different for the people one rung above us, and the people one rung above that, and the ostentatious winners at the top of the ladder.

First, that grossly uneven distribution: In September 2022, the nonpartisan Congressional Budget Office published a report titled "Trends in the Distribution of Family Wealth, 1989 to 2019." It examined changes over that thirty-year period in the United States, and it found that while total wealth in the country tripled, the effects weren't at all the same for the most affluent versus the less and least affluent families. "Family wealth increased more in the top half of the distribution than in the bottom half," the report said. "Families in the top 10 percent and in the top 1 percent of the distribution, in particular, saw their share of total wealth rise over the period. In 2019, families in the top 10 percent of the distribution held 72 percent of total wealth, and families in the top 1 percent of the distribution held more than one-third; families in the bottom half of the distribution held only 2 percent of total wealth."

In March 2023, Matthew Desmond, the Princeton University sociologist whose 2016 book, *Evicted*, won the Pulitzer Prize for general nonfiction, published a follow-up, *Poverty, by America*, that looked in part at increases in income inequality in the United States over recent decades. It noted that wage earners in the bottom 90 percent of income were, on average, making about 24 percent more annually, in inflation-adjusted dollars, than they had been four decades earlier. But the income of people in the top 1 percent of wage earners had gone up more than 100 percent—meaning it had doubled and then some. The book also noted an enormous and persistent wealth gap between white and Black Americans. In 2019, Desmond wrote, the net worth of the median white household was about $188,000. The median Black household? Just over $24,000.

Peter Turchin, the author of the 2023 book *End Times: Elites, Counter-Elites, and the Path of Political Disintegration*, captured the gross disparities of wealth in the United States with a different example. "Back in 1983, 66,000 American households were worth at least $10 million," he wrote in an adaptation of *End Times* published in the *Atlantic* shortly before the book's release. "That may not sound like a lot, but by 2019, controlling for inflation, the number had increased tenfold." There'd been huge increases as well, Turchin said, in households worth $5 million and in millionaires—increases that far outpaced population growth.

That would seem at first glance to be terrific news, he acknowledged. "But at whose expense did elites' wealth swell in recent years?" he rhetorically asked. "Starting in the 1970s, although the overall economy continued to grow, the share of that growth going to average workers began to shrink, and real wages leveled off." And that, he explained, is a recipe for civic trouble according to "a database of hundreds of societies across 10,000 years" that he and his research team built to identify the conditions in which political crisis occurred. It was fueled by not only widespread economic frustration but also what he called a "top-heavy" social pyramid that renders the stakes of rising high versus falling short so great. In the United States, there's yet another volatile factor: over recent years, the population of Americans with college educations, advanced degrees, and other credentials that they've been told are passports to the uppermost percentiles of income and realms of respect expanded much more than the population of that exalted and exclusive class. "More and more people aspiring to positions of power began fighting over a relatively fixed number of spots," Turchin wrote. "The competition among them has corroded the social norms and institutions that govern society."

Our worries about the shrinking pie only sharpen our awareness and resentment of income inequality. But so, paradoxically, does our liberation from even direr concerns, and the present iteration of inequality exists in precisely such a charged, oxymoronic context of pessimism and plenty. As the Congressional Budget Office noted, there was a tripling of national wealth over those thirty years; as

Desmond pointed out, incomes in the bottom 90 percent *did* rise during that time. And that's consistent with the fact that broadly and historically speaking, many of those of us in the richer nations of the world have it good, our most basic needs met and some of the more immediate and overwhelming threats that faced our forebears eliminated, at least for the time being.

Yes, there's a nonstop stream of the depressing news and grave harbingers that turn contemporary life for many people into an accretion of letdowns. Yes, there has been less social mobility in the United States over recent decades than in periods before then, and in the middle class there has been a sort of economic stasis. Below the middle class, there are unacceptable levels of poverty, homelessness, and even hunger in the United States, especially given our resources. Climate change has terrifying implications. Mass shootings mean that today's schoolchildren participate in active shooter drills the way some schoolchildren more than a half century ago girded for the possibility of a nuclear bomb. The Great Recession at least temporarily wiped out the savings of tens of millions of Americans between 2007 and 2009, causing many of them to lose homes whose mortgages they could no longer pay. A decline in American manufacturing has hollowed out many cities and towns between the coasts and contributed to the deadly epidemic of opioid abuse. The Covid pandemic exacerbated economic and social ills. And Russia's invasion of Ukraine in early 2022 and the war between Israel and Hamas in late 2023 provided heartbreaking, terrifying reminders of global instability, tribal hatred, and how profoundly we Americans might be affected by such bloodshed.

But we don't fear that missiles will be raining down on us, not in any real and immediate way. We haven't been engaged in the kind of military conflict that necessitated a draft since the Vietnam

War. The Great Recession wasn't the Great Depression, the likes of which we haven't seen since its end in 1941, just like we haven't seen anything remotely similar to the Second World War since *its* end in 1945. What we've observed instead is astonishingly swift scientific progress, including medical advances that have alleviated our suffering and technological strides that have created efficiencies, conveniences, and amusements that were once the province of futuristic fiction. Back in 1945, according to the Digital History project of the University of Houston's College of Education, "nearly a third of Americans lived in poverty. A third of the country's homes had no running water, two-fifths lacked flushing toilets, and three-fifths lacked central heating. More than half of the nation's farm dwellings had no electricity. Most African Americans still lived in the South, where racial segregation in schools and public accommodations was still the law." We think of the 1950s as a boom time in the United States, and it was, but at the end of that decade, more than 20 percent of Americans still lived in poverty, according to the US Census Bureau. By 2021, according to Census Bureau figures, which typically lag several years behind, fewer than 12 percent did.

Those strides help explain a strain of thinking—of counterpessimism—captured in Steven Pinker's 2011 book, *The Better Angels of Our Nature: Why Violence Has Declined*, and reflected anew in a 2018 book by the Swedish physician and statistician Hans Rosling, *Factfulness: Ten Reasons We're Wrong about the World—and Why Things Are Better Than You Think*, which made not only a fan but also an evangelist of Bill Gates, who offered to provide a copy of it to any 2018 college graduate who requested one. Those strides also informed a frequently cited speech that Obama delivered in Hanover, Germany, in April 2016. At that moment, in the last of his eight years as president, he pulled back from the sorts of struggles and squabbles that might dominate a given news cycle and took the long view:

"We are fortunate to be living in the most peaceful, most prosperous, most progressive era in human history. That may surprise young people who are watching TV or looking at your phones and it seems like only bad news comes through every day. But consider that it's been decades since the last war between major powers. More people live in democracies. We're wealthier and healthier and better educated, with a global economy that has lifted up more than a billion people from extreme poverty and created new middle classes from the Americas to Africa to Asia." He went on to mention the remarkable eradication of once-devastating diseases. Then, as a sort of summary, he said, "If you had to choose a moment in time to be born, any time in human history, and you didn't know ahead of time what nationality you were or what gender or what your economic status might be, you'd choose today."

That appraisal came, obviously, before the ascendance of Trump, before the spread of his conspiracy theories and his nihilism, before the intensifying appeal and power of autocrats, would-be autocrats, and autocratic impulses around the world. It came before Covid, which caused tens of millions of deaths globally and depleted the financial reserves of many, many more people than that. It came before war in Ukraine, before the slaughter in Israel on October 7, 2023, and Israel's subsequent bombing of Gaza.

But none of that erases Obama's assessment or renders it obsolete. The astonishingly rapid invention and distribution of vaccines against Covid and treatments for it essentially make one of his points. A rational assessment of our affairs, not some cracked Pollyanna complex, prompted the writer Chris Taylor to posit in an article in *Mashable* that "the data suggests that right here right now in 2020 is literally the best time we could possibly be alive, with the greatest opportunities available to the greatest number, and the lowest threat of death, Trump and the climate notwithstanding." The longtime political analyst George F. Will made a similar argument. "Progress, a wit once said, was fine for a while but it went on too long," Will wrote at the start of a column in the *Washington Post* in November 2022. And at the end of that column: "The fundamental economic problem of attaining subsistence having been banished by plenty, many hyper-politicized Americans have filled the void in their lives with the grim fun of venting their animosities."

Nichols's take, in *Our Own Worst Enemy*: "Had anyone said forty or fifty years ago that everything from energy to clothing would be cheaper and better, that food would be so plentiful that we wouldn't know what to do with most of it, that the Soviet Union would vanish peacefully and that we would dismantle tens of thousands of nuclear weapons, or that diseases that once struck fear into us were curable, most people would have burst out laughing at such utopianism. This is the twenty-first century. We were supposed to be choking on overpopulation, eating Soylent Green, and joining gangs in the wasteland to protect our supplies of water and gasoline. Instead, we're put out when the Wi-Fi goes down on our flights to Orlando."

And we're put out because of *expectations*. That word—that dynamic—is key. People's degrees of happiness and unhappiness typically have less to do with their circumstances per se than with their circumstances measured against what they'd reasonably aspired to, what they'd been encouraged to hope for, what they'd deemed possible. Generally rising wealth in the United States from the 1950s through the 1990s upsized Americans' expectations, while our desires were whetted by marketing that grew ever cleverer at making consumers want, want, want. When a country fills people with longings while telling them that only a shortfall of initiative stands between them and material satisfaction, it's a breeding ground not just for achievement but also for disappointment, which is its own special, bitter circle of discontent. In today's America, that circle is large indeed.

Those yardsticks include all those perks the Joneses enjoyed, which are representative of the highly visible and relentlessly multiplying badges of affluence all around us. While we have long advertised our places in the pecking order with our homes, cars, clubs, and clothes, there are now extravagances, fringe benefits, and microclimates of exclusivity that didn't exist before. The plane mirrors the sports arena, in which luxury boxes take up more space than they used to and there are other special (but not *as* special) entrances and dining options for spectators who can't quite ascend to that celestial level but have a purchasing power greater than the plebeians'.

When I was a teenager in the late 1970s and early 1980s and went to the big concerts of major performers, different sections of seating had different prices, but they fell into a few general categories. A person's proximity to the stage often had less to do with her financial reserves than with how quickly and heroically she'd acted to get her tickets. I once showed up at the box office of what was then called the Hartford Civic Center at three in the morning, in pitch darkness, to be in place when tickets for a Queen concert went on sale several hours later. That was the surest path to the best seats—my friends and I ended up in the eighth row, where I caught Freddie Mercury's tambourine when he threw it into the crowd at the conclusion of the band's final song—and there was something egalitarian about it. But the seating maps for various stops on Taylor

Swift's 2023 tour revealed scores and scores of price tags, tailored with extreme specificity to the precise desirability of the vantage point. The highest ones were many thousands of dollars above the lowest ones: a family of four or five posting photos of themselves among other ecstatic Swifties as showtime neared was in some cases announcing to the world its ability to drop ten thousand dollars or more on one night's entertainment. But while the price range for Swift exceeded the price range for a garden-variety superstar, the exacting tiering of the experience was a common phenomenon in the world of live music.

When I was a teenager, school essentially came in two sizes: public or private. Now, private is the starting point, with many costly but broadly applied add-ons: the tutors for special subjects; the separate tutor for standardized exams; the individual sports coach; the independent college admissions consultant who (for a hefty fee!) does more plotting and pacifying than the counselors already on the school's staff are able to. When I was a teenager, you were posh if you belonged to a private gym (versus, say, the YMCA); the brand of that gym and the level of your membership weren't relevant. Now? Planet Fitness and Equinox are solar systems of pampering apart. And at some of the Equinoxes of the galaxy, different clients pay significantly different sums for personal trainers, in accordance with that ab whisperer's determined gradation of expertise. Those clients can also pay a surcharge for a better locker room, a surcharge for certain other sanctums. And none of that is unnoticed by or unnoticeable to the other customers. Its noticeableness is perhaps part of the point; aspiration and perspiration go together. The emphasis of the American economy may have changed over the years from manufacturing to services. But one product we make in abundance is distinctions.

They show up everywhere—my favorite example, a richly emblematic one, being the Ironman XC. The *Times* wrote about it in late 2022, explaining that it's a small, privileged, pampered group of Ironman athletes within the larger field of people in the competition, which involves 2.4 miles of swimming followed by 112 miles of cycling capped off with 26.2 miles of running. You'd think that someone committing to such a herculean physical ordeal—someone investing and taking pride in hardship itself—would be frill-averse, or at least frill-self-conscious. You'd be wrong, as the existence of Ironman XC demonstrates. (XC stands for "executive challenge.") According to the *Times*, "A typical Ironman race field has about 2,000 competitors, and the entry fee is between $475 and $675. The XC pool in such a race is 10 to 15, and the fee ranges between $5,700 and $15,000. In addition to being a C-level executive, applicants are generally referred for consideration and sit for an interview, though it's less onerous than it sounds, more of a jerk filter than an admissions process."

An XC competitor gets a superior room at the hotel closest to the starting line, the better to begin the swim as fresh and focused as possible. That room has a minifridge stocked with the competitor's favorite fuels. There are helpers, like a bike mechanic, available to troubleshoot any last-minute problems with equipment or gear. Troy Ford, whom the *Times* identified as "XC's tireless, unflappable master of ceremonies," told the article's author, Devin Gordon, that his goal is to "take all the logistics, headaches, hassles and hurdles" out of the race and "make it really easy" on his clients. The photographs accompanying the article suggested that Ironman XC competitors are oddly comfortable with advertising that ease. One of them appeared in a swimsuit and a swimming cap that both prominently displayed the initials *XC*.

Back in the realm of flabby, fatigued mortals, Uber allows customers to specify, when booking a ride, precisely how regal and roomy the vehicle should be. If they see themselves in an SUV, then an SUV is the chariot in which others will see them, too. When people subscribe to many online newsletters, they're presented with levels of access and get more content, packaged as an insider's exclusive trove, when they pay more. Some streaming services hew to a similar pattern, allowing subscribers freedom from advertisements—and, thus, from interruptions—if they're able and willing to shell out for it. That captures another aspect of our tiered living: the inequality of time. On lower rungs of the economic ladder, people lose hours and hours of it; higher up, they're liberated in a manner that allows them even greater concentration on their paid work and thus gives them yet another advantage atop the advantages they already had. Like the Ironman XC competitor, they're closer to the starting line, in a position to sprint more readily and energetically into the task at hand.

And that's not hidden from the less fortunate. Quite the opposite. The family at the Swift concert epitomizes the way in which social media platforms present a nonstop stream of braggart postcards from other people's lives. Just as there are new echelons of coddling, there are new portals and peepholes, and they present a warped view. On Facebook, on Instagram, somebody is always raising a glass of champagne at a wedding in a tropical locale while the sun is setting in a gorgeous mosaic of colors. Somebody just bought the most amazing pair of impossible-to-find shoes. Somebody got a promotion. Somebody got into Yale.

The negative effect of social media's lacquered scenes on adolescents' and teenagers' mental health has been established, to a point where in May 2023, US Surgeon General Vivek Murthy issued a special advisory that warned young people and their parents about the proven harms of spending hours daily on social media. Those harms included the low self-esteem that can arise from comparisons to peers whose lives, thanks to the selective editing that social media makes possible, seem so effortless, so joyful, so blessed. But adults on social media also suffer from exposure to the Potemkin perfection of friends, neighbors, and colleagues. And it takes a toll on our *civic* health.

"Hyper-connection enables citizens to parade all of the worst aspects of an affluent culture—especially conspicuous consumerism—in front of each other in a game of perpetual one-upmanship," Nichols wrote. "Americans, permanently connected and constantly performing, now showcase an idealist version of their lives to each other every day, inundating each other with pictures of vacations, cars and other life achievements and trophies. Instead of building trust, we build enmity." Nichols noted that even "small differences in lifestyles become magnified over the internet," which is a cruel tool for measurement, producing the "deep and abiding envy and resentment that plagues life in the modern democracies."

Other facets of contemporary life abet and exacerbate social media's scarily efficient production of those emotions. We're self-obsessed in a manner that many of our ancestors weren't, and that's partly a result of our affluence: when your day isn't organized around survival, it can include ample self-care. Self-care, self-actualization, self-esteem: those are heavy-rotation hyphenates that were relatively obscure a half century ago, before the 1970s, famously dubbed the "Me Decade" in a 1976 cover story in *New York* magazine by Tom Wolfe. In retrospect, "Me Decade" was a misnomer; "Me Turning Point" would have been more accurate, because the period of time since has been a nonstop me jamboree.

In his 2022 book *Liberalism and Its Discontents*, which can be read to some degree as an explanation of why his declared *End of History* didn't quite work out that way, the political scientist Francis Fuku-yama nodded to all the modern talk of personal wellness and all the energy put into it, and he wondered how those preoccupations per-haps reflected—and degraded—our politics. "One might ask, what is so terrible about a society in which individuals seek to actualize them-selves in diverse ways, from yoga to health diets to Soul Cycling?" he wrote. He then offered a few answers to his own question, the first of which was that "belief in the sovereignty of the individual deepens liberalism's tendency to weaken other forms of communal engage-ment, and in particular turns people away from virtues like public-spiritedness." Indeed, attendance at religious services, engagement in other communal activities, and active participation in our commu-nities seem to be in perpetual decline—we are, as the political sci-entist Robert Putnam chronicled and presaged in the famous title of his keen 2000 treatise on community breakdown, *Bowling Alone*—but self-examination and self-definition are 24/7 occupations.

Do you put real milk, soy "milk," or oat "milk" in your coffee? To listen to people describe the decision-making process behind their morning beverage—be it coffee or tea, frothed or iced—is to realize that nutrition has little or nothing to do with it. It's a cultural state-ment. An act of identity. So is how people exercise, what they binge-watch, which hobbies they take up. All those choices are the building blocks of their personal brands (and are also, not coincidentally, fod-der for their Facebook posts and Instagram stories). To attend to those brands is to privilege the private over the public, to gaze inward rather than outward, and that's not a great facilitator of common cause, common ground, compromise. But it's a road map to grievance, which sometimes lies at the confluence of pessimism and narcissism.

One of Jean Twenge's early books, written with another psychologist, Keith Campbell, is titled *The Narcissism Epidemic*, and it argues that we live in a time of extraordinary selfishness and entitlement, marked by "the odd perpetual adolescence of many American adults." She and Campbell name several principal reasons. One is the internet, including social media, which has given us a means to withdraw from real, physical engagement with others—the kind that forces us to consider them as much as we do ourselves—and to lavish attention on our own personas, which are now manipulable, marketable, and measurable with a whole new set of tools. A teenager on Facebook, Instagram, or TikTok creates content that's aimed at eliciting a positive reaction—"likes," shares—from as big an audience as possible, then monitors the odometer of approval, feeling little jolts of pride as the numbers climb.

Another reason for runaway narcissism is a parenting style over recent decades that focuses on affirmation—be stinting with punishment, generous with praise—and an analogous educational approach that emphasizes validation, protection, comfort. Children and young adults shouldn't be unsettled or provoked by what happens at school; they should be placated. Everyone should get a trophy. Participation—not winning or losing—matters most. No one should feel "less than," a suddenly ubiquitous phrase that requires no object, its voguishness obviating any specificity. Many high schools have dispensed with valedictorians: acknowledging one student's achievement as superior means telling many other students that their achievements are inferior. In early 2023, it emerged that more than a dozen schools in northern Virginia hadn't told students that they'd achieved National Merit awards, determined by their performances on a standardized test, in time to mention that coveted distinction on college applications. School administrators supposedly didn't want word of the students' good fortune to distress or disappoint peers who hadn't done as well.

The social psychologist Jonathan Haidt and the lawyer and free-speech advocate Greg Lukianoff examined that kind of thinking in their 2018 book, *The Coddling of the American Mind: How Good Intentions and Bad Ideas Are Setting Up a Generation for Failure.* I'm glad they put "good intentions" in the title: I don't think there's any nefariousness in wanting to tamp down the most cutthroat competition in society, in recognizing the vulnerability of boys and girls still lurching toward adulthood, in wanting to carve out at least a few places and a few moments ungoverned by sorting, ranking, rating. But when do those impulses and the actions that arise from them become a denial of reality and rejection of maturity? When are they unhealthy both for the individuals in question and society at large?

Those were among Haidt's and Lukianoff's concerns as they marveled at college campuses where lists of "microaggressions" kept expanding, "safe spaces" multiplied, and professors issued "trigger warnings" about content in books and discussions that might upset students. They wrote of "three Great Untruths that seem to have spread widely in recent years: 1. The Untruth of Fragility: *What doesn't kill you makes you weaker.* 2. The Untruth of Emotional Reasoning: *Always trust your feelings.* 3. The Untruth of Us Versus Them: *Life is a battle between good people and evil people.*"

Based on my experience since July 2021 as a professor at Duke University, I can say that campus life everywhere hasn't been subsumed entirely by these untruths—not even close. But seriously affected? Indeed. If a writing assignment includes the option of autobiography, most students will choose autobiography. They want to investigate their own emotions. In papers and in class discussions, many (though by no means all) students emphasize feelings, the bruising of which, no matter the cause or context, is terrible. And many students have an absolutist view of political right and political wrong, with progressive students, who constitute the majority at Duke, instantly drawn and potently attached to any policy or demand that's tucked under the rubric of "social justice." They're on patrol for "white supremacy" and "transphobia" in particular, and when they detect it, they demonstrate less interest in analyzing and understanding what they're seeing than in eradicating it. It is an us-versus-them, good-versus-evil take on the world.

One of my students once insisted that Republicans opposed to abortion rights were motivated by white supremacy; according to her, white women were more likely to have abortions than Black women, so Republicans wanted to preserve white numbers and white dominance. When I corrected her, citing statistics that Black women were nearly four times as likely to have abortions as white women, she was shocked into silence. I might as well have been telling her that the world was flat after all, or that I'd just spotted the Yeti dipping into the Duke Chapel for a prayer service. Several of my students recoiled at a guest speaker who, in a discussion about Caitlyn Jenner's decision to be photographed in *Vanity Fair* as a sexpot in a bustier, raised interesting questions about who gets to define womanhood and how. The students affixed the TERF tag (trans-exclusionary radical feminist) to the speaker, essentially putting a big red X over her. No point in rummaging through her ideas, in engaging with, poking at, and testing them. She was a fossil and a bigot.

As for the primacy of feelings, I have been present, in different professional settings, for long discussions about the need to address how a group of people within an organization were feeling or might feel that barely or never paused to ask whether those feelings were warranted or legitimate. The presumption was that any such assessment was too subjective—or, in some cases, too prone to bias—to be meaningful. Feelings had to be dealt with, period, and dealing with them meant yielding to them, lest a person be insulted, estranged, or harmed in some other way. While that kind of coddling is most prevalent among people on the left, the triumph of a feeling-shaped, feeling-centric, feeling-governed reality isn't contained to any one ideological predisposition or political party. It's plenty vivid—and has wrought damage aplenty—on the right.

One of my favorite deconstructions of the January 6 insurrection was the NPR podcast *Will Be Wild*, which was released in mid-2022 and took its title from a tweet with which Trump, in the waning days of his presidency, summoned his supporters to the nation's capital. ("Statistically impossible to have lost the 2020 Election," he wrote on December 19, 2020. "Big protest in D.C. on January 6th. Be there, will be wild!") The first of the podcast's eight parts introduced Natalie Jangula, a sunny-sounding woman who answered Trump's call. She lived in Nampa, Idaho, a city of about a hundred thousand people in the Boise metropolitan area. She worked in a financial management firm. She had two children who, according to a biographical sketch that she later posted online, "have provided her with a bachelor's degree in dealing with roller coaster emotions, a master's degree in wiping up water on the bathroom floor, and a PhD in laundry folding and calendaring." She'd been crowned Mrs. Idaho in 2015. To accompany her to Washington, she chose two other former Mrs. Idahos. From what I could tell, fate hadn't dealt her a terrible hand. She hadn't been cheated.

But she somehow *felt* that she had. Asked why she made her pilgrimage from Idaho, she told NPR's Ilya Marritz that "it felt like something was taken from us." She said that "these feelings just continue to compound—of frustration." She began to wonder, in her words, "what can I do to be part of a movement to represent how we are feeling?" *Felt, feelings, feeling*—she didn't define the "something" taken from her and didn't present a substantive case for her support of Trump and her attendance at his rally immediately before the storming of the Capitol, which she didn't join. She presented a diffusely emotional one. But that ambiguous blob of *feelings* was enough for a cross-country flight and a show of solidarity.

Four months after the insurrection, Marjorie Taylor Greene addressed an "America First" rally in Mesa, Arizona, at which the journalist Robert Draper was present. Draper later recounted, in a long profile of her for the *New York Times*' Sunday magazine, her remarks from the stage. They were *feel*-y in the extreme.

"Who do you think won Arizona on November 3?" she asked the crowd, referring to the 2020 presidential election.

People chanted, "Trump, Trump, Trump."

"That's how we feel in Georgia, too," Greene concurred. "As a matter of fact, that's how Michigan feels. Pennsylvania. Wisconsin. I think that's how at least seventy-four million people feel."

She did not emphasize evidence. She emphasized feelings. If so many people felt that way, there had to be something to it. It had to matter. And it couldn't be ignored.

When you give people the message that their feelings are paramount, that they should be protected not only from harm but also from disappointment, and that the world is a morally simple place, how could they *not* react to unfulfilled desires and unpleasant developments with a sense of grievance?

"There's a kind of infantilization in our society," Nicholas Christakis told me, landing on the same word that ricocheted around my mind. Christakis is a celebrated professor of sociology at Yale who has distilled his trailblazing work on how our social networks shape us into a TED Talk and, in 2009, made *Time* magazine's list of the 100 most influential people. But to many Americans, he's best known not for what he has accomplished but for what he was subjected to: taunts and insults from Yale students who swarmed him in a campus courtyard one day in 2015. The video of the encounter went viral.

Beforehand, his wife, Erika Christakis, who was then also teaching at Yale, had circulated a memo in which she questioned a university edict against culturally insensitive Halloween costumes, suggesting that students could police themselves and should have both the freedom to err and the strength to cope with offense. She wrote that her husband concurred. Outrage ensued. Hundreds of students signed an open letter denouncing her and hundreds demanded that the couple be punished. There were protests. And when Nicholas Christakis went to talk with and answer questions from angry students in that courtyard, one young woman, who happened to be Black, seemed to lose control. She *shrieked* at him, and her focus was telling: he and his wife lived among students in a quasi-supervisory role in one of Yale's residential units, Silliman College, and the student wanted him to know that he had befouled what was supposed to be—her words—a "safe space." "Stay quiet!" she yelled when he tried, with admirable calmness, to interject. "It's your job to create a place of comfort and home for the students who live in Silliman," she continued, her voice rising and rising. A few seconds later, she added: "Who the fuck hired you?" And then, shortly after that: "You should not sleep at night! You are disgusting!"

I first met him four years later, in 2019, when he was promoting a new book, *Blueprint*, which wasn't about the Yale ugliness but contained a few obvious allusions to it, including the assertion: "I have seen the effects of overidentifying with one's group and witnessed mass delusions up close." *Blueprint* is an argument for the essential

goodness of human beings—of the evolutionary necessity of that—
and we spoke at length about how strangely that paired with the
two hours he'd spent being pilloried in that courtyard at Yale, which
Erika felt compelled to leave but which remained his employer and
later awarded him the Sterling Professorship, the school's highest
faculty honor. "I do not want to be defined by that event," he told
me. Nor did he want his world to be.

We remained in loose contact, and when I asked him in early
2023 about how quick Americans are to feel aggrieved—not just
young Americans but all Americans—he made that "infantilization" comment. He remarked on how averse to hardship, how *offended* by hardship, so many of us have become, and how negatively
we respond to circumstances that aren't contoured to our liking. As
I listened to him, that enraged-cum-deranged young woman in the
courtyard came back to me. I thought about how representative she
might really be.

"People have been led to believe that they are owed something,
and it's very difficult to accept that they might not be," Christakis
told me. "Maybe it's an aftershock of the American century, the
prosperity, the safety—we take things for granted. We're almost a
victim of our success."

When I later revisited and reflected on his remarks, I found myself focusing not on how overwrought, unnuanced, and downright
cruel the students' treatment of him and his wife had been but on
how illogically it fit its environment. The students were society's
winners, any way you sliced it. They were at a university as storied as
universities come, one with an acceptance rate below 8 percent and
a record of launching its graduates into coveted jobs and dream careers. And the Yale edict with which Erika Christakis had taken issue
reflected an era of greater openness to and promotion of diversity,

both on and beyond the Yale campus. But the students' gilded, charmed environment had failed to yield fully and precisely to their ideals and desires. A crack had opened between their expectations and their reality, and the size of it had no bearing on their fury over its existence. They were not getting what they felt they were owed and had been promised.

Six

Chaos, Clicks, and Catastrophe

It's likely those Yale students had spent considerable time on so-cial media. Ditto for the dozens of students at Evergreen State College in Washington who, in 2017, screamed at and demanded the firing of Bret Weinstein, a biology professor, because he'd dared to raise questions about the method and message of a scheduled Day of Absence during which Black students wanted white students to vacate the campus. Ditto for the hundreds of students at Oberlin College in Ohio who, a year before that, staged protests outside a local bakery and branded its owners racist because they'd brought charges against a Black student whom they'd caught shoplifting wine. (Those owners ultimately sued Oberlin, whose administrators supported the protests and badly damaged the bakery's business, for defamation, and the college agreed to pay a settlement of more than $35 million.) Show me a group of people claiming a degree of offense disproportionate to its supposed justification, demanding a remedy that's similarly out of whack and communicating all of that histrionically, and I'll likely show you a group of people who have been whipped into their frenzy at least in part by what they see on social media—because what they see validates their complaint and models the most impassioned expression of it. That applies not only to the screechers on college campuses. It applies to the screechers on Fox News. To the screechers in state legislatures. To the screechers storming the Capitol on January 6, 2021. To screechers the world over.

Although these matters aren't neatly quantifiable, social media's most significant contribution to the age of grievance surely isn't as an engine of envy. It's as an incubator for anger. That incubation begins with how most of us use social media—and how we let it use us. When we're registering our approval of and sharing content we find on social media, when we're choosing whom to follow and what to invite into our feeds, most of us don't aim for a varied diet, one with the informational and ideological equivalent of this much protein, this much vegetable, this much fiber, this much fat. It's all saucy ribs or all naked tofu. It's one slender band of flavors, one tiny cluster of nutrients.

That's a reflection of our relationship to all media—to entertainment, to news, to knowledge itself. Never before have we had such a buffet to sup at. Never before have we had this much say. The changes in television news in the United States over the past half century perhaps best exemplify that: Once upon a time, for a significant stretch of time, television news meant the evening newscasts of ABC, CBS, NBC, and, to a lesser extent, PBS. Those programs occupied a finite time block, so their producers and anchors couldn't obsess over a given story and turn their viewers into similar obsessives, the way that MSNBC and CNN did with Trump and "Russiagate." (Remember those epic Rachel Maddow monologues?)

The newscasts of yesteryear weren't narrowly aimed at discrete demographic groups, so they sought to be of "general interest," providing a mix of topics—international, national, politics, sports, entertainment, lifestyle—to what they hoped was a mixed audience. Governed by the federal government's Fairness Doctrine (interred in 1987), they had an obligation to present competing viewpoints. And they were for the most part staffed, often robustly, with seasoned journalists who were at least familiar with certain standards and guidelines and thus acted as gatekeepers, albeit imperfect ones, who ideally kept junk information and unabashed partisan advocacy at bay.

All of that hardly added up to some news paradise: there was a profound lack of diversity in who produced and presented the news (white men, for the most part), enormous cultural blind spots in their reporting, and a sort of monolithic determination of what the public did (and didn't) need to know. But Americans got vetted information of a cooler temperature, with less brazen commentary, less self-promoting punditry. They received—and operated from—a common set of facts, which they could speak or spar about with a shared vocabulary. Contrast that to the situation in which Fox News found itself in late 2020, when its executives and its anchors realized that if they contradicted Trump's claim that the election had been stolen from him and accurately chronicled Joe Biden's victory, many of Fox's viewers would jump to one of several smaller cable or internet "news" operations that would confirm their dark suspicions of voter fraud and corrupt election officials. Truth had become a marketplace lousy with merchants, its barrier to entry not just lowered but essentially abolished by the all-permissive internet. Anybody with connectivity and a keypad could shout from the rooftops of cyberspace, broadcasting takes that were often tirades. Anybody could establish presences on YouTube, Facebook, Twitter (since renamed X), Instagram, TikTok. The gatekeepers were gone because the gate itself was gone.

Whom to listen to? To follow? We have a reflexive attraction to what we recognize, what's familiar, what assures us that we've figured out the world and that we belong to a community of the like-minded. And once social media's algorithms kick in, serving us meals precisely like the ones for which we've demonstrated an appetite, there's even less chance we'll expand our taste buds. The internet isn't really rigged to give us right or left, conservative or liberal, at least not until we rig it that way. It gives us more of the same. So if we've been marinating in conservative outrage, we'll get more and more concentrated marinade. Likewise for liberal outrage. Social media tells us how virtuous we are as it also tells us how victimized we should feel.

"Anger and hate is the easiest way to grow on Facebook," Frances Haugen, the Facebook "whistleblower" who disclosed tens of thousands of internal company documents to the government and the *Wall Street Journal*, said when she testified before the British Parliament about the company's practices in October 2021. She was referring in part to how Facebook, trying to build engagement, began prioritizing the content shown to a given user based on which previous posts the user had connected with strongly enough to go beyond the old-fashioned "liking" of it and to assign it one of five emojis that Facebook made available: "love," "haha," "wow," "sad," or "angry." Although some Facebook employees had warned that privileging content prone to elicit "angry" feedback might encourage the purveyors of hate speech and misinformation and lead to the proliferation of both on the platform, Facebook forged ahead with "angry" anyway.

The ethics and impact of that decision aside, it reflected a sound understanding of what got traction. As Max Fisher, the author of *The Chaos Machine: The Inside Story of How Social Media Rewired Our Minds and Our World*, explained in an interview with NPR's Ari Shapiro upon the book's publication in September 2022, Facebook posts, tweets, and YouTube videos that infuriate us "are most engaging to us because they speak to a sense of social compulsion, of a group identity that is 'under threat.' Moral outrage, specifically, is probably the most powerful form of content online."

Fisher elaborated on that in the book itself, a chilling portrait of profit-minded, audience-obsessed tech entrepreneurs devising formulas for engagement often antithetical to the values essential for democratic societies. He described social media as "a machine engineered to distort reality through the lens of tribal conflict and pull users toward extremes." He noted that the metabolism of social media—its bursts of elliptical and selective information, its encouragement of instantaneous reaction—demands that users "rely on quick-twitch social intuition over deliberative reason. All people contain the capacity for both, as well as the potential for the former to overwhelm the latter, which is often how misinformation spreads."

And Fisher wasn't hopeful. "Remember that the number of seconds in your day never changes," he wrote in *The Chaos Machine*. "The amount of social media content competing for those seconds, however, doubles every year or so, depending on how you measure it. Imagine, for instance, that your network produces 200 posts a day, of which you have time to read about 100. Because of the platform's tilt, you will see the most outraged half of your feed. Next year, when 200 doubles to 400, you will see the most outraged quarter; the year after that the most outraged eighth. Over time, your impression of your own community becomes radically more moralizing, aggrandizing, and outraged." Content that appeals to comity, to civility and fusty, cool-headed concepts like that can't compete, their light rendered faint, even invisible, by the crasser, brasher company, "like stars over Times Square."

Among scholars who study social media's effect on political life and review the academic literature about it, there's considerable disagreement about how much blame to place on social media—among various other forces in society—for sorting people into more rigidly partisan camps and blotting out opposing and potentially moderating views. In June 2022, the *New Yorker* published an article by Gideon Lewis-Kraus, "How Harmful Is Social Media?," about what is and isn't known in this regard. Lewis-Kraus used Jonathan Haidt as the principal witness for the prosecution of social media, distilling a few of Haidt's conclusions: "He believes that the tools of virality—Facebook's Like and Share buttons, Twitter's Retweet function—have algorithmically and irrevocably corroded public life. He has determined that a great historical discontinuity can be dated with some precision to the period between 2010 and 2014, when these features became widely available on phones." Lewis-Kraus quoted from an essay that Haidt had recently written for the *Atlantic*, in which Haidt asserted that the rise of social media "unwittingly dissolved the mortar of trust, belief in institutions, and shared stories that had held a large and diverse secular democracy together."

One of my colleagues on the faculty at Duke, Chris Bail, the author of the 2021 book *Breaking the Social Media Prism: How to Make Our Platforms Less Polarizing*, was one of the main witnesses for the defense. Bail didn't contend that social media was benign but said that there wasn't a whole lot of compelling, definitive evidence in academic research that it was walling off and radicalizing a large percentage of users in some singular and exclusive fashion. "A lot of the stories out there are just wrong," he told Lewis-Kraus. "The political echo chamber has been massively overstated. Maybe it's three to five percent of people who are properly in an echo chamber." Lewis-Kraus added that "research indicates that most of us are actually exposed to a wider range of views on social media than we are in real life, where our social networks—in the original use of the term—are rarely heterogeneous. . . . And too much of a focus on our intuitions about social media's echo-chamber effect could obscure the relevant counterfactual: a conservative might abandon Twitter only to watch more Fox News."

Matthew Gentzkow, a Stanford professor who has studied both polarization and digital addiction, told Lewis-Kraus that while there are examples of social media galvanizing small numbers of people in hugely destructive ways—"ethnic violence in Bangladesh or Sri Lanka, people on YouTube mobilized to do mass shootings"—those cases have little or nothing to do with "how social media affects the *average* person." "Much of the evidence broadly makes me skeptical that the average effects are as big as the public discussion thinks they are," he said.

Even so, there *are* those mass shootings. There *is* Bail's "three to five percent." And while it's possible, I suppose, that relatively few people are politically transformed by social media in and of itself, that doesn't rule out social media's interplay with other factors that are making us more stubborn and meaner. Social media can be a coarse realm with a coarsening effect that numbers, percentages, and the like don't capture. Most people don't spend much time on X, but the people who do also spend plenty of time *outside* of X, whose ethos surely follows some of them into, and contaminates, that wider world. That ethos is petty, preening, and peevish, and has seldom been described better than in a December 2022 article in *Vox* by Rebecca Jennings, "Every 'chronically online' conversation is the same." Jennings wrote:

> In October, a woman named Daisey Beaton made a huge mistake: She tweeted about her personal life. "my husband and i wake up every morning and bring our coffee out to our garden and sit and talk for hours," she wrote. "every morning. it never gets old & we never run out of things to talk to. love him so much."
>
> If you felt a creeping sense of dread while reading about Daisey and her husband enjoying coffee in their garden, it's possible you spend too much time online. That's because despite its seeming innocuousness, Daisey's post has all the markers of Twitter rage-bait, and by rage-bait I mean a person sharing an experience that may not be entirely universal.

Jennings noted that Daisy was quickly pelted with angry replies that took issue with her presumed affluence (a garden!) and privileged ability to "sit and talk for hours." There were then replies to those replies, including an especially clever one from Ben Collins, an NBC News reporter, who tweeted: "I wake up every day fully engulfed in flames and being eaten alive by wolves. The fact that your tweet doesn't represent my experience is a personal affront." Collins nailed the sense of grievance with which so many people on Twitter patrolled the platform, itching to find missives that they could read through the prism of that grievance and use as an opportunity to air it. Case in point: "When indie rocker Mitski tweeted that she'd prefer it if her fans didn't film her the entire time she's onstage, some fans claimed that her request was insensitive to people with memory-related disabilities," Jennings wrote.

That's the offense-primed, finger-pointing, *j'accuse* world of Twitter, in which, perhaps inevitably, some tweets in fact elicited death threats, reflecting Twitter users' eerie "thirst for punishment," as Jennings wrote. Jennings noted that on Twitter (now X) and other "platforms where controversy and drama are prioritized for driving engagement," users are actually "rewarded for despising each other."

Twitter/X is, yes, its own special circle of hell. But many politicians have lingered there, looking to be noticed, rallying the troops, quickly recognizing that the most strongly or snidely worded missives get the most comments and retweets, and adjusting their language accordingly. Twitter has left a mark on them. The same goes for the many journalists who have loitered there, trawling for new fans, ratcheting up their public profiles, knowing that a big Twitter following and widely seen tweets can help with book deals, speaking engagements, and more. And the messy and frequently divisive first drafts of many public narratives were written on Twitter, which reporters monitored, editors took cues from, and media personalities sprinted to so they could land a quip or throw a dagger before actual newspaper articles and television reports crowded the public discussion—before there was such a magnitude of material that no individual's witticism or wickedness stood out.

"You watch politicians on Twitter, I mean, they're pushing themselves in the same way that social media influencers do," Sean Illing told Ezra Klein on an episode of Klein's podcast in July 2022. "You have a lot of politicians now who are basically just professional shit posters. And they're just on there to say things that will get engagement and that will trend." Illing is a former academic with a doctorate in political theory who switched to journalism and, at the time of his conversation with Klein, was writing and podcasting for

Vox. He was also promoting a just-published book, *The Paradox of Democracy*, that he'd written with Zac Gershberg.

And he noted that Twitter had been as bad for journalists as for politicians. "I think it has been very toxic for our business," he told Klein, explaining that it "blinkers our intuitions. It creates anxieties and pressures that bleed into our work, certainly mine. And for individual writers, it's kind of become a platform for just personal brand promotion, and that carries its own kinds of perverse incentives."

He could have had any number of examples in mind, including the coverage of students from Covington Catholic High School in Kentucky who attended the antiabortion March for Life in Washington, DC, in January 2019. Some of those students, in red "Make America Great Again" caps, crossed paths outside the Lincoln Memorial with a group of Native Americans from the Indigenous Peoples March, and an ambiguous video snippet of the encounter included details that suggested—or allowed the interpretation—that the students were harassing and ridiculing those demonstrators. One student in particular, Nicholas Sandmann, seemed to have planted himself smack in front of a Native American elder, Nathan Phillips, who was drumming and chanting, and stared at him, his lips set in what looked like a smirk. The snippet was short; it gave rise to more questions than answers. But that didn't stand in the way of it becoming an instant magnet and stage for grievance.

"Honest question: Have you ever seen a more punchable face than this kid's?" Reza Aslan, a popular writer and commentator about religious issues, tweeted beneath a photograph of Sandmann. That was one of the milder rants. Erik Abriss, who wrote for *Vulture*, tweeted: "I've truly lost the ability to articulate the hysterical rage, nausea, and heartache this makes me feel. I just want these people

to die. Simple as that. Every single one of them. And their parents."
Kurt Eichenwald, a journalist who had worked for the *Times* and
Vanity Fair, weighed in with the wish that "this MAGA thug and his
friends" be named and shamed and "denied all work in perpetuity.
Their bullying of a Native American veteran matches the taunting
of Jesus." And Kara Swisher, who was then doing a podcast for the
Times, connected the snippet of the Covington students to a controversial commercial exhorting men to rise above "toxic masculinity."
She tweeted: "And to all you aggrieved folks who thought this Gil-
lette ad was too much bad-men-shaming, after we just saw it come
to life with those awful kids and their fetid smirking harassing that
elderly man on the Mall: Go fuck yourselves."

Death wishes, Jesus's crucifixion, fetid, fuck—to monitor Twitter during one of these paroxysms was to behold a wild, dizzying,
terrifying crescendo of condemnation and profanity. It's like a digital stoning, with each person who joins it hurling a bigger rock than
the last person did. You're that furious? I'm *this* furious. You're that
mean? You ain't seen nothin' yet!

And in the case of the Covington students, the first round of accounts and analysis from actual news sources indulged a similar rush
to judgment. "Boys in 'Make America Great Again' Hats Mob Native
Elder at Indigenous Peoples March" was the headline on one of the
initial *Times* articles. The *Washington Post* was quick with an ostensibly relevant sidebar: "The Catholic Church's Shameful History of
Native American Abuses." News organization after news organization extrapolated from that one video snippet—from a *maybe* smirk,
a church affiliation, and MAGA apparel—to grand pronouncements
and keening lamentations about white supremacy, white privilege,
male privilege, class entitlement. It was a full-on, fill-in-the-blank
freak-out.

Until, well, we actually *learned* something about what had happened. More video emerged—hours of it. Reporters went out and reported. It turned out that the true hecklers, who taunted both the Native Americans *and* the Covington teenagers, were several members of an extremist sect called the Black Hebrew Israelites. They were there at the Lincoln Memorial not only preaching but also denigrating and trying to provoke the Native Americans, who walked over to the Covington teenagers—not the other way around—to get away from the abuse and defuse the situation. At some point during this dance, several of the Covington teenagers indeed performed mock tomahawk chops, moving and gesturing in ways disrespectful to the Native Americans. But there was so much confusion and so much tension that it was difficult to know what to make of any individual's behavior. As Caitlin Flanagan wrote in the *Atlantic*, the students from Kentucky "wandered into a Tom Wolfe novel and had no idea how to get out of it." Sandmann's frozen posture and cryptic expression could have been nerves, bafflement, an odd-looking bid for calm—or, yes, derision. We'll never know.

Some of the people who'd tweeted so rashly after seeing just that first video snippet deleted what they'd written—Swisher not only did that but also issued an emphatic apology. Exemplifying the adjustments that all news organizations made, the *Times* did a follow-up article with a much different headline: "Fuller Picture Emerges of the Viral Video of Native American Man and Catholic Students." Sandmann went on to file defamation lawsuits against more than a half dozen news organizations and, in 2020, reached financial settlements of undisclosed amounts with NBC News, CNN, and the *Washington Post*. And right-leaning publications and figures exulted in the mainstream media's comeuppance, disregarding how suggestive that initial video snippet had indeed been and not realizing how vividly their schadenfreude demonstrated their *own* sense of grievance.

Summarizing the whole mess in *Vox*, Zack Beauchamp wrote: "The left, which sees white supremacy as one of its fundamental enemies, was quick—in some cases, too quick—to identify Sandmann and his classmates as villains. The right's reaction, in turn, revealed several of its core animating assumptions that white Christians are persecuted minorities, that overzealous social justice warriors represent an existential threat to a free society, and that the media is on their enemies' sides."

"It's tempting to view this incident as a sideshow, a social media kerfuffle with no real significance," Beauchamp added. "But read properly, it provides a sort of skeleton key to our increasingly identity-focused politics, explaining the real ideological divides that animate much of modern American politics." Let me simplify: grievance jousted with grievance, befogging and befouling whatever the truth was.

The Covington episode was anything *but* a sideshow if only for what it said about the evolution of the traditional media, which has been affected not just by social media—it's impossible to separate the two, to treat social media as its own discrete phenomenon—but also by other technological advances and by economic and cultural forces that put a premium on speed, attitude, boldness, loudness. The internet altered everything. It gave advertisers more efficient ways to reach consumers than through publications and television news programs, taking a fatal bite out of the revenues of many news organizations, especially local ones. But it also markedly decreased what it took for someone to stake a media presence of sorts: no big investment, professional credential, or finely honed skill was required to create an online publication or blog—to assemble a website, lickety-split. And the cheapest way to get into the content-creation game wasn't to hire a platoon of journalists who did extensive, objective on-the-ground reporting that commandeered serious time and racked up serious expenses: flights, rental cars, hotel rooms. It was to hire writers who puzzled over and pontificated about the material that richer organizations were airing and publishing. And for cable news networks such as CNN, which debuted in 1980, and MSNBC, which joined the fun and the fray in 1996, filling all twenty-four hours of programming every day with truly fresh information was (and is) logistically undoable. The solution: to have anchor after anchor, guest after guest, panel after panel hash over and riff about the same basket of information, with the look of the set and the lineup of talking heads changing every ten or thirty or sixty minutes. The solution was commentary. The solution was opinion.

I can't overstate how many of the changes in the news business since I took my first full-time newspaper job in 1988 have increased the presence and pointedness of opinion in journalism. Many of the online publications I just referred to donned partisan colors, in the way so many print publications in Europe always have. They made no bones about presenting news and commentary through a liberal or conservative lens. The line between neutral and opinionated journalism in news outlets that offered both began to blur, as articles that offered "analysis" created a space for subjectivity behind a fig leaf of objectivity and as the whole model and morality of objective reporting—in its classical form and according to its traditional definition—came up for debate. And the opinion sections of news outlets that did all kinds of journalism grew, largely because of another new technological wrinkle: the ability to measure what online readers, who represent the overwhelming majority of readers of the

Times and similar news organizations, are looking at and responding to. Turns out they especially like columns, commentary, essays with a distinct point of view. So they're getting more of that.

I don't think many people outside the news business appreciate the revolution in a news organization's ability to monitor its online readers. I don't mean *individual* readers—there's none of that, no nanny-camming of what a specific person, by name, is up to. But how a given piece or kind of content performs? In the old days, which weren't all that long ago, a newspaper or magazine had to conduct surveys or convene focus groups to know what its subscribers were reading, and it had to rely on their self-report. In the digital era, the *Times* can tell which articles have been viewed by the most people, how many people have viewed them, how long those people tended to stick with a given article, and whether they found their way to it through the home page or a social media post or a Google search. Editors have all this information and more, and writers can access it, too. I've always avoided visiting those byways in the *Times* digital universe where I could look at and dwell on my "numbers," and while I like to tell myself that that's a matter of journalistic principle, it's as much a matter of mental health. But I nonetheless know whether something I've written has found an especially large audience, because what I do sometimes check—and what any subscriber can, too—is the online "trending" list of the thirteen "most popular" articles at a given moment in time.

One striking aspect of that list, which updates several times an hour, is the disproportionate presence of articles generated by the Opinion section. In terms of the staff whom the section employs and the amount of content it publishes, it accounts for significantly less than a fifth of the *Times*'s editorial operation, which has separate units for local news, national news, international news, culture, sports, business, food, travel, and more. But articles from the Opinion section will often claim half or more of the "most popular" list. That's a quantitative fact. Here's a qualitative one, less obvious to outsiders but clear to me and anyone else who writes regularly for the section: A column or essay is more likely to be widely read and end up on that list if it packs a specific punch. If it radiates a passion. If, in other words, it has an especially sharp point of view.

I'm using the *Times* as an example because it's what I know best, but I'm describing dynamics that are industry-wide, and what's also true industry-wide is that the hyperabundance of different voices online and on television prods many of them to establish, and stick to, a particular brand aimed at a particular audience who can be relied on to come back for more of the same. It's not the only economic model for a journalist trying to make a splash, but it's the most convenient and probably the smartest one—if you want a bigger footprint on social media, if you want a television contract. Those cable news panels, after all, aren't three or four smart and lively people whose opinions about an issue are a matter of suspense. They're three or four smart, lively, and *predictable* people chosen and assembled to make sure that certain ideological and tonal marks are hit. There's the person who sees sexism everywhere, the one on patrol for racism, the one railing against the woke tyranny of it all—or whatever the panel calls for.

In 2012, after a big story by Jason Horowitz in the *Washington Post* about Mitt Romney's high-school bullying of an effeminate classmate, I got booked and then unbooked to discuss it on an MSNBC panel. The booker came to me because I'm a gay man who'd written many columns spotlighting antigay discrimination and advocating for gay rights; the booker dismissed me after I said, in a preinterview, that I was loath to condemn Romney unconditionally because the incident had occurred more than forty-five years earlier, in a much less enlightened world, and many of us behaved, as children, in immature and terrible ways that have no bearing on who we became as adults. That assessment, apparently, wasn't on brand. And I, as a result, wasn't on air.

Pundits are now legion, our written wares are among the most conspicuous and popular features of the news landscape, and, as I wrote in the *Times* in June 2021, when I went from a full-time to a part-time role there in order to join the faculty at Duke, "Too many columns are less sober analyses than snarky stand-up acts or primal screams. The stand-up and the screams sell." I wasn't making my job change because of that, but the change—and a column in which I was informing readers of it—seemed to me a logical moment to take stock, to reflect. I wrote:

> I worried, and continue to worry, about the degree to which I and other journalists—opinion writers, especially—have contributed to the dynamics we decry: the toxic tenor of American discourse, the furious pitch of American politics, the volume and vitriol of it all.
>
> I worry, too, about how frequently we shove ambivalence and ambiguity aside. Ambivalence and ambiguity aren't necessarily signs of weakness or sins of indecision. They can be apt responses to events we don't yet understand, with outcomes we can't predict.
>
> But they don't make for bold sentences or tidy talking points. So we pundits are merchants of certitude in a world where much is in doubt and many questions don't have one right answer. As such, we may be encouraging arrogance and unyieldingness in our readers, viewers, and listeners. And those attributes need no encouragement in America today.

That's hardly the only manner in which the media contributes to a climate of grievance, raising a temperature that's better lowered. Another way, also connected to how much the vast real estate of cable television and the infinite territory of the internet have stiffened the competition for attention, is the negativity and melodrama of so much of today's journalism, which puts considerably greater emphasis on problems than on solutions, amplifies conflict while shrugging at conciliation (the little bit of it that exists), and takes a five-alarm-fire approach to minor blazes as well as raging infernos. In a crowded marketplace, in a jangled world, five-alarm fires seem to generate the most discussion and garner the most clicks, so our breathlessness can be attributed as much to consumers—without whom we lack the revenue to provide *any* news, sunny or stormy— as to us. Which came first: the doomscrolling or the doom? Regardless, they're intertwined at this point, each rewarding and ramping up the other.

Of course, a certain degree of alarmism is in keeping with our mission. It has always been our way. It's necessary: you have to name the problems *before* you can present solutions, and the noble function of watchdogs—which good journalists are—is to bark at signs of incoming danger. But how consistently? How loudly?

Amanda Ripley, the author of the 2021 book *High Conflict: Why We Get Trapped and How We Get Out*, wrote an essay for the *Washington Post* in 2022 in which she confessed sheepishly that she, a journalist, had been avoiding the news. She found that when she stayed on top of it, the way she felt she was supposed to, "I was just marinating in despair." She couldn't take it anymore.

"I tried to toughen up," she recounted. "I gave myself stern lectures: 'This is real life, and real life is depressing! There is a pandemic happening, for God's sake. Plus: Racism! Also: Climate change! And inflation! Things *are* depressing. You *should* be depressed!'" I'm usually not a fan of that many exclamation points, but every one of Ripley's was wisely deployed, because that's how the news has been coming at us since 2016, in an indiscriminately exclamatory fashion. Ripley provided some evidence of that. "New data from the Reuters Institute showed that the United States has one of the highest news-avoidance rates in the world," she wrote. "About 4 out of 10 Americans sometimes or often avoid contact with the news."

"If so many of us feel poisoned by our products," she asked, "might there be something wrong with them?" She noted that therapists were treating patients for what they called "headline stress disorder." And she quoted something that Krista Tippett, the creator and host of the popular *On Being* podcast and the author of the 2016 book *Becoming Wise: An Inquiry into the Mystery and Art of Living*, once said about the ceaseless blasts of joyless updates coming at us in more ways through more devices than ever before: "I don't actually think we are equipped, even physiologically or mentally, to be delivered catastrophic and confusing news and pictures, 24/7. We are analog creatures in a digital world."

As it happens, one of the other best and most haunting laments I've read on the debilitating, addling effect of all the bad news hurled at us also appeared in the *Post*'s Opinions section, written in the early spring of 2023 by the columnist David Von Drehle, who likewise built his essay around an admission: he'd been staring at a cardinal on a tree outside his window, and his "heart swelled" at the beauty of it, but then he worried that he shouldn't feel that way, what with all that he'd been told about the crises that birds face courtesy of human rapaciousness and heedlessness.

"To know this, and to see a bird outside the kitchen window, should darken my mood, should it not?" Von Drehle wrote. "A look

at one bird—even a plump, handsome fellow feeding unconcern-
edly on the block of seeds and suet I keep dangling from a tree limb
through winter—ought to make me think of all birds, right?" He
should be remembering the "threatened and dying birds" throughout "the ravaged globe," he added, half in sarcasm, and should also
be reflecting on climate change, assaults on democracy, assaults on
free speech, the insidious impact of social media, the insidious impact of inequality, the national debt, drug overdoses. The length of
his list underscored the magnitude of our negativity.

"The news calls us to think constantly on a very large scale about
problems to which no individual holds the key," he wrote. "And to
feel jejune if we slip from that lofty, arid plane to delight in something here and now. The starry sky itself could contain the asteroid
that will kill us all."

On a gorgeous day a little more than two months after I read
Von Drehle's column, I was walking in the woods with a friend and
neighbor who's one of the least easily ruffled, most adaptable people I know when she announced that she was going to have to stop
watching NBC's *Today* show. Not some purposely somber newscast,
not some prime-time shout-fest, but the kind of morning television
program that was designed to be a somewhat soothing, somewhat
energizing, mostly pleasant get-the-day-going mix of entertainment-
world buzz, human-interest stories, sports updates, yummy recipes,
book recommendations, and yes, important news, definitely some
important news, but not too much and not too glum. What was turning my friend and neighbor away? *Al Roker and the weather.*

Lately, she said, Roker had been paying special attention to extreme weather events around the globe and would often quantify
how many millions of people were being displaced, distressed, or
diminished by the stubborn drought, the record heat, the fires, the

floods. He was doing so, she understood, to raise awareness of climate change, and that suited her politics. But it didn't complement her morning tea. Couldn't she wake up fully first? "And what am I supposed to do with that?" she asked me. She'd already installed solar panels on her roof. She'd decided that her next car would be fully electric or at least a hybrid. Roker's reporting wasn't giving her fresh ideas for bolder action. It was making her feel defeated.

We need hope, Von Drehle pointed out in his essay. We need "a sense of agency," Ripley wrote in hers, adding: "Feeling like you and your fellow humans can do something—even something small—is how we convert anger into action, frustration into invention. The self-efficacy is essential to any functioning democracy." But most of the news streaming at us—*screaming* at us—doesn't provide that feeling. One response is to tune out, as Ripley had found herself doing for a while, and as some 40 percent of Americans, according to the Reuters Institute, were doing. Another, overlapping reaction is to become numb. A third is to live in a state of permanent agitation. To marinate in the despair that Ripley felt before she tuned out. To stay in the clutch of an anger that's never converted into action, because the means for that transformation is never specified. To make friends with frustration and not make the acquaintance of invention. And that *absence* of self-efficacy is antithetical to any functioning democracy.

Fox News stands out from other major news operations in many ways, including the magnitude of recklessness that led to its $787.5 million settlement of the Dominion Voting Systems defamation suit. But one of its boldest distinctions is a mood and outlook even bleaker than the modern journalistic norm. The America it describes is disintegrating so rapidly that there soon won't be any hope of reversing the process. It communicates those dire circumstances with a signature disgust.

I'm not sure I've beheld any television figure who radiates the peculiarly manic disdain that Jeanine Pirro, a longtime fixture in the Fox News daytime lineup, does; Cecily Strong's martini-swilling impersonation of her on *Saturday Night Live* is much too benign (and a criminal insult to martinis). And watching the nighttime trinity of Tucker Carlson at eight o'clock Eastern (until he was yanked in April 2023), Sean Hannity at nine, and Laura Ingraham at ten was like being served a triple-decker Apocalypse Burger with patties that hadn't all been cooked to precisely the same temperature. Hannity was medium. Ingraham was medium-rare to rare—more savage, messier. Carlson was just about raw. And the meal certainly wasn't garnished with the kind of constructive, hopeful counsel for which Ripley rightly yearns. Not unless you considered the urging of extra contempt for liberals, extra resentment of immigrants and minorities, and extra firearms for all to be an inspiring and unifying agenda.

The trinity's obsession with immigrants and minorities—Carlson's obsession in particular—points to another distinguishing feature of major news organizations today that's additional grist for grievance, extending well beyond Fox News and right-wing media but not in incarnations of such monumental nastiness and rank bigotry: more and more reporting and commentary mirror or even upsize identity politics in their implicit and explicit categorization of Americans into discrete groups suffering their own indignities, facing their own threats, pressing their own agendas, fending for themselves. More and more provide Americans who are already inclined to feel wounded with an inventory and analysis of their wounds.

On his Fox News show, which ran from November 2016 to April 2023, Carlson performed a version of that so hyperbolic and histrionic that it achieved the aspect of burlesque; the one or two times a month when I forced myself to watch him, I kept waiting for him to break out in laughter, to fess up that he was doing some new-millennium homage to Archie Bunker in *All in the Family*. But, no, he was selling hate straight up, to a point where many major advertisers fled the show and never returned. He had "constructed what may be the most racist show in the history of cable news—and also, by some measures, the most successful," Nicholas Confessore wrote in a three-part series about Carlson in the *Times* in 2022 that reflected Carlson's undisputed crown as the king of cable news, whose nightly average of more than 4.3 million viewers in the second quarter of 2020 made *Tucker Carlson Tonight* the highest-rated cable news show in history.

The *Times* series was titled "American Nationalist." The headline atop the first part was "How Tucker Carlson Stoked White Fear to Conquer Cable." And Confessore explained: "Night after night, hour by hour, Mr. Carlson warns his viewers that they inhabit a civilization under siege—by violent Black Lives Matter protesters in American cities, by diseased migrants from south of the border, by refugees importing alien cultures, and by tech companies and cultural elites who will silence them, or label them racist, if they complain." In America according to Tucker Carlson, those cultural elites were doing more than just silencing the audience to whom Carlson appealed. They were working hard—by deliberately failing to police the southwestern border of the United States, by cheerleading for more permissive immigration policies, and by pushing amnesty and citizenship for people who'd entered the country illegally—to make sure that longstanding, pale-skinned Americans were physically outnumbered by newer, darker-skinned ones who'd be loyal to the Democratic Party.

That specter is known as "replacement theory," and while Carlson didn't use those exact words or sketch out the whole conspiracy in detail, he routinely presented pieces of it. He got the gist across, as when he told viewers in April 2021 that Democrats were importing "more obedient voters from the third world" to "replace" the less obedient ones already here. Confessore's three-part series documented more than four hundred episodes of *Tucker Carlson Tonight* during which, in Confessore's words, Carlson "amplified the notion that Democratic politicians and other assorted elites want to force demographic change through immigration." Carlson would continue to amplify that notion after Fox exiled him. In November 2023, he assailed Jewish donors who were protesting university officials' tepid response to Hamas's invasion of Israel the previous month; those donors, he complained, had done nothing over the past decade as faculty and students on the left were "calling for white genocide."

And Carlson was by no means whistling in the wind. An Associated Press poll released in May 2022 showed that about one in three American adults believed that there was an ongoing effort "to replace native-born Americans with immigrants for electoral gains." According to the poll, that belief was especially popular with the audiences of right-wing media outlets such as Fox News and Newsmax. It had unequivocally taken root with violent extremists: the shooters involved in the massacres of the Jewish people in that Pittsburgh synagogue in 2018, of the Mexican people in an El Paso Walmart in 2019, and of the Black people in a Buffalo supermarket in May 2022 made references, either in their interviews with law enforcement officials or in remarks or writing before they opened fire, to their fury at the prospect of immigrants and nonwhite people taking over the United States.

There are phrases for the thought structure that Carlson was (and still is) pitching, and for the type of pitchman that he embodies. That those descriptors appear prominently in Barbara F. Walter's *How Civil Wars Start* signals their dangerousness. What she describes as "ethnic nationalism" is exactly what Carlson promoted on *Tucker Carlson Tonight*. And the role he played was that of an "ethnic entrepreneur." Ethnic nationalism and ethnic entrepreneurship, Walter explained, splinter a country with particular efficiency.

"Countries that factionalize have political parties based on ethnic, religious, or racial identity rather than ideology," she wrote, an observation with special relevance given Fox News' mammoth sway over Republican politics, reflected in the composition of the network's audience, 93 percent of whom identified as Republicans or indicated an affinity for the Republican Party in a 2019 survey by the Pew Research Center. (The same survey found that 95 percent of viewers who relied on MSNBC for their television news belonged to or sympathized with the Democratic Party.) "The citizens of the former Yugoslavia could have organized themselves around their political beliefs—they could have coalesced around communism, as Tito had encouraged, or liberalism, or corporatism," Walter observed, homing in on the region of the world where, in the early 1990s, the Bosnian War raged and there were horrific incidents of "ethnic cleansing." "Instead, leaders chose to activate ethnic and religious identities."

"Ethnic nationalism, and its expression through factions, doesn't take hold in a country on its own," she further explained. "For a society to fracture along identity lines, you need mouthpieces—people who are willing to make discriminatory appeals and pursue discriminatory policies in the name of a particular group. They are usually people who are seeking political office or trying to stay in office. They provoke and harness feelings of fear as a way to lock in the constituencies that will support their scramble for power. Experts have a term for these individuals, ethnic entrepreneurs." Slobodan Milošević, the president of Serbia from 1989 to 1997 and then of the Federal Republic of Yugoslavia (which is what Serbia became) from 1997 to 2000, perfectly fit the bill. Vladimir Putin in Russia, Viktor Orbán in Hungary, Recep Tayyip Erdoğan in Turkey, and Narendra Modi in India inhabit this role to varying degrees. So, to an extent, does Trump, and it's no accident that despite the emergence in mid-2023 of text messages in which Carlson confessed to despising him, the two have played public kissy-face for many years now. They're peacocks of an ethnic nationalist feather. And they're ethnic entrepreneurs by Walter's definition; they "make the fight expressly about their group's position and status in society."

Note the trio of adjectives that kept company in Walter's appraisal: racial, ethnic, and *religious*. Entwined with the ethnic nationalism to which Trump and Carlson appeal is Christian nationalism, which has drawn more attention and concern in the United States over the past few years, especially given the elevation of Mike Johnson, a Republican congressman who seems to embody Christian nationalism, to the position of House speaker in late 2023 and the involvement of conservative Christian activists in the rollback of abortion rights, in the censoring of books that make reference to homosexuality or transgenderism, and in the allowance, in some states, for parents to use publicly funded vouchers to enroll their children in schools run by religious groups. A Supreme Court decision in 2020 blessed that application of vouchers, and Oklahoma in June 2023 went a nervy step beyond it by approving the first religious charter school in the United States, an online academy, St. Isidore of Seville Catholic Virtual School, to be run by the Roman Catholic Archdiocese of Oklahoma City and the Diocese of Tulsa. Although there can be confusion about the nature of charter schools among people who aren't in the educational know, charters aren't private. They're established and run with taxpayer money, Oklahoma's use of which for St. Isidore so blatantly disregards the separation of church and state that even some Republicans cried foul.

It's difficult to say exactly where ethnic nationalism ends and Christian nationalism begins, or vice versa. That's evident in much of the recent writing about Christian nationalism in the United States: it has sometimes been as much about ethnic nationalism *among* conservative (and especially evangelical) Christians as about some expressly theocratic plot. When Susan Stubson, a disenchanted longtime member of the Wyoming Republican Party, wrote an attention-getting essay, "What Christian Nationalism Has Done to My State and My Faith Is a Sin," that appeared in the *Times* in May 2023, she bemoaned Wyoming Republicans' racism and overwrought allegiance to Trump in a manner that didn't make entirely clear whether their Christianity's relationship to those phenomena was causative or correlative. I couldn't tell how much culpability "Christian nationalism" per se bore or precisely what her definition of Christian nationalism was.

But as Allyson F. Shortle, Eric L. McDaniel, and Irfan Nooruddin wrote in an article in the *Washington Post* based on their 2022 book *The Everyday Crusade: Christian Nationalism in American Politics*, Christian nationalist ideologies, which they define as a vision of the "American identity as exclusively White and Christian" and the desire "for a government that favors that group's beliefs," have grown more apparent over the past few years. "Far-right leaders have ramped up their calls to take back Christian America through violence," the authors noted. Even "Republican elites," they added, increasingly use the rhetoric of religious war, possibly making it "easier for Christian nationalist extremists to mobilize followers, gain adherents, and build coalitions to gain political power." One such member of the elite: Ron DeSantis, who has said that Republicans should "don the full armor of God" in their fight against Democrats, language that casts the contest between the parties—and the stakes of it—as fundamentally religious. "Full armor of God" has lately become a staple locution among Republican politicians along with godly verbiage in general. As part of DeSantis's campaign for a second term as governor of Florida, he released an ad that portrayed him as divinely chosen to hold office at this moment in time. "God made a fighter," stated the ad's narrator over and over, a grandiose pronouncement accompanied by beautifully shot, carefully chosen images of DeSantis that gave him a heroic sheen.

Many of the January 6 rioters waved Christian flags, toted Christian banners, and cradled Bibles. The ReAwaken America Tour, a traveling road show that puts right-wing conspiracy theorists and provocateurs before crowds of Christian activists, is sponsored by *Charisma News*, a Pentecostal Christian publication, and it brims with violent language and imagery. In a September 2023 article for the *New Republic*, Katherine Stewart recounted a recent stop of the tour in Las Vegas, where she noticed that "the T-shirts are getting nastier." One said "Size Matters" over big bullets. Another showed Trump with a long rifle, while yet another "featured dozens of white male soldiers and the words 'Diversity is Destruction' across the bottom," Stewart wrote. "There was the old standby, 'God, Guns and Trump.' And then there was 'BLITZKRIEG.'"

Regardless of Christianity's role in the rightward lurch of many rural Republicans, their rage has intensified and, in the manner of modern grievance, become less and less tethered to the actual dynamics of their daily lives. It is linked instead to a broader sense that their status and the esteem for them in the United States are diminishing. That was the part of Stubson's *Times* essay about Wyoming that most forcefully grabbed me. She wrote that right-wing candidates in her state in 2022 ran ads that warned about "government overreach, religious persecution, mask mandates, threats from immigrants and election fraud."

"None of those concerns were real," she added. "Our schools largely remained open during the pandemic. Businesses remained open. The border is an almost 1,000-mile drive from my home in Casper, and the foreign-born population in the state is only 3 percent. Wyoming's violent crime rate is the lowest of any state in the West. Wyoming's electoral process is incredibly safe. So what are we afraid of?"

Seven

The Oppression Olympics

Unlike Wyoming, the United States has a substantial foreign-born population—it's nearing 15 percent of all Americans, and that's an all-time high. Decade after decade, the United States grows more ethnically and racially diverse; between 2010 and 2020, the population of white people in the country declined for the first time, and the nation maintained net growth only because nonwhite people made up the difference, according to an analysis of US Census figures by the Brookings Institution. The speed at which the number of nonwhite Americans is drawing even with white ones is sometimes exaggerated: many Americans were shocked, in the aftermath of Trump's election, to learn that more than 60 percent of the United States was still non-Hispanic white, because for years some of the commentary about the country's diversification gave the impression that we were on the cusp of a majority minority nation, with the non-Hispanic white share of it below 50 percent. We'll get there. But some current projections put that date as far out as 2045.

That's a profound change, especially for older Americans who grew up in a country so demographically different from today's, and news organizations struggle to make proper sense of it and to report on it in the most constructive fashion. For a long time, the chief problem was their disregard for minority groups and failure to recognize—and explode—the homogeneous, monolithic perspective I mentioned earlier. But over the past ten years, there has been a veritable revolution in that regard, at least among media outlets and media figures more high-minded than Fox News and Carlson.

To cite just a tiny example: At some point over those ten years, or possibly a few years earlier, editors began to stress in a whole new way that we writers had to be more conscious of the lineup of experts we quoted in our articles and of the mix of them. And I realized, with a pang of shame, how overloaded with white men my figurative Rolodex was. That probably said as much about the overrepresentation of white men in the ranks of experts as it did about my prejudices, but it also suggested a vicious cycle: if I yielded lazily to that overrepresentation, I'd help perpetuate it, and it would change much more slowly than it should. I began casting a wider net. I noticed many of my colleagues doing the same. And I was grateful for being pointed in that direction. It was not only the right way to go but also the way toward better work.

Similarly, many major news organizations have done much, much more reporting than in the past on the challenges and general life experiences of groups that have been marginalized and have suffered (and continue to suffer) discrimination. That, too, has been necessary and overdue, and it has led to much essential and superb journalism.

But some race-oriented, gender-focused, minority-conscious coverage, in its current form, has a reflexive, intellectually facile feel that does little to draw in the audience that would benefit most from engagement with it. Some of it insists on a predetermined framing and on preordained findings. And that accentuates the idea that we Americans exist not as one big tribe with shared interests but as dozens of little tribes with separate—and, worse yet, competing—interests.

A major event occurs, and the crop of articles about it includes specific examinations of what it means for—or what the public reaction to it says about—women or gay people or trans people or Black people or Latinos (who are often called Latinx people, even though the overwhelming majority of them chafe at that term) or Muslims. A candidate catches fire, and the aspects of his or her record and proposals that come up for exploration include their possible impact on voters in those and other demographic categories, as if those categories shape voters' outlooks and experiences more than anything else. For many people, that's indeed the case. For many others, it isn't. But the news media sometimes seems determined to spot the fault lines of race, gender, gender orientation, ethnicity, and more in everything it examines and to etch those lines as boldly as possible.

It wasn't long after Vladimir Putin sent Russian missiles and troops into Ukraine in 2022 that at least a few prominent journalists and articles in major publications detected or wondered about racism in the rapt attention to, and tears for, the plight of Ukrainians: Where was that swell of feeling for the casualties of war in developing countries in Africa and elsewhere? Were Ukrainians more sympathetic because they were white? For some news consumers, probably, and that's disgusting. But there were other dynamics at play. The invasion of Ukraine was getting intense coverage largely because the invading country was a nuclear superpower with an increasingly unhinged leader flexing what might be growing imperial ambitions; because the conflict was happening on NATO's door-step and, for that reason, might draw in NATO and thus the United States; and because Europe hadn't been a theater for this kind of war in many decades. All of that made what was happening exceptionally dangerous and exceptional, period. And for better or worse, news organizations have long favored the extraordinary over the commonplace.

The moment Jacinda Ardern resigned as prime minister of New Zealand at the beginning of 2023, I braced for articles positing that she'd relinquished her post in part because of sexism. In short order, those articles came. They weren't especially persuasive, and that's not because sexism doesn't exist or even because she miraculously escaped it. It absolutely exists, and I doubt *any* woman escapes it. But that doesn't make it the dominant narrative at every juncture and in every corner of her life. In addition to being a woman, Ardern was unusually young for a national leader. She governed during the stresses and political crosscurrents of Covid. The price of housing in New Zealand skyrocketed under her watch, causing broad frustration and bitter recriminations. Sexism wasn't necessarily the driver of her political fate, nor did it have to be a prominent theme in her biography.

Major news organizations nonetheless treat sexism, Islamophobia, homophobia, transphobia, and especially racism exactly that way, and they raise the specter of white supremacy whether its imprint on a given circumstance is abundantly clear or entirely questionable. And there's at least a threefold risk in that. One, readers and viewers grow inured to such analyses, and fail to recognize and reckon with white supremacy at its most evident and destructive. Two, it dwells on our divisions, sorting us, labeling us, and telling us that our labels are our destinies, a message that's the enemy of both incentive and accountability. Three, it puts some of the people at whom it's targeted on the defensive. They don't hear a summons to be better than in the past. They hear a demand that they feel awful in the present. Many of them may deserve that indictment. But it can be a road to grievance as much as to redemption.

Andra Gillespie, a political scientist at Emory University, told me that we may not have taken that into proper account, and we haven't carved out "a middle ground where you can actually try to bring people along." Gillespie, whose books on Black politics in the United States include, most recently, *Race and the Obama Administration*, said: "The idea that somebody might learn in school that their ancestors weren't the best people in the world, and that they took things, and what that meant is that their descendants were going to be privileged and other folks' descendants were going to have to work harder to even kind of make the same baseline of comfort— you know, that is a radical notion to people who have been on the privileged side of that lived experience, and perhaps we shouldn't be surprised that we have seen the backlash that we've had."

Is the cause of ending discrimination against Asian Americans served or undermined by grafting a discussion of such discrimination onto events where it's not conclusively present? Immediately after a white gunman rampaged through three massage parlors in Atlanta in March 2021, fatally shooting eight people, including six women of Asian descent, there were articles, tweets, and other public comments galore that mentioned or alluded to a Covid-exacerbated resentment of Asian Americans, a rise in hate crimes against them, white nationalism, and white supremacy. But a portrait of the gunman and his motives was only just emerging, and it harbored more evidence that he was a sexually tormented religious zealot lashing out at the objects of his desire—he'd apparently been a customer at two of the spas—than it did proof that he hated Asian Americans.

Commentary about the horrific killing of Tyre Nichols, a Black man, at the hands of five Black police officers in Memphis in early 2023 accommodated mentions of or allusions to white supremacy, crediting it with the violent and degrading system in which the Black officers were operating. Along those same lines, the *Washington Post* published an opinion essay in early 2021 in which a New York University professor explained that Trump had improved his standing with Black and Latino voters between 2016 and 2020 and that there were people of color among the January 6 rioters because of "multiracial whiteness." In other words, Black and Latino voters' aspirations to whiteness, or at least to its privileges, motivate them to behave as callously and savagely as white people, who are ultimately to blame.

That essay came to mind when, midway through 2023, the *New Yorker* published an article that pondered a recent mass shooting in which a thirty-three-year-old Mexican American man who had expressed white-supremacist views killed eight people at an outlet mall in Allen, Texas. The headline: "The Rise of Latino White Supremacy." Apparently sensing how nonsensical that cluster of words sounds, the author wrote, in the first paragraph: "In fact, Latino white supremacy isn't an oxymoron, and carrying out a premeditated mass shooting in the United States is one of the more American things a Latino could do." I understood what the author was saying. I also understood how cynical and selective that willed logic was, and I understood the agenda behind it: to preserve the progressive, race-obsessed taxonomy of oppressors and oppressed—evildoers and those to whom evil is done—by finding a way to apply it even to events that resist or contradict it. The author went further than that, saying that the events she was looking at *validated* white supremacy if you just knew how to look at them in the proper way.

The subhead of the article was as revealing as the headline. "At a time of increased racial violence," it said, "Latinos are potential perpetrators and potential victims." That's a pointless statement of the blazingly obvious—*of course* Latinos can fall into either role, because *people* can fall into either role—unless both author and reader inhabit a world in which Latinos are supposed to be only the objects of harm. The supposed "news" here was that they can be the agents of harm, too: four of the twenty-two mass shootings in Texas by that point in 2023 had been committed by Latinos, the article reported. Then it chastised anyone whose eyes widened at that statistic, because that eye-widening was, well, more white supremacy: "Expressing surprise or disbelief at the fact that Latino white-supremacist shooters exist marks them as outsiders, as many Latinos before them have been marked. But it should be the shootings that we see as un-American, not the shooters themselves." Wait, wait: the author had said earlier that mass shootings were *quintessentially* American, to the point where the commission of one is an act of assimilation. Here, as in too much journalism today, grievance was supplanting coherence.

I'm not surprised that writers trying to capture racial dynamics and explore the overt and oblique wages of racism in the United States sometimes end up twisted into intellectual knots. This work is knotty stuff. But that's why it's all the more important that we acknowledge as much, that we not forcibly squeeze every set of circumstances into the same box, and that we show some respect for the subtleties of human nature and human relationships. It would be helpful as well to recognize that most individuals in the United States, for all the country's flaws, maintain at least some agency, some choice, and that what they do with it is in part a matter of character. The conservative writer Andrew Sullivan communicated that eloquently in a 2023 edition of his Substack newsletter, the *Weekly Dish*: "We live in the freest, most multiracial democracy in the history of the planet. Of course traditional prejudices linger, ebb and flow, and the past has helped define the present. But they do not come near to definitively describing the infinitely fascinating interactions between all of us, in every possible combination, our shared humanity, the cross-racial friendships and marriages, our individual personalities, our different upbringings." He added that "reducing our entire world to these allegedly irreconcilable abstractions of 'hate' is a pathological distraction from reality."

The "most multiracial democracy in the history of the planet"—that superlative is correct, and it points to the fact that no other country has ever attempted what we're attempting in the United States. There's no exact antecedent. No instructive template. No model that reassures us that we can be successful and endure. "The world has not actually seen a full-scale, wholly diverse, wholly inclusive, multiracial, democratic republic like what we are trying to become," Pete Buttigieg said when he and I talked about our country's challenges—and about the primacy of grievance—in May 2023. I broached the topic with him not chiefly because of his presence in President Biden's cabinet, as the US transportation secretary, but because of how often I'd heard him speak—in private conversations when I first got to know him nearly a decade ago and from the stump when he campaigned for the Democratic presidential nomination in 2020—about the vital importance of forging common ground, common goals. I knew he worried and cared about the forces pulling us apart.

"There are obviously very healthy social democracies in Northern Europe," he added. "Indonesia is pluralistic in one way, but maybe less so on a religious dimension, and arguably not as democratic also. I don't think you can actually point to anywhere that has established, at the scale that we're trying to do it, a truly representative democracy with this level of racial, religious, and other diversity."

Representative Ro Khanna, a California Democrat whose national profile has risen sharply and steadily since his first election to the US House of Representatives, put it to me this way: when his parents arrived in the United States from India in the late 1960s and early 1970s, they were anomalies; most of the immigrants then coming into the country were European. "Today, it's less than fifteen percent," he said. That reflects the multiracial arc of the country, as do the backgrounds of the fellow lawmakers all around him in the House. "It's a remarkable Congress where you can have Rashida Tlaib (a Michigan Democrat), whose family members have personally faced actions that she disagrees strongly with from the Israeli government, sitting with people who trace their heritage back to survivors of the Holocaust," Khanna said. "There's a reason the temperature in our politics is higher—it's because what we're trying to do is so difficult." That difficulty, he added, is what gives him hope. There's great confidence, great intention, and great purpose in "the grandeur of the project that we're trying to achieve."

Buttigieg expressed similar sentiments. The United States, he said, stands as "the most important democracy, the most consequential democracy" on the globe, not only for its current wealth, power, and cultural reach but also because it introduced "representative, republican democracy to the world," inspiring other countries and showing them the way. "If, two hundred and fifty years later, we could do the same thing for *inclusive* democracy: that's as big a contribution to humanity and as novel a one as anything we achieved out of the Revolution," Buttigieg said. "I think we'll either get it done or we'll fail to get it done decisively in our lifetimes. And the prospect of achieving it is wildly exciting. But there are major, major antibodies to getting it done."

Those antibodies fascinate Yascha Mounk, a political scientist at the Johns Hopkins University School of Advanced International Studies who has devoted his three most recent books to the challenges that Western democracies face. Mounk focused on populism in the first of them, *The People vs. Democracy*, published in 2018, and on diversity in the following two, *The Great Experiment* (2022) and *The Identity Trap* (2023). And he has repeatedly emphasized that what the United States and many other Western democracies are doing, in terms of creating large multiethnic democracies, is "a historically unique experiment," as he said once on German television. The fuss that his "experiment" remark stirred—especially among people who thought he'd just fessed up to the real liberal agenda—confirmed for him what multiethnic, multiracial, multicultural democracies were up against. In *The Great Experiment*, he stated, bluntly: "The history of diverse societies is grim."

Mounk used *The Great Experiment* for observations too seldom made or appreciated—observations that speak to how mature and careful we need to be about getting this experiment right, because we *must* get it right, as he also stressed. He was urging mindfulness, not making excuses. But he noted that "only in the past five or six decades have most democracies embraced erstwhile outsiders as compatriots on a significant scale. At the end of World War II, fewer than one in twenty-five people living in the United Kingdom had been born abroad. Today, it is one in seven. Until a few decades ago, Sweden was one of the most homogenous countries in the world. Now one in five Swedish residents have foreign roots. Countries from Austria to Australia have undergone similarly rapid changes." He name-checked France, Denmark, Germany. "None of these countries intentionally chose to turn themselves into diverse democracies, and so none of them ever developed a coherent plan for how to deal with the key challenges they would face." Yes, he wrote, the United States and Canada "thought of themselves as nations composed of immigrants from their inception." But that's different from being open, in practice, to immigrants of all kinds and colors and from setting out to weave the ethnic and racial tapestry of the United States now. The United States enslaved Black people and, once chattel slavery ended, failed to protect them from horrific abuse and domestic terrorism and continued to bar them from full participation, with equal rights, in American life. It favored people from Europe and even from northern Europe over those with darker skin from southern Europe and certainly from Asia. We were not, from 1776 onward, good-naturedly, high-mindedly, consciously, and conscientiously laying the path to the diverse country of the present. But the diverse country of the present *is* consistent with what we've told ourselves and told the world our values are. It's special. It's exhilarating. And it can and should be the kind of global beacon we have long called ourselves, but the stability and harmony that such a role requires aren't served by some of what grievance is wreaking.

They aren't served by what I referred to in a 2017 column in the *Times* as the oppression Olympics, with various groups insisting that the distinctiveness and magnitude of its challenges—the singularity of its experience, usually meaning its suffering—be given discrete recognition and even be ranked vis-à-vis the experiences and suffering of other groups. There's an inherent divisiveness to that approach.

There's a bluntness that banishes complexity, often disregards the particulars of a given sequence of events, or privileges one stretch of history over another. And there's sometimes even a cruelty to it, evident in the way that many people on the left moved so quickly to condemn rather than console Israelis and their Jewish allies in the United States after October 7, 2023. Yes, the scope, intensity, and duration of Israel's retaliation in Gaza—and the civilian deaths and desperation that it caused—could be deemed excessive and demanded debate. But some protests of it reflected the moral logic of the oppression Olympics: Israelis and Jews had more power and wealth than Palestinians and Muslims, and all empathy and solidarity should be meted out accordingly. A similar logic seemed to haunt the justly derided testimony of the presidents of Harvard, the University of Pennsylvania, and MIT during a congressional hearing in December 2023 about anti-Semitism on college campuses. The presidents gave squishy, lawyerly answers to the question of whether "calling for the genocide of Jews" constituted impermissible bullying and harassment, though, as lawmakers and commentators later pointed out, their institutions and other universities made vigorous efforts to purge their environments of anything offensive to, say, Black or transgender students.

Not long ago I took an antiracism seminar during which the instructor showed us a pyramid. "Racism Defined" were the words in big letters beside it, and smaller letters near those explained that the pyramid illustrated "white supremacy" at work. As for the pyramid: At its pinnacle was the word "white." Below that, after a huge gap, in the center of the pyramid, was a tight cluster of other races: "Japanese," which was above "Chinese," which was followed, in descending order, by "South Asian," then "Latinx," then "Pacific Islander," then "Arab." After "Arab" came another big gap, and at the very bottom of the pyramid, "Black."

One of the two instructors leading the seminar said that the history of the world, and of the United States, could be understood in terms of the oppression and exploitation of people lower on the pyramid by people higher on it. One of my fellow students raised his hand. How, he asked, were we to think about and integrate the brutal experience of Koreans, who'd been given no place on the pyramid, at the hands of Japanese people during World War II, when female Koreans were, for example, forced into service as "comfort women" for Japanese soldiers? Where was the white supremacy in that? He might as easily have asked about other examples of Japanese imperialist aggression in the past. Or about whether South Asians would agree that they all belonged to one race and were treated with more respect than were Hispanic people in the United States and other Western countries. To any of those inquiries, though, he would probably have received the same answer as the one he got about Japanese-Korean relations: the instructor said that on this day and for the purposes of this course, those relations were irrelevant. The instructor hustled us onward, to various destinations, including the assertion that one of the United States' most significant exports to the world was racism, a statement that confounded me, given that people of different races have been treating one another abominably for much longer than our country's roughly 250-year existence.

What happened in that seminar was a tiny and relatively harmless version of a shutting-down that occurs all the time, and in much more serious ways, and that contradicts and undermines the supposed spirit and purpose of the larger project: respect for everyone, a voice for everyone, inclusion. Yes, some of our sins warrant an especially bright spotlight and their own atonement, and some of our persistent shortcomings cry out for redress more urgently than others do. But shouldn't that still leave room for what Bo Young Lee, who had been the head of DEI at Uber since 2018, did in mid-2023?

She moderated an employee event titled "Don't Call Me Karen," which acknowledged that "Karen" had become a derogatory term for a white woman who, in all her privilege and entitlement, was supposedly prone to calling law enforcement officials on Black people or lodging complaints with store managers, especially about minority workers. "Karen" was a slur and a stereotype, so Lee decided that a discussion of the term and how it made white women feel fit with her diversity mandate. Wrong. Many Uber employees complained that fretting over "Karen" was insensitive to people of color. "You are in pain and upset," the company's chief executive, Dara Khosrowshahi, wrote in a contrite company-wide email to them. He placed Lee on a leave of absence.

There's a hierarchy of oppression, and in certain sectors of American life, including many corporations and most universities, questions about or challenges to it are often met sternly, censoriously, in a manner that seems designed, albeit unintentionally, to till a whole new set of grievances and a whole new class of the aggrieved. The hierarchy of oppression—it's sort of like the pyramid from the seminar I took, only inverted—frequently presumes that people who occupy one tier of it can never truly understand the people who occupy another tier. That belief explains much of the uproar over fiction writers creating protagonists or taking on the voices of characters outside their demographic group. It explains the way some people begin statements of their opinions with a qualifier about the vantage point from which they're speaking: "as a lesbian trans woman of color," "as a cisgender heterosexual white man."

Phoebe Maltz Bovy noticed and rued those qualifiers early: in her 2017 book *The Perils of "Privilege,"* she mocked the inevitable juncture in a certain kind of essay "where the writer (probably a cis White Lady, probably straight or bisexual, probably living in Brooklyn, definitely well educated, but not necessarily well-off) interrupts the usually scheduled programming to duly note that the issues she's describing may not apply to a trans woman in Papua New Guinea." Those self-definitions and disclaimers act as credentials or anti-credentials that supposedly shape—or warp—entire worldviews. But they're also traps, both for the individual and for society: If we can't relate to people who aren't just like us, if empathy is an illusion and attempts to muster it are insults, if we're a hodgepodge of rival grievances rather than a team of unified aspirations, how can we prosper and how can we endure?

We've let the kind of sensitivity we lacked in the past and very much need in the present morph, in many instances, into a hypersensitivity so strange and even illogical that it's a kind of insensitivity all its own. Take some of the media coverage and public discussion after the fatal shooting of six people, including three children, at a Christian school in Nashville in March 2023. The shooter, it turned out, was transgender, and several prominent news organizations pivoted from that detail to stories about the discrimination that transgender people face, the forces arrayed against them in a state like Tennessee, and how keenly transgender people in Nashville feared a reaction to the shooting that would vilify and imperil them. During a panel discussion along those lines on MSNBC, the chyron "Transgender Americans under siege" appeared at the bottom of the screen. Madonna announced that she was going to add a concert in Nashville to her upcoming world tour, and that it would be a fundraiser, with a portion of the proceeds going toward transgender rights organizations. In an accompanying statement, she decried the "oppression of the LGBTQ+" and how that was making "America a dangerous place for our most vulnerable citizens, especially trans women of color."

America *is* dangerous for trans women of color. Many transgender people in general *do* endure discrimination. The media should (and does) write about that, and Madonna should raise as many millions for the cause as she can. But is the plight of trans Americans the conversation to be having following a massacre that yields more logically, readily, and aptly to discussions, no matter how tired, about Americans' easy access to guns—the shooter owned three of them, and fired off 152 rounds before being shot and killed by police—and about the conversion of our schools into shooting galleries? And did none of the reporters, editors, and producers creating the coverage about the terrible treatment of trans Americans not worry that it might seem tactless, to say the least, in the context of those dead children? Or, worse, that it would come across as some kind of exoneration of the shooter, a shift of blame from assassin to society that might well have some merit but also distinguished the reporting on this bloodbath from some of the reporting on other ones?

I don't believe that empathy is unattainable, but I do believe that some of today's social-justice warriors perform pantomimes of it that are driven more by buzzwords and fashionable poses than by serious consideration of the precise message they're sending, the eye rolls it's bound to elicit, and the counterproductive effect of that, which is to make skeptics tune them out. Consider what happened at Johns Hopkins University in June 2023. Someone leaked screenshots of an "LGBTQ Glossary" that had been posted as a resource on the website of the university's Office of Diversity and Inclusion, and that glossary recommended a new definition of "lesbian" as "a non-man attracted to non-men." It explained: "While past definitions refer to 'lesbian' as a woman who is emotionally, romantically, and/ or sexually attracted to other women, this updated definition includes non-binary people." In other words, if people think of themselves as neither women nor men, and are attracted to people who think of themselves as neither women nor men, they can rightly call themselves, and be referred to as, lesbians.

Was "gay man" subject to a similar reassessment? No. The glossary defined that phrase as "a man who is emotionally, romantically, sexually, affectionately, or relationally attracted to other men." So the drafters of the glossary, in trying to include and accommodate nonbinary people, *excluded* women by erasing womanhood from the word for woman-woman partnerships or marriages while preserving manhood in the word for man-man partnerships or marriages. In the realm of same-sex attraction, there were now men and "non-men." That discrepancy was indeed noticed—widely. "Lesbian was literally the only word in English language that is not tied to man—as in male-feMALE, man-woMAN," the tennis great Martina Navratilova, who is lesbian, tweeted. "And now lesbians are non men?!? Wtf?!?" Wtf indeed. Having no good answer for that, a spokesperson for Johns Hopkins released a statement saying that the new definition of "lesbian" had not been reviewed by top officials with the Office of Diversity and Inclusion before its posting online and that "the language in question has been removed pending review."

That it got there in the first place exemplifies the hypersensitivity I'm talking about. It was an especially loopy manifestation; a more sadly representative one was the dismissal, in late 2022, of an adjunct art history professor at Hamline University who had shown her class a painting of the Prophet Mohammed. A few students at Hamline, a liberal arts school in St. Paul, Minnesota, complained that what the instructor had done was unacceptably offensive to

Muslims, many of whom believe that depictions of the prophet are sacrilegious. Senior school administrators agreed.

But not all Muslims subscribe to that thinking. There's no prohibition on such depictions in the Koran. And the painting shown by the instructor, Erika López Prater, was nothing like the mocking cartoon of Mohammed that the French satirical magazine *Charlie Hebdo* once famously published, to violent effect; it's a widely acknowledged masterpiece. As an article about the instructor's ouster in the *New York Times* by Vimal Patel noted, "It is housed at the University of Edinburgh; similar paintings have been on display at places like the Metropolitan Museum of Art. And a sculpture of the prophet is at the Supreme Court."

López Prater apparently gave students several trigger warnings, even letting them know that they could be excused from class if they felt that the painting would upset them. What's more, the painting could have been regarded, even heralded, as a welcome complement to the countless canvases of Jesus, Mary, Joseph, and the other Christian characters who populate art history courses. Didn't its inclusion reflect the kind of diversity that we rightly ask universities and their faculty to embrace?

Not in the eyes of a Muslim student in the class. After being exposed to the image, she lodged a formal complaint. Why she hadn't objected ahead of time or chosen not to attend this session of the class was unclear: she declined an interview with the *Times*. Maybe she wanted the provocation, having felt so marginalized for so long that she craved and seized an opportunity to broadcast her hurt and demand accountability. Some of her and her fellow Muslim students' comments at a community forum that was prompted by the classroom incident and described in the *Times* article suggested as much, and she later said publicly that "it breaks my heart to stand here to tell people and to beg people to understand me, to feel what I feel."

But was that classroom incident so awful? Was the instructor really any kind of villain? And were the outcry over her actions and her subsequent dismissal fitting responses to what had transpired? For the student, for several top school officials, and for local Muslim allies, such concerns paled beside the larger wrongs to be righted.

In this instance as in so many related ones on dozens of campuses, an overarching grievance—and the imperative of being or seeming exquisitely sensitive to it—left little if any room for guilt, innocence, and proportionality. At the forum, Jaylani Hussein, the executive director of the Minnesota chapter of the Council on American-Islamic Relations, declared that the instructor's showing of the painting had "absolutely no benefit," as if knowledge, scholarship, *education* were irrelevant.

Mark Berkson, a religion professor at Hamline, pushed back. According to the *Times* article, he pointed out to Hussein that "there are many Muslim scholars and experts and art historians who do not believe that this was Islamophobic." Weren't those scholars relevant? Didn't their views matter? Hussein dismissed them as marginal, extremist, and indicative of the broad spectrum of legitimate and illegitimate opinion on any issue. "You can teach a whole class about why Hitler was good," he said, thus likening the display of the painting to the extermination of millions of Jews during the Holocaust. When grievance flowers, perspective withers.

And other intellectual contortions take root. Following the media coverage of what happened at Hamline, its president at the time, Fayneese Miller, released a lengthy public statement (while declining interview requests, at least up to that point). Miller took issue with the idea that López Prater was dismissed per se but gave no specific explanation for why she wasn't being asked back to teach again. Miller also challenged the notion that Hamline was sacrificing important educational and civic principles. "To suggest that the university does not respect academic freedom is absurd on its face," she wrote. "Hamline is a liberal arts institution, the oldest in Minnesota, the first to admit women, and now led by a woman of color." The second of those sentences was a non sequitur—and a revealing one. It implied that a liberal arts institution that blazed trails for women and had racially diverse leadership was inherently virtuous across the board and thus obviously a tribune for freedom of speech and thought. In doing so, it promoted the popular and perverse grievance-era reasoning that the oppressed cannot, ipso facto, behave oppressively.

That reasoning isn't true to how our lives and our societies work, and the further we travel from truth, the deeper we stray onto terrain where everyone's motives are suspect, fewer and fewer people trust one another, and a spirit less collective than competitive prevails. There was a funny take on that spirit in the 2022 movie *Bros*, which cast the gay comedian and actor Billy Eichner as the lovelorn head of a new LGBTQ+ history museum in the making. The members of a staff assisting him in that endeavor represent the different consonants in that cluster and, in a scene given prominent placement in the trailer for the movie, they harp that they're being slighted vis-à-vis the other letters.

"This happens to be Bisexual Awareness Week," says an apparently bisexual man at the conference table, adding, in a full-throated, full-throttle bellow: "No one has acknowledged it!"

"Lesbian History Month was in March!" responds the requisite lesbian, her voice growing as loud and her manner as enraged as the bisexual man's. "Nobody said a goddamn thing!"

The bisexual man fires back: "Of course lesbians get a month and we get a week!" Eichner's character slumps in frustration. It's one of the movie's best moments, not because it's outlandish but because it's on the mark. Grievance is so ambient that it's no longer the lode for docudrama. It's the grist for rom-com.

Much less humorously, I keep thinking back to the contest for the 2016 Democratic presidential nomination and to a stretch of time midway through 2015 when two of the three leading candidates for it—Hillary Clinton and Martin O'Malley—drew swift and stern condemnation for linguistic sacrilege. They committed the same sin. "All lives matter," they said.

In isolation, that has to be the least objectionable message imaginable, a moral no-brainer. And it shouldn't have been an especially big deal even under the circumstances then: Clinton and O'Malley uttered those three words as Black Lives Matter was on the rise. But many activists in the movement or supportive of it reacted furiously, treating "all lives matter" as a belittling correction and blatant insult.

To go characteristically bonkers over Clinton's use of the phrase, the indignity sentries of Twitter had to disregard the occasion and setting of her remarks: she was at a historic Black church in Florissant, Missouri, a location chosen in part as an expression of solidarity with the Black denizens of Ferguson, Missouri, just five miles away, where the fatal shooting of a Black teenager, Michael Brown, by a white police officer had sparked more than a week of protests. The indignity sentries also had to ignore the precise fashion in which "all lives matter" tumbled from Clinton's lips. She didn't say it in connection with police violence, choosing "all" as a pointed alternative to "Black." She said it as the coda to a brief reminiscence about her mother's struggles and stoicism. "I asked her, 'What kept you going?'" Clinton remembered. "Her answer was very simple:

kindness along the way from someone who believed she mattered. All lives matter."

"Hillary Clinton was telling a story about her mother," Donna Brazile, whose role at the helm of Al Gore's 2000 bid for the White House made her the first Black woman to manage a major presidential campaign, noted in a tweet defending Clinton against all the other tweets. Brazile added that Clinton had previously said that "we can stand up together & say 'yes Black lives matter.' Stop hating!"

To rage at O'Malley, activists had to edit out the fact that before he said "All lives matter," he answered "yes" to the question of whether, as president, he would "advance an agenda that will dismantle structural racism in this country." They had to edit out the fact that the person asking that question was one of several dozen Black protesters whose chanting was a deliberate disruption of his onstage conversation with a progressive immigration reform advocate, Jose Antonio Vargas, at the Netroots Nation convention in Phoenix. And they had to edit out the fact that he *did* say "Black lives matter" but just didn't give it the discrete, unchallenged space that activists insisted on its having.

"Black lives matter, white lives matter, all lives matter" were O'Malley's exact words. He was booed nonetheless, and the ruckus continued when Bernie Sanders took the stage, to a point where Sanders told the protesters: "If you don't want me to be here, that's okay. I don't want to out-scream you." He didn't muck up the special status of "Black lives matter" on that day, but as various journalists and other political observers analyzed Clinton's and O'Malley's transgressions, a few of them realized that in an interview with NPR the month before the Netroots Nation convention, Sanders had said, "Black lives matter, white lives matter, Hispanic lives matter."

That, too, was deemed unideal. "Black lives matter" shouldn't have a comma after it. It should have a period. Or, better, an exclamation point.

Sanders stopped talking that way. Clinton watched her language more carefully. O'Malley apologized profusely. And the idea that "Black lives" and "all lives" were somehow in conflict with each other persisted: at a Democratic primary debate in October, the candidates were asked, "Do Black lives matter or do all lives matter," a surreal question if you step just a few paces back from it, a suggestion that there's some binary here, that a choice between the two must be made, and that "both" is a flatly unacceptable response. It wasn't the answer that Sanders, Clinton, or O'Malley gave. They knew better by then.

I understand—and agree—that "Black lives matter" is a necessary reminder and lament that Black lives in particular have been treated as disposable, insignificant. The phrase has purpose and power. But the occasional assertion by political *allies* that "all lives matter"—that the overarching goal is for everyone to be accorded respect and a full complement of rights regardless of color or creed—is outrageous only if you're intent on outrage, only if you've traded the language of inclusion for the impulse to categorize, only if you're measuring each category against the others.

And only if you're as interested in tearing down the people who aren't speaking and behaving in accordance with your dictates as you are in lifting yourself up. Five years after Clinton, O'Malley, and Sanders inadvertently or disobediently strayed from the prescribed talking points, Leslie Neal-Boylan, the dean of the school of nursing at the University of Massachusetts Lowell, reflected on the murder of George Floyd by Minneapolis police officers by distributing a statement to her colleagues and her staff that said:

I am writing to express my concern and condemnation of the recent (and past) acts of violence against people of color. Recent events recall a tragic history of racism and bias that continue to thrive in this country. I despair for our future as a nation if we do not stand up against violence against anyone. BLACK LIVES MATTER, but also, EVERYONE'S LIFE MATTERS. No one should live in fear that they will be targeted for how they look or what they believe.

"How they look" or "what they believe": those phrases sound like an effort to reach out and be as inclusive as possible, to console and fortify Hispanic, Asian American, Muslim, and Jewish people as well as Black people. Given that Neal-Boylan began her statement with references to "people of color" and "a tragic history of racism," I can't read the whole of it as some diminution or dilution of concern for the Black victims of police violence. I can even make the case that by drawing connections between those victims and others, and by alluding to the stake that every marginalized group—that everyone, period—has in a society without bias-driven violence, she's trying to push the cause of Black victims forward, not showing it disrespect.

But a nursing student tweeted her upset over Neal-Boylan's statement, calling it proof of "narrow minded people in lead positions" and warning the dean that "your words will not be forgotten." Within weeks of that tweet, Neal-Boylan was removed from her job. While Fox News and others on the right attributed that development to her "EVERYONE'S LIFE MATTERS" addendum to her "BLACK LIVES MATTER" proclamation, the school vaguely contested that version of events (without volunteering an alternate one), and some of the less ideologically driven reporting on the matter noted several unanswered questions about it. Neal-Boylan didn't publicly present her own account of her ouster.

But what's indisputable is that top university officials felt the need to use the university's official Twitter account to console the upset student, writing: "Thank you for bringing this to our attention. The university hears you and we believe black lives matter." And Neal-Boylan released a *second* statement, atoning for the first. It reads like a parody of penance. "I am writing to apologize," it begins. "I am embarrassed," it goes on to say. "I am personally committed to continue to reflect, learn and grow from any mistakes I make as I, imperfectly, seek to advocate for equality, peace and justice with my words and actions," it concludes.

Is that the mea culpa of someone who has had the scales fall from her eyes? Or of someone performing the dance that she must in an age of elaborate and sometimes illogical choreography? Hardly a week goes by when I don't hear or read a statement of supposedly earnest principle and ask myself that question while also asking myself what's accomplished if what so many people say and do is merely dutiful, prophylactic, an insurance policy against, metaphorically speaking, that one aggrieved student who lies in wait.

Throughout June 2023, people in higher education and students and parents on the cusp of the college application process held their breaths, monitored their inboxes for news bulletins, and otherwise watched closely for any sign, any word, any murmuring of a ruling that could upend college admissions and alter campus life. The Supreme Court had heard arguments regarding two cases—one involving Harvard, the other involving the University of North Carolina at Chapel Hill—that challenged the use of affirmative action, meaning the consideration of applicants' race, in deciding which applicants gained admission to selective schools, and the denouement had to come before the end of the month, when the court closed up shop for the summer. On the last week of June, the court indeed spoke: In a 6–3 ruling, it declared the race-conscious admissions programs at Harvard and UNC—and, by implication, similar programs at other schools—to be unconstitutional.

That ruling of course reflected the ideological composition of the court, with its conservative majority. And it reflected how persistently and enterprisingly opponents of affirmative action had worked not just to get a big case but to get the *right* case before the Supreme Court: the lawsuit against Harvard, filed by Students for Fair Admissions, focused on the negative impact that race-based decisions were allegedly having not on white students but on Asian American ones. "There was a lot of organization at the grassroots level in terms of finding plaintiffs to bring this case forward," Andra Gillespie, the Emory political scientist, recalled, adding that prominent conservatives and conservative groups "have actually been trying to recruit folks for years," especially nonwhite folks. "It's not unusual for conservative movements to try to demonstrate their multiracial chops in some way, shape, or form."

But the court's ruling and the timing of it reflected other factors, too. As Christopher Caldwell noted in an essay in the *New York Times* several weeks beforehand, they spoke to how much the nature and stakes of the college admissions game had changed with the country's racial diversification. That diversification meant a pool of Asian American applicants big enough for extensive data about their admissions and rejections to exist and enough affected people to draw increased attention to affirmative action from the public and the courts. It meant bigger pools of multiple racial and ethnic groups, too, and Students for Fair Admissions argued in part that preferential treatment for people of color *other* than Asian Americans translated into discrimination against them. According to the organization's analysis, Asian Americans would make up more than half of the student body at Harvard if their numbers weren't being deliberately suppressed.

Caldwell recalled that in the early days of affirmative action, in the 1960s and 1970s, its intended and actual beneficiaries were limited in number; their enrollment, in turn, affected an equally limited number of white applicants. "The trade-offs in weighted admissions were relatively small, and the affected parties were hard to identify," he explained. That arithmetic didn't forestall debates over affirmative action, which were constant and often heated, but it kept the temperature of them below the boil that brought the Harvard and UNC cases before the nation's highest court. By the time of the court's June 2023 decision, however, colleges were carefully considering—and, with affirmative action, boosting the percentages of—Latino and Native American and Pacific Islander students as well as Black ones. When you added Asian American students to the mix, you ended up with a student body like Stanford University's. White Americans were just 22 percent of its class of 2026, according to Caldwell.

The new math created a situation in which some white people felt more protective than ever about the slots that they still occupied, and in which the percentages of other racial groups were high enough that any increases or decreases had readily discernible effects on everyone else. "In today's admissions systems," Caldwell wrote, "all racial groups' relative outcomes are scrupulously tallied, and all trade-offs among groups are conspicuous. The claim of Students for Fair Admissions is that significant numbers of Asians are being lopped off admissions rolls to serve the goals of racial balancing, securing admissions for Black, Latino and probably also white students."

It's a muddle, a scramble, and perhaps that's why a YouGov poll taken just before the Supreme Court's ruling on June 29 showed not only that more white Americans and more Hispanic Americans opposed the consideration of race in college admissions than supported it, but also that more Black people were opposed to than in favor of it. Among white Americans, the split was 71 percent to 21 percent, with 8 percent undecided. Among Hispanic Americans, the split was 57 to 23, with 19 undecided. And among Black Americans, 47 to 38, with 15 undecided.

David Malcolm Carson, a half-Black, half-Jewish man profiled by the *Free Press* on the eve of the ruling, personified the fluid feelings and serious misgivings about affirmative action in the United States. He'd once been a fierce and involved advocate for its use in school admissions, but he felt conflicted about how the suits against Harvard and UNC should be resolved. "When affirmative action was conceptualized, it was to right past wrongs," he told the article's author, Rupa Subramanya. "Then, it became sort of endless. It wasn't just African Americans. It was Native Americans and Hispanics. And then it was women, LGBT, etc., and that wiped out the moral imperative of it a little, because diversity is not quite as strong a claim as correcting past wrongs."

In the realm of college admissions—where just-grow-the-pie-bigger bromides won't work, given the ceiling on the size of an incoming class—marginalized groups aren't aligned with one another. They're in competition with one another: I lose when you gain, and vice versa. That dynamic exposes the sloppiness and even silliness of the "people of color" catchall, whose shortcomings are also revealed by the disparate degrees of attachment that Black, Latino, and Asian American voters feel to the Democratic Party. It has shown up in arenas other than higher education. And it threatens to fragment

American life even further, as it introduces new us-versus-them sub-sets and new strains of grievance to go along with them.

Look at that sordid mess with the Los Angeles City Council in late 2022. An audio recording of a meeting of three Latino mem-bers of the council and an influential Latino labor leader leaked to the media. On it, the council's president, Nury Martinez, could be heard comparing the Black child of a white council member to a monkey and complaining about how often that council member carried the boy around in public, as if showing him off and trying to score points. The context for her racist remark made it all the more revealing: the four political players were discussing how the districts that compose the council should be redrawn, a process fraught with Latinos' frustrations that their representation on the council, where they then held just four of its fifteen seats, was out of sync with their numbers in Los Angeles, where they accounted for nearly half of the population. Martinez and the three others were talking about power and, specifically, the jostling and *competition* for it, a preoccupation evident in one of her other vulgar com-ments: she disparaged and dismissed the city's Cuban American district attorney, George Gascón, by saying, "Fuck that guy—he's with the Blacks."

So much for rainbow coalitions. So much for the rainbow flag, too? I ask not because of that fictional scene in *Bros*. I ask because there is ample and growing tension in the LGBTQ+ consonant clus-ter, though many Ls, Gs, Bs, Ts, and Qs are understandably and, in some ways, commendably loath to discuss it, lest each component of the coalition and the whole of it suffer. It's a complicated, even painful matter. But it's caused in part by increasingly specific rec-ognitions of subgroups, and of subgroups within those subgroups, each believing that unless it is singled out, its particular persecution spotlighted, its needs and demands recognized on their own, it is being denied justice. It is being erased.

The Human Rights Campaign, a major force over the years in the fight for gay rights, has had a gigantic sign outside its Washington, DC, headquarters with the same words as those emblazoned on a T-shirt for sale on its website: "Black Trans Lives Matter." Are those lives not included in the Black Lives that Matter? Or in the Trans Lives that Matter? Or in All Lives that Matter? And when you splinter groups to spotlight them, aren't you also, in a fashion, segregating them? What message comes across?

Mounk wrote in *The Great Experiment* that as he "traveled the world and studied its history," he came to believe "that a generalized hostility to any form of collective identity is a misguided way to build tolerant societies." As I scrolled through *all* the T-shirts on the Human Rights Campaign website, I came upon one that arguably obviated the others. It was simple. It was forceful. It was universal: "United Against Hate."

Eight

The Price Is Not Right

Throughout much of 2022 and early 2023, many concerned Americans who didn't support Trump nonetheless debated the wisdom of the various criminal investigations—by federal, New York, and Georgia prosecutors—into his conduct in the presidency and immediately afterward. They didn't doubt that he'd done wrong. He was *Trump*, after all. He'd almost certainly done wrong. But they worried about the precedent that those probes might be setting and about the possibility of future ex-presidents being pursued by their political opponents for much less reason or for no reason at all. They worried that in an era of such fiercely dueling realities, the investigations didn't—and any prosecutions that resulted from them wouldn't—have credibility with a sizeable share of Americans. They worried about partisan passions being inflamed even further, about political animosities somehow growing more intense still.

They also worried about violence—and with excellent reason, as the immediate responses to Trump's federal indictment in June

2023 on thirty-seven counts of criminal wrongdoing made clear. The provocateur Pete Santilli, who hosts an internet talk show popular on the far right, said that if he were in charge of the US Marines, he'd order them to hunt down President Biden and "throw him in freakin' zip ties in the back of a freakin' pickup truck" so that he could not return to the White House or preside over the United States any longer. In the same spirit, one of Santilli's guests fantasized aloud about confronting and shooting General Mark A. Milley, the former chairman of the Joint Chiefs of Staff, whom Trump had branded an enemy. On the Donald, a wild message board whose Trump-loving participants had been kicked off Reddit for their threats of violence and expressions of white nationalism, one person wrote: "We need to start killing these traitorous fuckstains." Someone else chimed in that attempts to crush Trump and the Americans he spoke for were "not gonna stop until bodies start stacking up."

Mainstream Republicans' language didn't hew quite as closely to a Quentin Tarantino script, but it went well beyond the norms of just a decade earlier. There were invocations of civil war, intimations of bloodshed. Kari Lake made her proud declaration, mentioned earlier, that Trump's eager defenders were a gun-loving lot with an ample trove of firearms. Donald Trump Jr.'s fiancée, Kimberly Guilfoyle, posted a picture of her father-in-law-to-be on Instagram and, over the image, the words "RETRIBUTION IS COMING." "Eye for an eye," tweeted an Arizona congressman, Andy Biggs. Among no small number of lawmakers in the time of Trump, the Code of Hammurabi was as relevant as any code of conduct.

And violence wasn't merely in the air. It was at the Capitol, where four people, including a police officer, were killed as a direct result of the January 6 rioting and five police officers who'd been on the job and on the scene died later, four by suicide. It was inside the Wisconsin home of John Roemer, a retired judge who was zip-tied to a chair and fatally shot in June 2022 by a man whom he'd once sentenced to six years in prison for burglary and who carried a list of other public figures he was apparently targeting. It was near the Maryland home of Supreme Court Justice Brett Kavanaugh days later, when a man who'd threatened Kavanaugh's life was found with a gun and a knife and arrested on a charge of attempted murder. That same year violence came for Paul Pelosi, Nancy's husband, with a hammer in San Francisco, and for Representative Lee Zeldin, a Republican congressman running for governor of New York, with a knife in upstate New York. He was onstage at a campaign event when his assailant, who was foiled, came at him.

Violence showed up in polling, too. After the January 6 insurrection, pollsters and researchers began burrowing more deeply and frequently into how Americans felt about violence against the government, and while a majority of them disapproved, the minority who could see the need for it was disturbingly large. A poll by the *Washington Post* and the University of Maryland released days before the first anniversary of the January 6 insurrection found that 34 percent of Americans said that violence against the government could be justifiable, a figure that, according to the *Post*'s main article about the survey, was "considerably higher than in past polls by the *Post* or other major news organizations dating back more than two decades." Republicans and independents were almost twice as likely to find violence justifiable as Democrats, 23 percent of whom could nonetheless envision circumstances that warranted violence.

A separate survey conducted shortly before the 2022 midterm elections by YouGov and States United Action, a nonpartisan organization that promotes fair elections, found not only that 37 percent of Americans condoned some degree of violence if their presidential candidate of choice ended up losing in 2024 "because of unfair actions" by political rivals, but also that 20 percent could imagine violence being "a little" justified even if that candidate lost "after all eligible voters were counted fairly." Another of the survey's findings was especially ominous in retrospect, given many of Trump's supporters' assessment of his federal indictment for mishandling (to say the least) classified documents, which they saw as no worse than the discovery of classified documents at President Biden's home, even though Biden promptly returned all of them. About 30 percent of respondents said that violence was "always" or "frequently" acceptable if "leaders from the party in power disobey the laws while prosecuting their political opponents who disobey the same laws." Another 19 percent said that under such circumstances, violence was "occasionally" acceptable.

According to polls, significant majorities of Americans had come to expect violence following an election. Americans assumed that would be the case with the presidential contest in 2024, just as it had been with the presidential contest in 2020. We were looking at the possibility of becoming inured to political violence. Or maybe we already *were* inured. The fatal shooting of eight people at a mall in Allen, Texas, in May 2023 by a gunman whose attire and social media history flagged anti-Black, anti-woman, and anti-Semitic beliefs got less intense and sustained coverage than comparable incidents had before, as Michelle Goldberg noted in a column in the *New York Times.*

In years past, she recalled, a massacre with such a toll and such a trigger "would have brought the news cycle to a halt and forced politicians to respond. When the white supremacist Dylann Roof murdered nine parishioners in a South Carolina church in 2015, it was so shocking that the governor at the time, Nikki Haley, removed the

Confederate battle flag from the State House grounds." But not only had mass shootings become unsurprising ("the background noise of life in a country coming apart at the seams," Goldberg wrote), mass shootings by gunmen with ideologies like Roof's and the Texas assassin's were also familiar. According to a report in early 2023 by the Anti-Defamation League, all the killings in the United States in 2022 that were clearly tied to extremism were committed by right-wing extremists of some kind.

"It's hard to think of a historical precedent for a society allowing itself to be terrorized in the way we have," Goldberg reflected, under the headline "Timothy McVeigh's Dreams Are Coming True." McVeigh was one of the two antigovernment, gun-fetishizing, right-wing extremists responsible for the bombing of a federal building in Oklahoma City in 1995 that killed 168 people, and Goldberg was referring in large part to how little we've done to keep guns away from dangerous people. She was also nodding to *Homegrown*, a 2023 book by Jeffrey Toobin about McVeigh, in which Toobin wrote: "In the nearly 30 years since the Oklahoma City bombing, the country took an extraordinary journey—from nearly universal horror at the action of a right-wing extremist to wide embrace of a former president (also possibly a future president) who reflected the bomber's values."

And here we are. American society's propensity for political violence shows up well beyond such high-profile tragedies as what happened in Allen, Texas. Well beyond the 2017 shooting at a Republican practice session in Alexandria, Virginia, for the annual Congressional Baseball Game. Well beyond that synagogue in the Squirrel Hill neighborhood in Pittsburgh the following year and that Walmart in El Paso and that supermarket in Buffalo over the years after that. It showed up in a growing number of antisemitic attacks in the United States in late 2023 and in a similar increase in gruesome threats against American Jews. Cornell University canceled classes for a day as students, faculty, and administrators there sought to make sense of the arrest of a Cornell junior charged with posting online messages that called for violence against Jews. On campuses around the United States, confrontations between pro-Palestinian and pro-Israeli demonstrators grew so common and tense—and Jewish and Muslim students were so acutely on edge, so genuinely scared—that the federal government in mid-November 2023 opened discrimination investigations into half a dozen schools.

As the extensive reporting for the *New York Times* Opinion section's series on political violence in late 2022 and for Adrienne La-France's cover story on the same topic in the *Atlantic* in early 2023 made clear, participants in political demonstrations are increasingly likely to be armed. Paramilitary groups have been growing. White nationalists with stockpiles of firearms appear to be ever more numerous and ever less abashed. Threats to federal lawmakers have risen.

In the candid interviews that Mitt Romney gave the journalist McKay Coppins for the 2023 book *Romney: A Reckoning*, Romney disclosed that following the January 6, 2021, rioting at the Capitol, he started spending five thousand dollars a day on private security for his family. Romney was alone among Republican senators in voting to convict Trump after *both* of his impeachments by the House, and he spoke to Coppins of a whole new fear he sometimes felt at public events, including one in his home state, Utah, where Trump diehards were waiting for him. "As a former presidential candidate," Coppins wrote in an adapted excerpt from the book in the *Atlantic*, "he was well acquainted with heckling. Scruffy Occupy Wall Streeters had shouted down his stump speeches; gay-rights activists had 'glitter bombed' him at rallies. But these were Utah Republicans—they were supposed to be his people. Model citizens, well-behaved Mormons, respectable patriots and pillars of the community, with kids and church callings and responsibilities at work. Many of them had probably been among his most enthusiastic supporters in 2012. Now they were acting like wild children. And if he was being honest with himself, there were moments up on that stage when he was afraid of them."

Coppins wrote that before Trump's second Senate trial, on charges of inciting that January 6 riot, a fellow Republican senator of Romney's who was a member of the party's leadership in the chamber said that he was leaning toward a vote to convict Trump. "You can't do that, Romney recalled someone saying," Coppins recounted. "Think of your personal safety, said another. Think of your children. The senator eventually decided they were right." Party loyalty and political self-preservation weren't all that kept Republican lawmakers solidly behind Trump. At least a few of them feared physical harm if they strayed.

And the specter of violence has trickled down to public officials and public workers well below the level and visibility of members of Congress. Rioters, in some instances armed, have invaded statehouses. In 2020 and again in 2022, law enforcement officials braced and sketched out plans for violence at the polls on Election Day. State election officials and local election workers have been harassed or downright terrorized, some receiving death threats, some forced into hiding. There have been attacks or bomb threats against abortion clinics, antiabortion pregnancy centers, and places that provide medical care to transgender children. School officials and librarians have been harassed and threatened by parents who disapproved of the instruction being promoted or the books being made available. And on and on.

None of that is normal. None of it is healthy. None of it bodes well. As LaFrance wrote, "In recent years, Americans have contemplated a worst-case scenario, in which the country's extreme and widening divisions lead to a second Civil War. But what the country is experiencing now—and will likely continue to experience for a generation or more—is something different. The form of extremism we face is a new phase of domestic terror, one characterized by radicalized individuals with shape-shifting ideologies willing to kill their political enemies. Unchecked, it promises an era of slow-motion anarchy."

What's radicalizing them are grievances puffed up beyond all rationale, swollen by contemporary life and modern politics to the size of a zeppelin. Political violence is the consummation of grievances that gargantuan. LaFrance's checklist of optimal conditions for it tracks dynamics that nurture grievance almost exactly: "highly visible wealth disparity, declining trust in democratic institutions, a perceived sense of victimhood, intense partisan estrangement based on identity, rapid demographic change, flourishing conspiracy theories, violent and dehumanizing rhetoric against the 'other,' a sharply divided electorate, and a belief among those who flirt with violence that they can get away with it." Our grievances, unchecked, aren't just ugly. They're deadly.

Grievance stalks the federal government from without, and grievance undermines the federal government from within. It does that in ways lamented in countless articles and many books over the past few decades, by calcifying lawmakers' positions and aggravating the enmity between parties to a point where many members of Congress are unwilling to compromise—at least not with the scoundrels across the aisle—and uninterested in common ground. They care as much for bipartisanship as they do for shingles, so when there isn't one-party control of the Senate, House, and White House, there isn't much of a path to ambitious legislation or, for that matter, to doing the nation's basic business and fixing its fundamental problems with anything approaching expedition. For that matter, there's barely any decorum. During a committee hearing in the Senate in late 2023, Senator Markwayne Mullin, an Oklahoma Republican, challenged the president of the International Brotherhood of Teamsters, Sean O'Brien, to a brawl. Representative Tim Burchett, a Tennessee Republican, said that Representative Kevin McCarthy, the former House speaker, had intentionally shoved him in a crowded Capitol hallway—and he chased after McCarthy. A headline in the *New York Times* declared: "Fight Club Erupts on Capitol Hill." A month later, a *Politico* article by Mia McCarthy that reflected on 2023 bore the headline "Farewell to one of the dumbest years in congressional history" and quoted Representative Patrick McHenry, a North Carolina Republican who had decided not to run for reelection, on all the melodrama. "A very actively stupid political environment," he called it.

Although measuring the productivity of various Congresses is a beloved political pastime, it's an imperfect science, at least as done by most journalists. The number of pieces of legislation enacted doesn't take into account their heft, complexity, and import. And who's to say that the amount of legislation brought up for significant debate isn't more important? Or that, in the cases of some Congresses, the amount of legislation thwarted isn't of more vital service to the nation than an assembly line of successfully passed but shoddily conceived bills? Even so, reasonable metrics chart, in general, a worrisome lack of productivity over the past few decades (with a bit of an uptick in President Biden's first two years, given that he had Democratic majorities in the Senate, if you counted Vice President Kamala Harris's tie-breaking vote, and the House during that period). And reforms that enjoy broad public support (the elimination of the carried-interest loophole in the tax code, a more comprehensive and reliable system of background checks for gun purchasers) languish. Congressional constipation has become a predictable motif of political journalism. My favorite highlight of such coverage was a September 2014 article in the *New York Times* about a surprising burst of activity from the 113th Congress, which had previously seemed to be on track for ignominy: "Congress Avoids Being Least Productive Ever." Whew! Close call.

But it's not just sclerosis that grievance has brought to the halls of Congress. It's silliness, too. Yuval Levin, the founding editor of the policy journal *National Affairs*, has traced the devolution of Congress from a place of lawmaking to a place of theater with a troupe of actors more interested in grievance than governance. "We now think of institutions less as formative and more as performative, less as molds of our character and behavior and more as platforms for us to stand on and be seen," he said in an interview on NPR's *Morning Edition* in 2020, on the same week as the release of a new book of his, *A Time to Build*, that looked at all that had been torn down or degraded, including many crucially important institutions such as Congress.

"We see people using institutions as stages, as a way to raise their profile or build their brand, and those kinds of institutions become much harder to trust," he continued, saying that the institutions inhabited by politicians were perfect examples—Congress in particular. When various Republican members of Congress took to the stage of the House floor in October 2023 to argue for or against House Speaker Kevin McCarthy's removal from his post,

Representative Kelly Armstrong, a McCarthy supporter, rendered an assessment identical to Levin's. "Let's be clear why we're here—because the incentive structure in this town is completely broken," she told her fellow lawmakers. "We no longer value loyalty, integrity, confidence, or collaboration. Instead, we have descended to a place where clicks, TV hits, and the never-ending quest for the most mediocre taste of celebrity drives decisions and encourages juvenile behavior that is so far beneath this esteemed body."

That juvenile behavior was perfectly exemplified by a ludicrous series of symbolic votes that the Republican House majority insisted on taking in late 2023. For alleged crimes of indolence, incompetence, wokeness, or simply having the temerity to serve a president they abhorred, House Republicans voted to cut the annual salary of Defense Secretary Lloyd Austin to $1. Then they voted to cut the annual salary of Transportation Secretary Pete Buttigieg to $1. Neither Cabinet member actually needed to fear such impoverishment: the votes didn't have that actual force or effect. They were antics. They were tantrums.

And they were at once results of our grievance culture and perpetuators of our grievance culture, belonging to a doom loop of legislative unseriousness and inertia that was described as such by Larry Hogan, the former two-term governor of Maryland, when I spoke with him in mid-2023. I'd interviewed and written about Hogan several times over the years, fascinated by his outsize popularity—he maintained approval ratings above 70 percent—as a Republican in one of the bluest states in the country. And I'd noticed that while he indeed had a typical politician's ego, he did not have a typical politician's style, perhaps because of his mathematical need to do what most other politicians could neglect to and appeal across the political divide. He didn't sprint, in the hope of extra media attention, toward divisive cultural issues. He didn't hurl gratuitous insults at political opponents. And as he saw how well that worked for him, he also saw how poorly the opposite tack worked for American democracy. "We've sort of created the environment that rewards bad behavior," he told me. "The crazier, the louder, the angrier you are, the more attention you get. That's true for some cable news personalities—and it's true of elected officials in both parties."

The country suffers. A Congress dedicated to and distracted by grievance leaves an enormous power vacuum, which is filled, imperfectly, by the president through controversial executive actions and the courts through judicial activism—both mechanisms that exacerbate partisan warfare. "Grievance politics is imbued with a fundamental sense of *negative civic energy*," wrote the political scientists Matthew Flinders and Markus Hinterleitner in a 2022 paper, "Party Politics vs. Grievance Politics," for the scholarly journal *Society*. Those italics are theirs, not mine. That's how much they wanted to stress that phrase and the phenomenon. "Traditionally, parties articulate and aggregate public preferences in party programs, compete for votes and office, and seek to transform preferences into policy; but the new breed of politicians merely transforms citizens' preferences into grievances and blame," they observed. That transformation isn't much of a magic trick. Those citizens are swimming in grievances even before the new breed of politicians deepens the pool. And those citizens are already eager to cast blame.

Our insufficiently questioned, inadequately modulated grievances endanger us in ways less obvious and final than violence, and they impede and diminish us apart from turning our governments into instruments clumsier, more ineffectual, and less honestly representative than they could and should be. They affect how, every day, we interact or fail to interact with one another. They affect the stories we tell about ourselves and about our world, ratcheting up the subjectivity of those narratives and corrupting the truth of them. They skew our perspectives. They skew *us*.

And they do the opposite of what, in their most constructive form, they're meant to, the opposite of what we believe, foolishly or disingenuously, we're trying to make happen. They don't hurtle us and those around us into actions that bear results; they strand us in a kind of inaction that just feels like something else because of all the noise that attends it. They trade motion for commotion. They turn us inward, as we focus on our wounds and what we're owed for them, rather than outward, where the possibility of some measure of the change we say we want exists. They isolate us in cliques of the like-minded, when it's in the diverse community of a larger America that lasting reforms and durable truces are made. They're agents of stasis in revolutionary drag.

They facilitate a retreat from responsibility, from accountability—from reality itself, guiding the people in their grip away from events and facts that would challenge their sense of victimization toward other events and "alternative facts" that keep their aggrieved takes intact. That was on display when the congressional committee looking into Trump's election lies and the January 6 violence held televised hearings to share their findings. Rather than reckon with the committee's painstakingly assembled conclusions and encourage their supporters to do likewise, right-wing commentators and conservative lawmakers labored to recast the rioting as relatively innocuous and to dismiss the committee's account of Trump's role in it. They did so not with their own, contradictory evidence. No such evidence existed. They instead fanned the flames of their supporters' grievances, telling them that the nine members of the House of

Representatives who composed the committee and that Democrats in general were exaggerating and weaponizing an ugly but dubiously remarkable incident to muffle their voices and sideline their values. *Nothing to see here, folks!* Nothing, that is, except the ways in which *you* are being disrespected and mistreated.

On the eve of the committee's first televised hearing, the comically pro-Trump website the *Federalist* published a commentary by the indefatigably pro-Trump congressman Jim Jordan with the headline: "The True Goal of the J6 Committee Is to Slander and Shame Conservatives Out of the Public Sphere." The paragraphs that followed were of an aggrieved piece with that. "Democrats want to use the violence of Jan. 6 to stigmatize conservative voices and delegitimize conservative ideals," Jordan wrote. "They've even talked— condescendingly, of course—about treating conservatives as 'cult' members who need to be deprogrammed." I suppose I should be comforted that Jordan acknowledged the violence. But that was merely in the service of identifying the much greater danger: haughty liberals.

Mollie Hemingway, the editor in chief of the *Federalist*, weighed in a week and a half later, after several of the televised hearings had taken place. "The January 6 riot was not unimportant," she wrote, her double negative perhaps a clue to her discomfort with giving her ideological adversaries so much as an inch, "but its importance has been blown wildly out of proportion by Democrats and their compliant media mostly because it's a vehicle to get rid of the politician they detest." She meant Trump, of course, who, in her telling, was the most unjustly maligned egomaniac ever to bring his grift to Washington, DC. The headline on her blame-deflecting screed: "The Corporate Media Aristocracy Is Completely Out of Touch on What's Important and Urgent."

Fox News was an emporium of similar sentiments, where Republican viewers could find comforting reassurance that *they*—not the injured and dead police officers, not the voters being discounted in Trump's schemes to overturn their will—were the besieged and besmirched parties. The popular right-wing radio host and podcaster Mark Levin told Sean Hannity that the nine lawmakers investigating January 6 were nothing more than "a rogue committee that is appointed by Nancy Pelosi to stop Donald Trump from running for president." Tucker Carlson's summary of January 6 was that "some guy in Viking horns wandered around on mushrooms and made weird noises." Media characterizations that made more of it amounted to "lifestyle liberal narcissism," he said. Peeved and aggrieved, he offered validation to viewers who felt the same way.

It was just as Trump wanted. It was Trump's signature way. Much as his allies and enablers told Republicans that they were the real targets and victims of the January 6 committee's work, he told Republicans that they were the real targets and victims of the FBI's search for—and recovery of—the classified documents that he had strewn throughout Mar-a-Lago, from ballroom to bathroom, and refused to part company with despite repeated entreaties of escalating impatience from federal officials. At a huge, raucous rally in Wilkes-Barre, Pennsylvania, less than a month after that August 2022 showdown, Trump told his audience: "They're trying to silence me and, more importantly, they're trying to silence you."

The Oscar ceremony during which Will Smith slapped Chris Rock on live television crystallized grievance's incursion into nearly all forums and facets of American life. Almost a year later, Rock's stand-up comedy special on Netflix amounted to a commentary on that. At one point during that show, *Selective Outrage*, he bemoaned

Americans' desire for attention, attention, attention, and he inventoried their strategies for getting it. One of the main ones, he said, was "to be a victim."

"Don't get me wrong," he cautioned. "There's no victim shaming going on—no, no, no, no, no. There are real victims in the world. There are people who are going through unspeakable trauma, and they need your love." But there are also "people that know good and goddamned well they ain't victims," he added. "Like white men! When did white men become victims? White men actually think they losin' the country. Did you see the Capitol riots? White men tryin' to overthrow the government that they run!"

The audience roared at that one. They didn't at a few lines he'd uttered a few beats earlier, not because those words were artless or off target but because they weren't crafted for laughs so much as for earnest reflection, and they captured something about grievance as eloquently as possible. "If everybody claims to be a victim," Rock said, "when the real victims need help, ain't nobody going to be there to help them, okay? And right now, we live in a world where the emergency room is filled up with motherfuckers with paper cuts."

Stated in cliché, grievance cries wolf. It's the enemy of perspective, proportionality, and nuance, all of which are necessary for honest conversation, for meaningful collaboration, for progress. And perspective, proportionality, and nuance are in trouble on the left as well as on the right. The entirety of *Selective Outrage* and Rock's recent history—he stopped doing shows on college campuses because he didn't want to navigate the minefield of microaggressions—make clear that "paper cuts" was an ecumenical admonition.

In some precincts of the social-justice left, the insistence that insults lurk everywhere, that even the littlest nicks do big damage, and that the only enlightened strategy is to rid the world of anything that anyone might deem offensive, isn't just humorlessly literal, needlessly absolutist, and vaguely paranoid. It's exhausting. It runs contrary to human nature. We can't be on guard all the time. We can't care about everything, as Amanda Ripley's and David Von Drehle's reflections on the all-Armageddon-all-the-time news media so intelligently argued. And if we're commanded to care that much, if we're hectored to patrol our every gesture and syllable, we're likely to care about less, not more, and to lapse into stillness and silence. The virtue police haven't taught us triage. They haven't given us a short list of top priorities.

They have given us Stanford University's Elimination of Harmful Language Initiative, a glossary much like the one by the Sierra Club that George Packer marveled at, thirteen pages of about 150 terms, including ones so benign in the eyes of any reasonable human that the people who put it together achieved little more than their own discreditation and the supply of ammunition to all the politicians, pundits, and publications railing against excessive wokeness. Like Johns Hopkins after the fiasco involving the definition of lesbians as "non-men," Stanford essentially disavowed the effort as soon as the public grew aware of it in early 2023. When a college sides with Fox News over its own staff, that's a good indication of grievance gone berserk, but then the glossary itself was indication enough.

It outlawed "brave" because some Native Americans had long ago been called Braves. Never mind that 99.9 percent of the English-speaking population considers "brave" a compliment and hears nothing more or less than that in it. Never mind that "brave" has been bestowed, over time, on civil rights pioneers, on gay rights pioneers, on marginalized people who were, um, bravely refusing to confine themselves to the margins. "Brave" had to go, as did "basket case," with etymological roots in the existence of limbless people transported by basket; "rule of thumb," with linguistic connection to long-ago guidelines for wife-beating; "hip-hip hooray," apparently a variant of a rallying cry used by German citizens during the Holocaust.

Those explanations, furnished in Stanford's glossary, underscored the document's nonsensicalness: a person could be offended by many of the prohibited words and phrases only once Stanford had told them to be and why. Is that not the creation rather than the elimination of insult? Interviewed about the semantic no-fly list for an article in *Inside Higher Ed*, a rabbi named Josh Yuter said that the dark nature of "hip-hip hooray" was news to him and, he suspected, to most of the Jewish people he knew. "I cannot speak to traumas experienced by actual survivors," Yuter said, "but I would be very surprised if 'hip-hip hooray' was passed down as intergenerational trauma to merit inclusion as being 'harmful' in any way."

Neither the scuttled Stanford glossary nor the Sierra Club's overzealous scrub of the English language are distant outliers. Around the same time that sensible people were puzzling over Stanford's peculiar contribution to contemporary discourse, they were treated to a tweet from the account of the Associated Press's stylebook on proper usage, "the gold standard for English-speaking journalism," as Nicolas Camut wrote in *Politico*. The tweet read: "We recommend avoiding general and often dehumanizing 'the' labels such as the poor, the mentally ill, the French, the disabled, the college-educated."

I'd argue that most readers or hearers of those phrases understand and experience them as synonyms for poor *people* or mentally ill *people*, even if "people" isn't spelled out or uttered. But in regard to those groups, I also acknowledge how the language flagged by the AP can possibly, over time, function as a concern-suppressing, emotion-dulling, dehumanizing abstraction. But the French? The college-educated? Even (forgive me) the French wondered at this impulse to preserve their humanity and bubble-wrap their feelings: the French embassy in the United States tweeted a screenshot of a mock new designation of itself as "the Embassy of Frenchness."

Funny. But, then again, not, as my *Times* colleague Nick Kristof nailed in a column: "The flap over the French underscores the ongoing project to revise terminology in ways that are meant to be more inclusive—but which I fear are counterproductive and end up inviting mockery and empowering the right. Latino to Latinx. Women to people with uteruses. Homeless to houseless. L.G.B.T. to LGBTQIA2S+. Breastfeeding to chestfeeding. Asian American to A.A.P.I. Ex-felon to returning citizen. Pro-choice to pro-decision. I inhabit the world of words, and even I'm a bit dizzy. As for my friends who are homeless, what they yearn for isn't to be called houseless; they want housing." Kristof, a columnist decidedly left of center, worried enough about the "liberal penchant for renaming things" that he revisited it in another column just four and a half months later, writing that it "leaves many Americans feeling bewildered and excluded." That second column delivered a blunt message to Democrats trying to keep Trump from returning to 1600 Pennsylvania Avenue or a Trump Lite Republican culture warrior from moving in: "The way to win elections is to engage voters rather than wag fingers at them."

I'm functionally blind in one eye and live with the elevated risk and fear of going blind in the other, and every time I stumble across some tsk-tsk about doing away with "blind study" because it's cruel to me, I want to scream. It's not. It's a succinct and evocative metaphor—nothing more. To go down that censorious road is potentially to arrive at a pedantic and joyless cul-de-sac where "having a vision" is verboten, because some people don't have actual vision, and where "you're not hearing me" is disrespectful to deaf people, who can *never* hear you or anyone else. "I don't feel seen" and its variants happen to be popular expressions among marginalized people and groups, but isn't "seeing" as the yardstick of recognition a worse disregard for people like me than "blind study"? We could end up in some kooky verbal quagmires. We *are* in some kooky verbal quagmires.

We jumble undebatable transgressions that indisputably matter and stuff of lesser if any consequence, and we do it with more than language. Flash back to the height of the #MeToo conversation in 2017 and 2018 and to the Shitty Media Men list, which circulated privately among women journalists for a while before its existence, along with many of the names on it, became publicly known and the subject of considerable news coverage and commentary. It was a crowdsourced compilation of men in media who'd allegedly acted abusively toward women or made the work environment a hostile or uncomfortable place for them. My characterization of the men's wrongdoing is verbose because the accusations on it sprawled incoherently from grave criminal offenses to behavior more in the realm of discourtesy, and that was at once one of its chief flaws and one of the principal ways in which it served as an emblem of the age of grievance. The Shitty Media Men list argued for attention to and redress of a serious problem—male bosses and colleagues doing physical and professional harm to the women around them—but made the universe of offenders and offenses so vast and muddled that major culprits blended together with minor ones, and the discussion of that core problem took a detour into an inevitable and mandatory debate over the threshold for inclusion on the list.

Should "weird lunch dates," which was one of the cited infractions, be keeping company with rape? Didn't the former minimize the latter? My answer is yes, and some of the eventual and predictable backlash to #MeToo and the petering out of talk about sexual abuse and sexual harassment were likely hastened by excesses like Shitty Media Men. And what of the list's granting of anonymity to accusers but not to the accused? And its allowance of accusation without evidence, conviction without trial? Defenders of the list and of similar overcorrections claimed that possibly ending the careers and savaging the reputations of some innocent men were acceptable prices for getting the guilty ones and protecting women. That's a moral calculation at blatant odds with our system of justice. It's a math undercut by the paper cuts of "weird lunch dates." And it lengthens the odds against any consensus about the remedies for the problem at hand by feeding defensiveness, justifying distrust, and giving people who'd prefer not to confront it a rationale for that—an exit.

The number and array of circumstances that many liberals brand "racist" and their elastic, expansive application of "white supremacy" to all aspects of Western culture risk a similar side effect. To go by a new cadre of antiracism evangelists, we essentially breathe white supremacist air, and the only real fix would be reinventing and rebuilding our societies from scratch. How is that a sellable, workable action plan? I'm an American football fan, so please forgive the American football metaphor: It moves the goal posts not just dauntingly far downfield but to a whole other end zone in a whole other stadium in a whole different ZIP code. They're unreachable.

Robin DiAngelo is one of the most prominent of those evangelists. She wrote *White Fragility: Why It's So Hard for White People to Talk About Racism*, which was a success out of the gate in 2018 and then, following the murder of George Floyd by Minneapolis cops in 2020, zoomed to number one on Amazon and became more than just an influential book with millions of copies in print. It became a religion. Its pages laid out the tenets, as did the training sessions DiAngelo conducted for corporations and universities and the public lectures she gave. As described by Daniel Bergner in a 2020 profile of her in the *New York Times Magazine*, she told her audiences that assertions and insinuations of white preeminence and Black insignificance "are raining down on us 24/7, and there are no umbrellas." "White supremacy," she explained, describes not only the mindsets of avowed white nationalists and proud neo-Nazis but also "the society we live in, a society in which white people are elevated as the ideal for humanity, and everyone else is a deficient version." "There is something profoundly anti-Black in this culture," she said, and she confessed that "internalized white superiority is seeping out of my pores." That was her way of telling her white listeners that it was seeping out of *their* pores, too, if only they had the self-awareness and self-effacement to recognize it.

While "white supremacy" was a tag once dedicated almost exclusively to clear beliefs that white people were intrinsically superior to other races and were thus entitled to live apart from and above them, and while "racist" was reserved for people speaking and acting in hateful and bigoted ways, antiracism evangelists use those terms for much, much more. The premium placed on polished written communication? There's racism in that. The insistence on punctuality and the veneration of objectivity? White supremacy. A graphic posted online in 2020 by the Smithsonian National Museum of African American History and Culture substituted "white dominant culture" for white supremacy; stated that it "refers to the ways white people and their traditions, attitudes, and ways of life have been normalized over time and are now considered standard practices in the United States"; and then went on to identify some of those ways as "rational linear thought," "hard work," "work before play," "plan for future," and "delayed gratification." (Like Johns Hopkins with "non-men" and Stanford with its language glossary, the Smithsonian later retracted and rethought the matter.)

When the heightened terminology of racism, white supremacy, and white dominance is used for situations significantly more ambiguous than the ones for which those words were coined—when workplace professionalism, school tests, awkward body language, and clumsy conversational asides are muscled under those rubrics—people who aren't versed in the proper catechism or have reasonable reservations about the faith avoid the church. They're alienated. And all of us are left at a loss for effective language when *actual white supremacists* voice and flex their noxious beliefs, as happened during the 2017 Unite the Right rally in Charlottesville, Virginia. News organizations rightly called the torch-wielding white men who chanted "You will not replace us!" white supremacists, white nationalists, neo-Nazis. But some journalists couldn't leave it at that: "White supremacist" and "white supremacy" had become so ubiquitous by then that they had to write separate paragraphs or articles distinguishing *these* white supremacists from, say, me. Or you. The stagers of the rally, journalists explained, openly embraced and actively promoted the idea of white superiority and were prepared to brawl over it. The rest of us unthinkingly perpetuated and were pacifically complicit in it.

"The gap between how the initiated express their ideological beliefs and how everyone else does seems larger than ever," John McWhorter wrote in an article in the *Atlantic* in early 2021. He had particular expressions in mind, as the subhead of the article made clear: "The word *racism*, among others, has become maddeningly confusing in current usage." McWhorter teaches linguistics at Columbia University, contributes a regular newsletter on language and race to the *New York Times,* and is the author of the 2021 book *Woke Racism: How a New Religion Has Betrayed Black America,* in which he argues, as he has elsewhere, that our infinitely broadening conceptions of racism and white supremacy work against the cause of a more equal and just society in multiple ways, including the alienation I mentioned above.

"Nearly every designation of someone or something as 'racist' in modern America raises legitimate questions, and leaves so many legions of people confused or irritated that no one can responsibly dismiss all of this confusion and irritation as mere, well, racism," McWhorter wrote in the *Atlantic* article. I don't know about "nearly every"—sadly, I still observe many political leaders in this country and elsewhere speaking and acting in manners that "racist" covers unquestionably well—but McWhorter's larger point remains, and he provided an interesting example of "racist" bloat, noting that people opposed to the filibuster had recently taken to calling it racist because it had been a tool of racists in the past. "This implies a kind of contamination, a rather unsophisticated perspective given that this 'racist' practice has been steadily supported by noted non-racists such as Barack Obama (before he changed his mind on the matter)," McWhorter wrote.

His prescription? He wrote that Americans should "go back to using *racism* to refer to personal sentiment" and veer away from such terms as "societal racism." Otherwise, he explained, too many people "will still either struggle to process racism both harbored by persons and instantiated by a society, or just quietly accept the conflation to avoid making waves." That quiet avoidance has been documented in many surveys, with Americans of all political persuasions telling pollsters and other researchers that they hold back from expressing and even working through their opinions for fear of

The Price Is Not Right

social sanction. Something they say might come out wrong. Something they say might be objectionable to someone around them.

Interestingly, it's college-educated Americans who are more likely to muzzle themselves in discussions of political issues. "In a surprising reversal of the usual trends of political participation, in which citizens who have more resources feel more empowered to take an active role in civic life, it is the urbanites and the highly educated who are most afraid to speak their mind," the researchers James L. Gibson and Joseph L. Sutherland wrote in a 2020 analysis for the online magazine *Persuasion*.

Beyond such muzzling, many scholars and researchers doubt the effectiveness of sweeping indictments of "white culture" and equally sweeping claims of white supremacy, which don't resonate with many of the people not already predisposed to accept them and can also come across as a personal blaming that they don't deserve—a visiting of the sins of their forebears on them. Or, worse yet, on their children. Over the past few years, several politically liberal white friends of mine have complained to me about some of the DiAngelo-inflected, white-supremacy-infused lessons that their children have been taught at school. They worry that their kids are hearing that their unchosen whiteness is cause for shame and are being made to feel bad about themselves. Many parents' upset over that has become a potent factor in American politics. It was an issue emphasized by Glenn Youngkin, the Republican governor of Virginia, along the way to his surprising triumph in 2021 over the much better known, much more politically experienced Democratic incumbent, Terry McAuliffe. DeSantis has made it a core part of his pitch to voters. Both men's political fortunes suggest that it has traction well, well beyond the culture warriors of the right: Virginia is bluer than it is red, and DeSantis's margin of victory in his election in 2022 to a second term as governor of Florida indicated strong support for him among moderate Republicans, independent voters, and swing voters in general. If that support didn't translate into much of a performance by DeSantis in the 2024 Repblican presidential primaries, well, that wasn't a repudiation of his culture-war tactics. It was a testament to his charisma deficit, which was more noticeable on a national stage than on a state one, and to the fact that he was running against a behemoth named Trump.

And there is, at best, inconclusive evidence that the kinds of diversity training and DEI workshops composed and conducted by antiracism evangelists have a significant positive impact on the institutions that use them, though, according to a March 2023 analysis by the management consultants McKinsey & Company, the global market for DEI initiatives was "estimated at $7.5 billion" for 2020 and "is projected to more than double by 2026." Bergner's profile of DiAngelo pointed to respected experts and studies raising questions about the return on that formidable investment. "Hundreds of studies dating back to the 1930s suggest that antibias training does not reduce bias, alter behavior or change the workplace," Frank Dobbin, a professor of sociology at Harvard, and Alexandra Kalev, a professor of sociology and anthropology at Tel Aviv University, wrote in *Anthropology Now* in 2018, which predated the efforts of DiAngelo and some of her contemporaries but spoke to that sort of approach. "We have been speaking to employers about this research for more than a decade, with the message that diversity training is likely the most expensive, and least effective, diversity program around." Why? In an earlier article by Dobbin and Kalev in the *Harvard Business Review*, they gave reasons, including this one: "Laboratory studies show that this kind of force-feeding can activate bias rather than stamp it out. As social scientists have found, people often rebel against rules to assert their autonomy. Try to coerce me to do X, Y, or Z, and I'll do the opposite just to prove that I'm my own person."

That suggests how the grandest claims for racism and white supremacy play with a portion of their white audience. But what about their Black audience? Mightn't the belief that society is *this* expansively, enduringly, intricately, and irredeemably constructed to subjugate anyone who's not white encourage a crippling, self-defeating sense of hopelessness and helplessness? Wouldn't that be a perfectly logical response? And mightn't a rejection of the merit of polished written communication, careful planning, and punctuality deprive people of the very tools that, for better or worse, help them achieve their goals and maximize their agency, at least until such day—which could be a *very* long time coming—when values less supposedly white-centric prevail?

In that context, I was drawn to some of the comments that Glenn E. Singleton, who founded and runs the diversity training firm Courageous Conversation, made to Bergner for his *Times Magazine* piece. "There's this whole group of people who are named the scientists," Singleton said. "That's where you get into this whole idea that if it's not codified in scientific thought that it can't be valid." Singleton wasn't maligning science on the grounds and in the ways that, say, anti-vaxxers malign it. He was identifying it as a tool of white supremacy, as a justification for disregarding the different methods and different hypotheses of nonwhite cultures, as "a good way of dismissing people" descended from those cultures. Pushing back at the sticklers for science, he said, was "one of the challenges in the diversity-equity-inclusion space. Folks keep asking for data. How do you quantify, in a way that is scientific—numbers and that kind of thing—what people feel when they're feeling marginalized?" He's right that you can't neatly measure emotions nor ace a tidy cause-effect analysis of them.

But the answer isn't to genuflect before them because they exist. Indiscrimination isn't the route out of discrimination.

In a 2016 essay in the *Los Angeles Times*, Thomas Chatterton Williams, the author of the memoir *Losing My Cool: Love, Literature, and a Black Man's Escape from the Crowd*, offered a retort to what he deemed a reductive conversation about race, one that made assumptions—good, bad, and in between—about people based on the category to which they were assigned, the label they were given to wear. "My black father, born in 1937 in segregated Texas, is an exponentially more worldly man than my maternal white Protestant grandfather, whose racism always struck me more as a sad function of his provincialism or powerlessness than anything else," he wrote. "I don't mean to excuse the corrosive effects of his view; I simply wish to note that when I compare these two men, I do not recognize my father as the victim."

I found my way to that essay, and quoted from it, when I wrote that column in the *Times* in 2017 about the oppression Olympics—and about an increasingly loud insistence by more and more people on the left that neither I nor any other white person had any standing to discuss matters of racial injustice because we'd never lived the wages of it. We should shut up. We should "check our privilege." I agreed then and agree now that I possess unearned privilege; that I should always bear that in mind; that I must factor it into what I say and write and do, not as a matter of etiquette or even as a matter of morality but as a matter of truth; and that I can't know what it means to have someone prejudge me by the color of my skin. But I have experienced the lesser bigotry of being prejudged by the objects of my romantic and sexual affections—of being accepted or rejected, esteemed or reviled, because I'm gay. I know something of marginalization: I was gay—and keenly aware of it—in the 1970s, when gay stereotypes went unchallenged, when gay jokes drew hearty laughter, when most gay people spoke of that part of themselves in carefully curated company and in whispers, when many of us trembled inside not just when we strayed into the wrong ZIP codes, but, well, everywhere. And I was gay in the 1980s, when AIDS spread and we wore scarlet letters as we marched into the public square to plead with President Ronald Reagan for help. Our rallying cry, "silence=death," defined marginalization as well as any words could.

So am I oppressor or oppressed? It's messy, and grievance isn't. Grievance tells the displaced white worker in what was once a thriving factory town with full employment that foreigners in China who demand less per hour are to blame for the hushed streets and barren bank accounts all around him, or that darker-skinned denizens of the big city a few hundred miles away are hogging federal aid that might otherwise flow to him and his neighbors and lessen their troubles, or that immigrants are the real problem, even if he hasn't fully worked out precisely how that's so. Grievance doesn't ask him to accept that the world is ever changing, and that its latest twists may call for adjustments in where he lives and what he trains himself to do—not because he has some error to correct, not because he has done anything wrong, but because life sometimes unfolds that way, and yelling at an image of Ilhan Omar on his television screen won't lead anywhere.

Grievance convinces one group of people that any talk whatsoever of Covid being unleashed by a laboratory experiment gone wrong is rank xenophobia and that anyone pondering that possibility and sternly demanding more information from China is a racist who should be shamed and gagged. Grievance convinces another group of people that a cabal of government insiders are in covert league with foreign powers and engaged in mass mind control. That a bunch of frazzled bureaucrats and frightened citizens of varied political stripes are bumbling across terra incognita—and making dozens of false assumptions and scores of mistakes along the way—is a less popular scenario, not only because it's less sexy but also because it's less useful. It doesn't sanction anyone's anger. It doesn't back up anyone's taxonomy of trustworthy and untrustworthy actors. Grievance likes its crises neat and tidy. It banishes shades of gray. That's driven home every time a prominent political figure dies, some partisans from the opposing party decide to spare a few kind words for the deceased, and their allies freak out at their apostasy.

That happened twice in 2018, first with John McCain's death and then with George H. W. Bush's just a little over three months later. McCain's detractors howled about any framing of him as a hero—*McCain*, a former US Navy pilot who was shot down over Vietnam, captured and, for years, tortured by the North Vietnamese, and refused early release unless his fellow prisoners were also freed. Upon news of Bush's death, Bryan Behar, a television writer whose Twitter followers knew him as a principled liberal, tweeted something respectful about having "never once doubted President Bush's love for his country." He called Bush "a good, decent man who lived a life of dignity." And Behar's followers lashed out at him so viciously that the whole episode became its own narrative on Twitter, a cautionary tale about steering even briefly and slightly outside of one's ideological lane, an illustration of too many Americans' inability to hold two thoughts at once.

Yes, Bush had blots on his record. In his presidential race against Michael Dukakis, he'd sanctioned that despicable Willie Horton ad, and that was hardly the first, last, or only time he'd empowered his political aides and allies to play dirty in the service of his ambitions. Also, he'd nominated Clarence Thomas to the Supreme Court. And he'd done much less than he should have in the face of the AIDS crisis, not able to see, from his lofty perch, how many people were suffering. But he'd also, to borrow one of his own favorite phrases, had points of light, so very many of them. He'd shown a willingness to compromise that most of the Republican leaders who came after him spurned. In my own limited interactions with him in 1999 and 2000, years after he'd left office, I encountered a man of uncommon courtesy, palpable kindness, and unrestrainable honesty—he and Barbara Bush disagreed (amicably) in front of me and didn't hide their surprise at George W.'s big political fortunes because they simply couldn't. To mention such qualities at the time of a person's death isn't an act of moral laundering. It's the essence of civility. But grievance has no appreciation of that. No patience for it. Grievance coarsens us.

Grievance threatens to consume us, too. It turns everything— beer, M&M's, Skittles, restaurant chains, theme parks, athletic teams, athletic competitions—into cultural battlefields. For many Americans, the war zone is infinite. For many Americans, a war posture is permanent. "The particular disputes over which we are supposed to be at each other's throats constantly shift and change," Yuval Levin wrote in *Comment* magazine in 2022. "Sometimes it's race and policing, sometimes immigration and borders, sometimes American history or education, cancel culture or some burgeoning fascism, free speech or hate speech, wokism or systemic discrimination, transgenderism, election integrity, vaccines, masks, or the latest careless proclamation of some ridiculous celebrity. Individually, these fights sometimes touch on genuinely vital questions. Yet seen together they appear as a vast sociopolitical psychosis. They are all one fight, and the fight is the point."

I have watched that vast sociopolitical psychosis—which is uncontrolled and uncontrollable grievance by another name—degrade some of my friends' and acquaintances' mental health as they doomscroll and shitpost (how do we even *have* these neologisms, let alone these phenomena?) the days away. We all have. We've seen relationships ruined by it. Rival grievances have estranged friends, riven families. That's part of what I mean by proportionality. We've lost the ability to control how much of our lives we surrender to grievance and to declare some areas off-limits. But if we're going to move past grievance, we're going to have to work a lot harder at that.

Nine

Don't Be a Stranger

If our descent into a society of metastasizing grievances has dozens of culprits large and small, it has at least as many cures. They span the echoing halls of Congress and the glowing confines of our tiny screens. They represent broad policy proposals and individual lifestyle tweaks, national programs that would take years to get going and personal fixes that each of us could implement today. An accretion of these modest fixes could have an immodest impact, and they're preferable to simply treading water and hoping that the ocean doesn't get too much choppier.

There's a common theme among some of the cures, and it's one worth keeping in mind, because doing that—always remembering it, continually making adjustments that nod to it—would help a lot: distance nurtures grievance. And distance in this sense has many meanings. I'm referring to our physical separation from other people, especially those in whom we don't instantly recognize commonalities; to our digital separation from them; to our psychological and emotional separation from them, created not only by those physical and digital separations but also by habits of mind that we've developed and don't fight back against. Just about every social psychologist and political scientist will say that it's easier to demonize people whom we don't know, who exist in caricature rather than flesh and blood.

I can't count the number of times over the three and a half decades of my journalism career when I've received an angry, insulting, or even wildly abusive email from a reader and, after I've responded with relative cool, received an apology. I was an abstraction to the reader until that point, and few people hesitate to attack an abstraction. But wait: I had manners? Feelings? I was an actual human? That changed the interaction.

I also can't count the number of readers who've contacted me to say that while they disagree with me about certain issues or about the entirety of what they perceive my politics to be, they subscribe to my weekly newsletter and feel a warmth toward me because of the tenderness and love with which I write about my dog. They're dog people, too, and, hey, dog people are never all bad. Or they've said that while I had too much respect for Barack Obama or too little for Hillary Clinton, I can be forgiven, because I've admitted my flaws and vulnerabilities, and shown guts and soulfulness, through my candid autobiographical accounts of coping with an eating disorder in my teens and twenties and learning in my fifties that I might go blind. It's in the details of our lives outside of politics that we become whole and comprehensible and valuable to others.

Of course that doesn't mean we discover at least a few pinpricks of fondness and respect for everyone we get to know. Many of us have neighbors, relatives, or coworkers whom we can't and will never be able to stand, relationships in which familiarity, hewing to that musty adage, breeds contempt. But those, I think, are the exceptions. I think we yearn, consciously and not, to find points of connection with the people around us, and I think we feel an incomparable sense of peace and safety when we've discovered those. Cooperation is humanity's great strength, the superpower that drives our progress. We are, to a remarkable extent, evolved to create strong bonds with our immediate neighbors. That's the sunny side of tribalism—and there *is* a sunny side of tribalism, if it's moderated, if it exists in balance with an awareness of its perils.

Here's the challenge: Most of the roughly 330 million Americans (or, if you live in a similarly roiled Western democracy, the 67 million Brits or 83 million Germans or 215 million Brazilians) aren't immediate neighbors. And they don't prattle on about their dogs, meals, and medical procedures in a venue as prominent as the *New York Times*. So we must find other venues and other methods to collapse the distance between us and them. We must integrate those methods into the structures and systems of our societies. And we must weaken the forces that get in their—and our—ways. Most of the following fixes would do that directly or indirectly.

Fixing Congress

In the summer of 2021, when Amanda Ripley received an invitation to meet with a group of lawmakers in the House of Representatives, she didn't have high expectations. Members of Congress have a well-earned reputation for performative dysfunction, and Congress itself has an approval rating to match. "I'd covered Congressional hearings before, and they often felt like a theater of the absurd," she wrote in her Substack newsletter, *Unraveled*. "The members of Congress were barely paying attention, if they showed up at all, and the back-and-forth was for the cameras, not for the country."

But Ripley had been invited to talk about her book *High Conflict: Why We Get Trapped and How We Get Out*. She had insights to share, lessons to impart—an opportunity, at least theoretically, to make the kind of positive impact that she sought to. And the elected officials who greeted her in the hearing room, all members of the bipartisan Select Committee on the Modernization of Congress, turned out to be genuinely interested in how they and their colleagues might escape the vortex of partisan grievance and actually govern. Instead of delivering political zingers for the C-SPAN cameras, the Democrats and Republicans on the committee spent two hours in a brainstorming session with Ripley and a group of other experts, commiserating about grievance politics. "We are not dealing with broken rules and procedures—we are dealing with broken norms," Representative Derek Kilmer, the Washington Democrat who was chairing the committee, said that day.

Those broken norms had led Congress into the "high conflict" that was Ripley's expertise and interest: a self-perpetuating cycle in which normal disagreement balloons into something big and uncontrollable. But Ripley brought hopeful news. "It is possible," she assured the committee members, "to shift out of high conflict and into good conflict." She had observed as much in her research, which encompassed bitter divorces, Chicago gang wars, even the civil war in Colombia, all instances in which aggrieved combatants found ways to tame or escape the misery of endless fighting. Where high conflict is personal and all-consuming, good conflict is substantive and structured, and is focused on issues instead of identities. There are dividends. Good conflict can be "strangely exhilarating," Ripley told the lawmakers. "You feel open, able to be surprised even as you fight for what you hold dear."

Ripley's book details how those gang members in Chicago

ended cycles of retaliation by instituting rules for dealing with slights and insults, essentially creating a space for cooling off and communicating with rivals before words turned into violence. It recounts ad campaigns during the Colombian civil war that sought to remind guerrilla fighters of their family ties, speaking to them as sons and daughters, brothers and sisters, to complicate the narrative of government versus rebels. Emphasizing people's fullest, most multidimensional identities—which are different from their identity groups—tells them that they're more than combatants and that conflict doesn't have to define them.

For Congress, de-escalating from high to good conflict means creating and promoting as many opportunities as possible for lawmakers to sit down with and listen to one another—to converse rather than speechify. "It turns out that basic practices you would use to prevent anarchy in any kindergarten classroom were not being followed in Congress," Ripley wrote in an essay in the *Washington Post* about her observations and prescriptions. So members sat in an open circle, where they could look one another in the eye, instead of sitting side by side on a raised dais, where they could pose and pontificate. They started conducting hearings in a more free-flowing, conversational style instead of allotting strict, five-minute blocks of time to each member. And they seated Republicans next to Democrats instead of dividing the room by party. "This means that when a member hears something interesting during a hearing, and they lean over to the member sitting next to them for discussion, they are sharing thoughts with someone from the other party," the committee recounted in its own report about its changed practices. Ripley's translation: "Turns out that fixing politics starts by rearranging the furniture."

But they went beyond interior decorating. Committee members

resolved to spend time together and did so—scheduling group dinners, holding brown-bag lunches, and organizing and attending listening sessions, facilitated by experts, during which members took turns sharing their experiences in Congress and speaking about their frustrations with the way it's run. Inevitably, they discovered common complaints and common wishes, which are patches of common ground. And they issued more than two hundred bipartisan recommendations for getting the entire Congress—not just their committee—out of high conflict and back to work, many along the lines of the new habits they were forming.

I don't live my life with the melody and lyrics of "Kumbaya, My Lord" running through my brain, where skepticism, I'm not proud to say, commands considerably more real estate than idealism. But I do think that half the trick to getting along is prioritizing and resolving to get along—pausing long enough to know that you want that and then pausing anew at determined intervals thereafter to remind yourself. I see that in my family and my friend groups, and I bet you do, too. Peace and harmony are decisions and values more than they are eureka strokes of good fortune. The new rituals that the committee developed were value statements, declarations of intent, exercises in discipline. They were the building blocks of a different culture.

Such a culture would have a better chance in Congress if the House weren't the product of egregious gerrymandering in many states. That gerrymandering produces ideologically homogeneous congressional districts that elect extremists or near-extremists who by nature have little interest in conciliation and compromise and whose constituents aren't pushing them in that direction or rewarding them for bipartisanship. And gerrymandering is getting easier, not harder, to do. "Although gerrymandering has existed for more than two centuries and is an activity in which both major parties partake, it has in recent decades, with the advent of new scientific and mathematical tools, become more commonplace and brutally effective," Our Common Purpose, a project of the American Academy of Arts and Sciences, reported recently.

My home state of North Carolina has been Exhibit A for gerrymandering over recent decades, during which Republicans in the state legislature have, in defiance of the state's purple hue, repeatedly succeeded in implementing maps that guaranteed them well over half of the state's seats in the House. In the 2018 midterm elections, the Republican-drawn map led to a North Carolina congressional delegation of ten Republicans and three Democrats, though Republican House candidates as a group received only 2 percent more of the statewide vote than Democratic House candidates did. The state supreme court had changed that map by the 2022 midterms, when North Carolina, now with fourteen congressional districts, sent seven Republicans and seven Democrats to the House, a balance appropriate for a state whose voters had twice chosen their second-term governor, Roy Cooper, a Democrat, over his Republican opponent. No matter: North Carolina Republicans are taking advantage of a changed, friendlier composition in the state supreme court to throw out the 2022 map and replace it in 2024 with one that will make that seven-seven split an impossibility.

States can fix this glaring breach of democratic norms by putting district maps in the hands of independent commissions or of bipartisan committees evenly split between Democratic and Republican lawmakers. The tall hurdle: whichever party is in power at a given moment perceives little interest in doing that. Why surrender their advantage, they reason, when their opponents wouldn't do so? They need to be pressured by voters to take the long view: at some point in the future, their opponents may well be in charge, and if a history and practice of gerrymandering are firmly embedded, with partisans instead of independent commissions making the decisions, those opponents will behave selfishly and undemocratically.

"It's eroding the public's trust in our political system," Larry Hogan wrote in the *Washington Post* in 2018, when he was still the governor of Maryland, where Democrats were the ones who'd done the (very aggressive) gerrymandering. During his two terms as governor, he waged a stubborn battle against the Democratic majority in the state legislature to change that, eventually taking Democratic lawmakers to court and getting a judgment in favor of what he was trying to do. Less gerrymandered maps took effect in Maryland in 2022.

Hogan also supports shaking up the primary system so that it's less beholden to partisans and party loyalists, who are most likely to turn out and who dominate it, favoring extremists and incumbents and disadvantaging less hidebound, more open-minded politicians. "It's one of the biggest problems we have in America today—a small subset of people are making the decisions," he told me. "What you have to do to win a primary is almost the exact opposite of what you have to do to win a general election. We get to the general election and it's like, 'Oh, my God, *these* are my two choices?'" Open primaries can make a difference, by inviting independents into the voting mix. Jungle primaries—in which all candidates from all parties compete to become the two in the general election—can have a positive impact as well. Both open and jungle primaries have flaws, and there has long been an argument that diminishing party officials' power in this fashion is dangerous, as those officials can essentially filter out candidates who are risky neophytes or beneficiaries of some mass hysteria. But Trump was the kind of candidate that party control was supposed to prevent. And once most Republican officials sensed his sway with voters, they went from sentries to sycophants.

We should also push for ranked-choice voting in more states than the relatively few where it's currently used. Some of the journalism about it makes it sound more complicated than it is, because that journalism focuses on how ranked-choice votes are counted, the multiple rounds of counting, and the uncertainty—given our small sample set of places where it already exists—of which sorts of candidates would and wouldn't benefit. But the voting itself is no ordeal: whatever the contest, voters list the candidates from most desirable to least. They give not just their first choice but also, if there are three candidates in the race, their second and third. That theoretically (again, our sample set is small) increases the odds of success for a moderate candidate, who may not be many voters' first choice but may be the second choice of a majority of voters and may, if none of the unyielding partisans in the race gets an outright majority of votes in the first round of counting, become the victor in a subsequent round. "Because second and third choices matter in the ranked-choice model, candidates have an incentive to speak to a broader group of voters," an analysis by Our Common Purpose explained. "The result: more moderate candidates and campaigns, a more welcoming environment for third-party candidates, and greater confidence among voters that their votes are not being wasted or distorting the outcome." The voters to whom Our Common Purpose referred are, say, Democrats in a majority-Republican district or Republicans in a majority-Democratic one. They might move the needle, and thus wind up feeling more engaged in the process, more invested in the results, more trusting.

We must also make it easier to vote, and by "easier" I don't mean dropping all ID requirements or giving incarcerated felons the right to vote where they don't have it; Democrats have at times and in places done the voting-rights cause a disservice by seeming to resist what seem to most Americans like perfectly sensible safeguards, even if they're safeguards erected without a substantial amount of evidence for their need. When I went to vote here in Chapel Hill, NC, in the 2022 midterms, a poll worker asked me for my name and address, and when those matched the entry for me on some multipage printout that she had, she handed me my ballot—no proof that I was me required. I think I should have been asked to show *something*. But with at least notional safeguards, voters should be able to vote by mail, they should be able to vote early, they should get the day or a half day off from work to vote, and nowhere should they have to drive hours away or stand in hours-long lines to vote. If Amazon can accomplish the feats of speedy delivery that it does, governments can make voting something other than an epic inconvenience. They just have to try. They just have to care. Grievance sups gluttonously on feelings of disenfranchisement.

Fixing Our Political Culture

Once elected, politicians could chip away at the most intense partisanship and polarization—and, by extension, grievance—by focusing on actual, measurable, and, in many cases, tangible improvements in voters' lives. For many politicians, that approach wouldn't be any great sacrifice: it dovetails with their self-interest in maintaining enough favor with voters to be kept in their current offices or to be promoted to higher ones.

It's no accident that four of the recent or current governors in the United States with the most consistently high approval ratings don't belong to the same political party as the significant majority of voters in their states. Because of that discrepancy, they couldn't or can't afford to emphasize their parties' national positions on the most divisive culture-war issues. Nor could or can they wallow in broad philosophical differences between liberals and conservatives. They've had to focus instead on so-called bread-and-butter concerns (jobs, housing, health care, school performance) and on results. And when voters in their own party saw them doing that, they forgave them any dearth of demonstrable passion on the Big Arguments, while voters in the opposing party discovered a fondness for them, too. It's an excellent model for governing.

I'm thinking of Andy Beshear in Kentucky, a Democrat whose approval rating has frequently topped 60 percent despite the vivid redness of his state, whose voters chose Donald Trump over Joe Biden in 2020 by a twenty-six-point margin. He has joined with other Democratic politicians in red or reddish states in "casting themselves as competent, good-government-minded bureaucrats focused on fixing kitchen-table problems," Zach Montellaro wrote in early 2023, assessing Beshear's chances to win reelection later that year (which Beshear indeed did, besting his Republican opponent by nearly five percentage points). I'm thinking of Phil Scott in Vermont, a Republican whose approval rating has crested 75 *percent* in a state whose voters went for Biden over Trump in 2020 by more than thirty-five percentage points. He has compared himself to "a mechanic" in terms of his technocratic approach.

"I left office with a seventy-seven percent approval rating," Hogan, another of these four highly rated governors, reminded me. "And it was over seventy with every single demographic." That was as a Republican in Maryland, which Biden won in 2020 by about thirty-three percentage points. I should pause here to acknowledge that American voters routinely approach presidential elections in a more tribal way—one that's an expression of cultural and ideological affinity—than they do elections for governor or mayor or even for the House or the Senate. But still, Hogan's, Scott's, and Beshear's success and popularity—and the success and popularity of the fourth governor I had in mind, Charlie Baker, a beloved Republican at the helm of deep-blue Massachusetts from 2015 to 2023—mean and teach something, which, according to Hogan, is this: "It turns out that an overwhelming majority of Democrats, independents, and Republicans—and everybody of every ethnicity—is sick of toxic politics." But because most primaries are closed, because so many districts are gerrymandered, because ranked-choice voting is rare, and because too few politicians are willing to abandon the bluster and bellicosity that seems to be working just fine for their peers, toxic politics is what we get. It depresses voter turnout, which then leads to yet more toxic politics, because the Americans most likely to vote are the most committed partisans, who choose dyspeptic candidates who mirror their dark mood.

There are plenty of politicians beyond Hogan, Baker, Scott, and Beshear who prove Hogan's point. Look at Governor Brian Kemp, the Georgia Republican. He had to win reelection in 2022 in a purple state, and he did that by generally ignoring Trumpian drama—and specifically ignoring Trump's denunciations of him for respecting the 2020 election results that gave Biden the victory there—and by talking about other matters, like employment. At a time when most Republican politicians treat "green energy" like an expletive, Kemp has made his state a leader in the manufacturing of electric car batteries and has brought electric vehicle (or EV) assembly plants to Georgia as well. "Since 2020, the state has scored more than 40 E.V.-related projects, which are expected to yield around 28,000 jobs and $22 million in investment, according to the governor's office," my *Times* colleague Michelle Cottle wrote in June 2023, noting that Kemp "frames things in terms of Georgia's economic future and, most especially, jobs."

It's arguable that the politician at the apex of America, Biden, also proves Hogan's point. He spoke much less provocatively than most of the Democrats with whom he vied for his party's 2020 presidential nomination. He took less polarizing positions. He talked constantly about healing and unity. And he beat his younger, more energetic, more articulate rivals in the end. I've been encouraged and impressed to see that since enacting that trillion-dollar infrastructure-plus bill, he has staged events to tout it not only in states where the 2024 presidential election might be close but also in states where he has zero chance of winning, because that's an important symbolic act and a statement of principle. It communicates to voters that we're not just warriors in a perpetual battle with one another. It also gives them a reason for faith in government by pointing at the *physical* bridges that government builds, the internet access it creates, the roads it expands, the public transit it improves, its potentially positive effect on daily and even hourly life.

Just as we'd be better off if we weren't so down on politics and *all* politicians, we'd be well served by not feeling so quickly and harshly negative about one another, and there are hundreds of scholars, activists, and nonprofit organizations working to understand and counteract the forces that drive polarization and grievance. With our tax dollars, with our own dollars, with our participation, and with our cheerleading, we can better fund and better encourage them.

One of the more interesting and seemingly effective groups is Braver Angels, a national nonprofit organization that emerged after the 2016 election and the shock of realizing just how little Americans understood about their political opposites. Braver Angels began convening workshops around the country of "reds and blues," hard partisans who felt misrepresented and often victimized by those on the other side. The group wagered—and says it has found—that if those partisans understood better why their ostensible foes held different positions, what those people's lives were like, and how familiar their aspirations sounded, they'd soften a crucial bit. Participants aren't just hearing people they've never listened to before. They're being heard, and *not* being heard is part of what hardened them in the first place.

We should fund a serious national service program. When Americans speak admiringly about what the US military has done and still does for this country, they're referring not just to the battles it has fought, the allies it has buttressed, the aggression it has deterred. They're referring to its creation of common purpose and common understanding among people drawn from all regions of the country and all walks of life. Luckily, we haven't had to require military service of young Americans since the Vietnam War, and nobody wants a return of the draft. But we could compel or incentivize other kinds of national service for young Americans as a way of recognizing how fractured the country has become, confronting the mistrust and misunderstandings that stem from that, and giving people of different geographic, socioeconomic, religious, racial, and cultural backgrounds familiarity with one another in the context of a shared mission that's simultaneously an investment in the country. That service might be the upkeep of public parks, work on initiatives to combat climate change, interventions with underprivileged children, visits to isolated elderly people, assistance of other kinds to other Americans in need, or a combination of all of that. It might guarantee student debt forgiveness. It might hold the promise of first crack at certain long-term jobs once the service is completed. Different politicians have floated different ideas. Most haven't really put all that much muscle behind those proposals.

I wrote "serious national service program" because there have been baby steps in that direction, such as AmeriCorps, but nothing commensurate with the strong belief among scholars and civic activists who study political polarization that shared endeavors are a promising corrective to it. "Anything that gives people the chance to work with other people who are different from them on something hard and get results matters, and it could help cut through pessimism or anger or division or polarization," said Buttigieg, who pitched national service frequently during his 2020 presidential campaign. He spoke from experience: he did a tour of duty in Afghanistan when he served in the US Navy Reserve after college and graduate school.

Fixing Cities and Towns

For all the time we spend online, what we know of one another, how we feel about one another, and how we then wind up treating one another are still very much shaped by the places we inhabit. Our neighborhoods, towns, cities, and metropolitan areas can encourage social connection or make it harder, narrow our worlds or broaden them. Eric Klinenberg, a sociologist at New York University, has thought and written extensively about that, and is a deep believer in the power of more smartly designed, better infrastructure to combat isolation, inequality, and polarization. "Social infrastructure is the missing piece of the puzzle," he wrote in his 2018 book *Palaces for the People*. "Building places where all kinds of people can gather is the best way to repair the fractured societies we live in today."

Klinenberg's first book, *Heat Wave,* published in 2002, was a "social autopsy" of the Chicago heat wave of 1995, which killed more than 700 people—most of them dying alone at home, even as countless others found the help they needed through friends, neighbors, community groups, and public services. Social connection can be a matter of life and death, and Klinenberg worries that a lack of dedicated investment in libraries, parks, school campuses, and inviting streetscapes imperils our democracy. "While social infrastructure alone isn't sufficient to unite polarized societies, protect vulnerable communities, or connect alienated individuals, we can't address these challenges without it," he wrote in *Palaces for the People.* Think about it. Private businesses—restaurants, retailers, fitness clubs—sort the people who use them by income and cultural affinity. That's often their very business strategy. Their brand. But the library? No. The park? If it's a big one straddling different neighborhoods, it's culturally and economically polyglot. The spruced-up urban plaza with nighttime lighting and peripheral buildings that create an atmosphere inimitable in the exurbs? That's an all-comers magnet. The great squares of Europe teem with diverse people for a reason, and that reason is instructive.

The shock of Covid lockdowns—and the reordering of urban life and workplace expectations that followed—have opened a window of opportunity to rethink what we want and expect from public spaces, and have given the urban planners, elected officials, and corporate chieftains who sculpt those spaces a chance to reconfigure our daily landscapes and push us toward richer interactions. "We could achieve, more comprehensively and more joyfully than before, the city's primordial aim: bringing people and ideas together," Edward L. Glaeser, a Harvard economist, and Carlo Ratti, an MIT urbanist, wrote in an essay in the *New York Times* in May 2023. The two scholars suggested ways in which emptied-out office districts could be repurposed to make way for a "playground city" that could bring together a diversity of people. "A healthy city makes space for the rich and poor alike," they wrote. "It generates positive interactions among people of all income levels."

"All income levels"—that's key, because Americans over the past few decades have been gravitating more and more to localities and neighborhoods of people with the same incomes, the same education level, the same politics. Bill Bishop noticed, analyzed, and warned about this back in 2008, when his book *The Big Sort: Why the Clustering of Like-Minded America Is Tearing Us Apart* was published. "The country may be more diverse than ever coast to coast," he wrote in his book. "But look around: our own streets are filled with people who live alike, think alike, and vote alike." We exist in "pockets of like-minded citizens that have become so ideologically inbred that we don't know, can't understand and can barely conceive of 'those people' who live just a few miles away."

Good public policy can fight this trend—with zoning laws that reflect social planning and not NIMBYism, with tax incentives for developers who create or rehabilitate public spaces as part of their projects, with grants to organizations that design and conceive of initiatives along these lines. We can open schoolyards for public use during evenings and weekends, make it easier for citizens to use existing public spaces for communal events. We can place new parks not so that they exist as bubbles within homogenous communities but, instead, so that they brush up against different communities, their borders on neighborhoods that aren't carbon copies of one another. We can locate community centers in the same fashion, and we can plot public transportation so that it passes through a diversity of neighborhoods whenever and wherever that's logistically sensible.

We can also make it so that big cities and big metropolitan areas—"superstar cities," in the parlance of economists and some other academics—don't gobble up and concentrate most of the best educated, most entrepreneurial people, widening the gap between urban centers and rural areas, between blue and red, and exacerbating class resentment, cultural misunderstanding, and the grievances fed by both. "For most of this century, large metros with a million residents or more have received all of the net gains from college-educated workers migrating around the country, at the expense of smaller places," Emily Badger, Robert Gebeloff, and Josh Katz wrote in a *Times* analysis in May 2023. "The dozen metros with the highest living costs—nearly all of them coastal—have had a uniquely bifurcated migration pattern: As they saw net gains from college graduates, they lost large numbers of workers without degrees." The MIT economist David Autor told the analysis's authors: "There's an incredible concentration of wealth in these superstar cities that is unhealthy. It also means a lot of the affluence that goes with that is very concentrated among a small set of people."

The rise of remote work has given us an opportunity to try to correct that—and, with it, the feeling among many working-class Americans geographically estranged from this cosmopolitan superstardom that their small cities and towns have been sacrificed to the gods of Big Tech, Big Finance, Big Consulting, and such. Already, in the wake of the Covid pandemic, there are signs of exodus and relocation from the most populous cities to less populous ones. Federal policy can support that with investments in transportation hubs, higher education, job training, and more. Maybe we can retire the dread phrase "coastal elite," or at least diminish the frequency and accuracy with which it's uttered.

Fixing Employment and Education

On his first full day in office in January 2023, Governor Josh Shapiro, a Pennsylvania Democrat, signed an executive order that dispensed with the requirement of a four-year college degree for 92 percent of positions in state government, meaning roughly sixty-five thousand jobs. That was smart and arguably self-interested politics: Democrats have lately been losing the votes of Americans without college degrees by large margins. But it was also fair and right: a college degree is no guarantee of competence, no exclusive proof of intelligence, and often less relevant to a given job than work and life experiences that have nothing to do with lecture halls. Above all, it was a step away from grievance, for which the "diploma divide," as it is now widely called, has become a powerful engine.

"Educational attainment is the new fault line in American politics," the political strategist Doug Sosnik wrote in an essay in the *Times* in April 2023. "It is increasingly the best predictor of how Americans will vote, and for whom." Those with college degrees see the Democratic Party as their home, while those without them favor the Republican Party, and each party has inevitably evolved to answer to and please those constituents. But there may be ways to collapse the diploma divide and the partisanship that goes with it, chiefly by not treating the attainment of a college degree as such a potent symbol of achievement and enlightenment, and by not making a diploma quite as strong a driver of income as it currently is.

I believe as fervently as anyone in the value of college not just as a path to professional opportunity but also as preparation for informed, thoughtful citizenship and as a tool for joyful living, one that can expose people to new pleasures, sharpen their curiosity about the world, speed them to knowledge, and show them how to enjoy that ride. I've written extensively about that, and I wouldn't take back a word. And there are indeed many lucrative careers that do and always will require a college education, which separates high and low earners like nothing else in American life, so I'd like us to bring down the cost of college and make it more available to those who want to go.

But not everyone *will* go, as a matter of circumstance or personal preference, so it's imperative that we not insist on this credential in those situations where there's no compelling reason to and that we not make it such a divisive emblem in our culture wars, especially considering that fewer than half of adult Americans have four-year college degrees. That's a majority of the population often being made to feel like second-class citizens. "The sharp bachelor's degree cutoff in America is divisive and unproductive," wrote the Princeton economists Angus Deaton and Anne Case in *Deaths of Despair*, which I mentioned in an earlier chapter. "The K-12 education system is largely designed to prepare people to go to college," they added, so "those who do not make it risk being branded as failures and left feeling either that they themselves are at fault or that the system is rigged, or both."

Economists of all political stripes have offered all kinds of proposals for elevating the wages of Americans without bachelor's degrees, improving their working conditions, and treating them with greater respect. We're not going to make much headway against grievance unless we do all of that. It begins with what Shapiro and a growing number of governors—in North Carolina, Utah, Alaska, Maryland, Virginia—are doing: They're urging or mandating that actual work and life experience be weighed at least as heavily as a college education when certain state jobs are filled. More state governments, local governments, and private companies need to follow suit and recognize what a group of scholars at Harvard's business school concluded in a report on "degree inflation" in 2017: "Many of the skills most often requested by employers in job postings that require a college degree are identical to those requested in job postings that don't require a college degree."

Byron Auguste, an economist and former McKinsey partner who served in the Obama administration and now runs an organization called Opportunity@Work, cites degree requirements as one of the key equity issues in American life, accounting for a big part of the wealth gap between Black and white Americans. As he explained in a 2021 interview on NPR's *All Things Considered*, "If you arbitrarily say that a job needs to have a bachelor's degree, you are screening out over seventy percent of African Americans. You're screening out about eighty percent of Latino-Latina workers, and you're screening out over eighty percent of rural Americans of all races. And you're doing that before any skills are assessed. It's not fair."

Alongside fewer degree requirements, employers should reinvest in the productivity and long-term prospects of their employees. In *Deaths of Despair*, Case and Deaton repeatedly mention, and rue, the fraying relationships between working-class Americans and their employers. Automation, outsourcing, soaring health costs, and a myopic focus on short-term earnings have led many companies to treat their frontline employees as essentially disposable, and those workers' sense of exploitation bleeds into how they perceive big institutions and American society more broadly. "Less educated workers live in a much more hostile world than did less educated workers of half a century ago," Case and Deaton wrote in their book. "The meaning that came from being part of an admirable enterprise, serving the public as well as its shareholders, has been lost for many less educated Americans."

There are signs that some companies' cold, dehumanized view of employment has begun to shift, with rising wages and the tighter labor market of the past few years forcing employers to think about more internships, apprenticeships, and on-the-job training programs to retain workers and boost productivity. The United States has long been a laggard among industrialized nations in workforce training, spending one-sixth of what Germany does on increasing the skills and opportunities of workers. Changing that would both improve the economy and create meaningful career paths for millions of people who feel stuck. "It's a scary place to be to need a job and not have the skills to get a good job," Commerce Secretary Gina Raimondo said during a White House briefing in 2021. "My view is if you have the guts in the middle of your career to go out and get some job training, to retrain yourself to get a new job, then we need to be there for you."

On the subject of education, our schools need to do much better with civics education, because they do miserably now: Americans of all ages fail basic civic literacy tests at staggering rates. That's both a betrayal of essential purpose—how can a *public* education not teach children about public life?—and an inexplicably self-defeating omission. But what's needed today isn't a revamp of *Schoolhouse Rock!*, so that every student can sing the branches of government and dance along as a bill becomes a law. We need civics education for the modern era, for an always-online generation that will inherit the most diverse America that has ever existed and figure out a way to make it function (or not).

"I have come around to the view that our very concept of citizenship needs to be revised, or better yet expanded," wrote the foreign policy guru Richard Haass in his 2023 book *The Bill of Obligations*. "Without a culture of obligation coexisting alongside a commitment to rights, American democracy could well come undone." That means understanding citizenship as equal parts entitlement and burden, blessing and responsibility, its gifts coupled with demands, including sustained engagement. "None of what is essential for a democracy to thrive is automatically passed on from generation to generation," Haass warned. "It needs to be taught, including its history, values, and obligations."

About that history: There's a vogue in many American schools to dwell on the crimes of our forebears, on the endless litany of ways—some of them, such as slavery, positively monstrous—in which our ancestors behaved immorally and failed to live up to the language in, and the spirit of, documents such as the Declaration of Independence. There's also a backlash that seeks not merely to launder that past but to ignore it altogether. What we need is a middle ground where we own our sins but never lose sight of how often the United States is and has been a force for good, where we never disregard our legitimate cause for pride and patriotism, neither of which is facile and neither of which needs to—or does—avert its gaze from the ugly parts of our story.

"My love must be sighted, not blind," wrote the Harvard political philosopher Danielle Allen in a 2020 essay in the *Atlantic* about why she reveres the US Constitution despite its compromises over slavery and its conversion of "the worth of my great-great-grandfather Sidiphus" and other enslaved people "into three-fifths' that of a free person." She went on to detail American political leaders' enshrinement of inequality over centuries and their betrayal, in some cases, of what they knew to be just and true. "So why, then, do I love the Constitution?" she asked. "I love it for its practical leadership. I love it because it is the world's greatest teaching document for one part of the story of freedom: the question of how free and equal citizens check and channel power both to protect themselves from domination by one another and to secure their mutual protections from external forces that might seek their domination." Allen has repeatedly observed that to forge some kind of solidarity among its citizens, a diverse nation such as the United States needs a compelling *and* inspiring national story. "An excellent civic education will cultivate reflective patriotism," she wrote in a 2023 essay for the *Washington Post* with the headline: "We hit rock bottom on civics education. Can we turn it around?"

Ro Khanna made a similar plea, in terms of our political discourse and journalism: it could and should incorporate more national pride and national purpose. "I've said to my party, 'You watch a group of us on television and sometimes you'd think nothing was going right with America,' and we've got to still believe in the possibility of this country," he told me. "A nation needs heroes. A nation needs to have aspirations." It needs confidence, too, he said, and Americans have cause for it. "We're doing remarkable things!" Grievance thrives on the idea that there's little good in and around us. But that's no less a myth than the insistence that the United States is a colorblind, classless utopia of unfettered opportunity.

What's more, civics education should incorporate lessons on media literacy. The internet can be a swamp of misinformation— and grievance loves misinformation—that's neither labeled nor easily detectable as such. Young people must be made more aware of that and given some pointers on what does and doesn't constitute a legitimate source with reasonably trustworthy facts. They must be made more vigilant, period: AI and deepfakes threaten to create a cyberspace where much is illusion and subterfuge. They must be equipped to distinguish propaganda from argument and argument from straightforward news. And they must be coached—as they are about food—on what a balanced news diet looks like and how it can be assembled. There are Americans who consciously do and always will stuff themselves only with news that feeds their prejudices, but there are also Americans who don't really intend to stack their plates that way and wouldn't if they were given reminders and tips.

A personal soapbox: We should also turn our backs on, and hasten the demise of, college rankings that are based largely on the selectiveness and "prestige" of institutions. I'm looking at you, *U.S. News & World Report*. Many Americans' obsession with elite college admissions is not only maddening but harmful, both to the individual students caught up in the quest to breach the sanctums of Harvard and Stanford (and Duke) and to the country itself. It buttresses the impression that we live in an emphatically tiered society of winners and losers, of superstars and also-rans, and that exclusivity and worth are synonymous. Talk about an engine of envy.

Fixing Social Media

When we picture some of the earliest printed volumes, we tend to think of Gutenberg and his Bibles or the first editions of Chaucer's *Canterbury Tales*. But much of what rolled off the presses in Renaissance Europe was vile dreck: pamphlets devoted to personal attacks and outbursts of religious bigotry. "Pamphlets were closely associated with slander or scurrility," wrote Joad Raymond, a professor at Queen Mary University of London, in *Pamphlets and Pamphleteering in Early Modern Britain*. "Pamphlets were small, insignificant, ephemeral, disposable, untrustworthy, unruly, noisy, deceitful, poorly printed, addictive, a waste of time." All they lacked were "like" and "share" buttons.

Queen Elizabeth I implemented a licensing regime to get a handle on all the blasphemy and sedition pouring out of English print shops in the sixteenth century, and Parliament eventually passed the Licensing of the Press Act in 1662. In the United States, jurisprudence around the First Amendment—copyright, libel law, obscenity restrictions, and much else—has evolved since the Bill of Rights was passed. And with the dawn of the new electronic media of radio and television came decades of trial-and-error regulation to bring those novel technologies at least somewhat in line with a healthy civic life. Although they existed primarily for entertainment, they were rightly saddled with public service obligations in exchange for access to public airwaves, the Fairness Doctrine being the best-known example of that.

There has been no such reckoning for online media. We're still in the larval stages of digital life; the laissez-faire impulse of the early, open, free-spirited internet has carried over to a corporate-dominated social media space where a tiny cluster of gigantic companies wield incalculable influence over our collective perception of reality. Congress has done a fine job of hauling Silicon Valley executives to Washington so they can be harangued in front of C-SPAN cameras, but so far none of those performative hearings has resulted in meaningful regulation, possibly because so many lawmakers don't even understand how social media operates. Mark Zuckerberg once famously had to explain the underlying business model of the internet to Senator Orrin Hatch, the Utah Republican, who was confused about how Facebook makes money for its "free" service. ("Senator, we run ads," Zuckerberg said, barely containing a smirk.)

TikTok may have finally broken the logjam. Now that a wildly popular social media app beloved by young Americans in particular is Chinese rather than Californian, there's a bipartisan appetite to get serious on tech regulation. I seldom find reason to concur with

and approvingly cite Justice Clarence Thomas, but even original-
ists like him have come around to the notion that Big Tech could
use a little oversight. "Today's digital platforms provide avenues for
historically unprecedented amounts of speech, including speech by
government actors," Thomas wrote in a much-noticed aside to an
otherwise insignificant ruling in 2021. "Also unprecedented, however, is the concentrated control of so much speech in the hands of a
few private parties. We will soon have no choice but to address how
our legal doctrines apply to highly concentrated, privately owned information infrastructure such as digital platforms."

We should regulate those platforms as we do publishers. I've
spent my entire professional career working for news organizations
that rely on the First Amendment and freedom of the press, which
are essential to the pursuit of truth and preservation of democracy.
But the power they give news organizations isn't unchecked. Those
organizations are held responsible for the truth or falsity of their
content. If Fox News—just a hypothetical!—started spewing non-
sense about metaphorical gremlins in voting machines, it'd be on the
hook for hundreds of millions. If I wrote a *Times* column trading in
salacious and unsupportable rumors about a neighbor who'd irked
me, the *Times* would probably be taken to court, and it would probably lose. That's why the *Times* would never publish that column in
the first place.

But Facebook can faultlessly host that rant, as can YouTube,
even though both can almost instantly reach an audience bigger
than any conventional news organization could dream of. They can
fan the flames of grievance not just with defensible political speech
but with fantastical political hooey. Google (which owns YouTube),
Meta (which owns Facebook), TikTok, X, Reddit, and other digital
platforms are essentially the largest publishers of our time, and yet

they skirt libel laws and legal exposure because they come under the protection of Section 230 of the Communications Decency Act. Passed in 1996, long before we saw what YouTube and Twitter/X could wreak, Section 230 says that "no provider or user of an interactive computer service shall be treated as the publisher or speaker" in regard to content they're hosting, sharing, disseminating—choose your verb—as opposed to composing or commissioning themselves.

Section 230 was about helping a nascent industry that promised to generate enormous revenue and create oodles of jobs grow. Section 230 was not about social media today. It sped these companies toward profitability. It didn't demand of them so much as a scintilla of thought about civic duty. That has to change. Everyone is entitled to free speech, but there's no entitlement to trafficking in reckless and predictably injurious falsehoods while the megaphone maker enjoys full immunity. The advent of ChatGPT and other AI tools only increases the urgency of filling that lacuna in the law.

New regulations must also compel social media platforms to share more information about how they operate, including about their algorithms. The black-box nature of those algorithms means that we're subjected to an aggressive manipulation of how we understand the world *without* understanding how that's happening. There's zero transparency, and that, too, is an indulgence too many for corporations that could be held to greater account. Publicly traded companies have their books audited so that stockholders can get a glimpse of what's really going on, so why shouldn't large digital platforms be required to divulge more information than they currently do?

In a previous chapter I mentioned my Duke colleague Chris Bail, the author of *Breaking the Social Media Prism: How to Make Our Platforms Less Polarizing*. Bail also runs a project at Duke called the

Polarization Lab, where he and other researchers gather as much data as they can about how people behave on social media: what motivates them, which cues they respond to, and more. But that data, he told me, is woefully incomplete. We've only begun to understand what social media is and what it could be, he said, and that's in part because we're dependent on what Big Tech companies are willing to share, which is limited. If they were prodded or forced to give researchers like him and his colleagues a closer look at what they do, we could try to tackle social media's corrosive effects with real knowledge as opposed to the theorizing and supposition that guide many of our discussions and debates about it.

Bail also believes that there are ways to make platforms more civic-minded and less divisive. "My view of social media is that it's primarily about gaining status," he told me. "So what kind of status do you want to incentivize? We can incentivize pro-social behavior. We can create different incentive structures for what allows us to gain status on social media." Right now, people on social media watch posts that like-minded people "like" and "share" go viral, and those posts tend to be strident, polarized content. But what if a platform gave the greatest visibility to content that was liked and shared by the greatest diversity of people—content that drew favorable responses from identified Democrats and identified Republicans both? What if the attainment of status hinged on the identification and promotion of areas of *consensus*? "All of a sudden," Bail said, "social media is not about taking down the other side."

Before Elon Musk bought Twitter, Bail was working with executives and programmers there on experiments along those lines, and those experiments, he said, revealed a definite appetite and market for such an approach. Most people don't want (or don't own up to wanting) the most toxic iteration of Twitter/X, but they haven't been shown or guided to a less toxic one. Such consensus-oriented engagement could be developed within existing platforms or could be the foundation of new ones in a market that changes rapidly. "Every year and a half, the dominant platform gets replaced," Bail said. "There's constant churn. People are innovating. Audiences are moving. And public appetite for innovation in social media right now is sky-high. Very few people say they love social media. What you hear is: Couldn't we do better?"

We could, and we might do better faster if there were public investment in, and other government incentives to create, online spaces specifically designed for healthier conversation and communication. Richard Culatta, the head of the International Society for Technology in Education, in his 2021 book *Digital for Good: Raising Kids to Thrive in an Online World*, envisioned a publicly owned or nonprofit social media platform that would aggressively moderate antisocial behavior while optimizing respectful, thoughtful engagement. "Creating constructive, civically engaging online communities is one of the most important, determining factors in whether our democracy will survive," he said in a 2021 interview with Stefanie Sanford for the College Board's website.

But even before those new, better platforms ideally emerge, we can take some smart steps, including one that enjoys bipartisan support on Capitol Hill: raise and enforce the age requirement for social media participation, so that the worst of it doesn't addle young minds so soon. Already, companies are supposed to bar children under thirteen from signing up for social media platforms without parental consent. That widely flouted rule can be better enforced: Bail noted that in Europe, companies trying to vet the ages of people using their websites or platforms are increasingly using facial-recognition software that's good at ascertaining how young someone likely is. And "under thirteen" is too permissive. Bans on users under sixteen or under seventeen would make more sense. "It's low-hanging fruit," Jean Twenge, who supports that, told me.

Also in that category, she said, is restricting the use of smart-phones—which are how young people access social media—in cir-cumstances where that's possible. "We could do no smartphones in school, bell to bell," she said. Then, she said, children would "talk to each other at lunch, there'd be fewer distractions in the classroom, you'd get better learning." Jonathan Haidt is an impassioned propo-nent of that. "All children deserve schools that will help them learn, cultivate deep friendships, and develop into mentally healthy young adults," he wrote in the *Atlantic*. "All children deserve phone-free schools."

Every moment that children can't stare at or escape into those digital interfaces is a moment when they're more likely to take no-tice of the other people around them. That's the collapsing of dis-tance that I mentioned at this chapter's start. It's also a pivot away from the self, and that movement is essential if we're to pivot, all of us, away from grievance.

Ten

The Antidote

I warn my students. At the start of every semester, on the first day of every course, I confess to certain passions and quirks and tell them to be ready: I'm a stickler for correct grammar, spelling, and the like, so if they don't have it in them to care about and patrol for such errors, they probably won't end up with the grade they're after. I want to hear everyone's voice—I tell them that, too—but I don't want to hear anybody's voice so often and so loudly that the other voices don't have a chance. And I'm going to repeat one phrase more often than any other: "It's complicated." They'll become familiar with that. They may even become bored with it. I'll sometimes say it when we're discussing the roots and branches of a social ill, the motivations of public (and private) actors, and a whole lot else, and that's because I'm standing before them not as an ambassador of certainty or a font of unassailable verities but as an emissary of doubt. I want to give them intelligent questions, not final answers. I want to teach them how much they have to learn—and how much they will always have to learn.

I'd been delivering that spiel for more than two years before I realized that each component of it was about the same quality: humility. The grammar-and-spelling bit was about surrendering to an established and easily understood way of doing things that eschewed wild individualism in favor of a common mode of communication. It showed respect for tradition, which is a force that binds us, a folding of the self into a greater whole. The voices bit—well, that's obvious. It's a reminder that we share the stages of our communities, our countries, our worlds, with many other actors, and should thus conduct ourselves in a manner that recognizes that. And "it's complicated" is a bulwark against arrogance, absolutism, purity, zeal. I'd also been delivering that spiel for more than two years before I realized that humility is the antidote to grievance.

The January 6 insurrectionists were delusional, frenzied, savage. Above all, they were unhumble. They decided that they held the truth, no matter all the evidence to the contrary. They couldn't accept that their preference for one presidential candidate over another could possibly put them in the minority—or perhaps a few of them just reasoned that if it did, then everybody else was too misguided to matter. They elevated how they viewed the world and what they wanted over tradition, institutional stability, law, order.

But lesser and less immediately destructive versions of arrogance inform every example, small and large, of grievance that I've mentioned in these pages, from Jane Campion's odd invocation of the Williams sisters to that Yale student's viral meltdown, from Ron DeSantis's fixation on mortifying his adversaries to Josh Hawley's conviction that liberalism is at odds with virility. A healthy measure of humility would have pointed all those people in a different, better direction.

Party leaders who consent to end gerrymandering are being

humble about what they can and can't predict about their future dominance and humble in their exercise of power. They're recognizing that there are issues bigger than the magnitude of their present spoils. Politicians who reexamine the necessity of college degrees are humbly compensating for our tendencies to extrapolate from our own backgrounds and success stories to what works best in the broad and diverse world beyond us. And people who attend bridge-building exercises, whether in the halls of Congress or the hills of Appalachia, are humbly making an extra effort to understand strangers with whom they don't usually meet and humbly accepting that civic repair is worth a personal investment of time and energy. They're the antonyms of the insurrectionists.

Humility comes up often in Jonathan Rauch's superb 2021 book *The Constitution of Knowledge*, a contemplation of truth and exhortation for free speech in the age of grievance. Rauch, a scholar at the Brookings Institution, defines the term in his book's title as a global network of "reality-based institutions"—universities, reputable media outlets, courts of law, scientific organizations—that are committed to finding truth through a structured process of conflict and debate. They are "liberalism's epistemic operating system: our social rules for turning disagreement into knowledge," Rauch wrote, noting that the defense of the reality-based world against a rising tide of purposeful disinformation and a sea of trolls is a constant struggle. It demands much of us, including, perhaps most important, intellectual humility, or what he calls "fallibilism"—the ethos that any one of us might be wrong, and we must therefore keep ourselves open to contradictory views and evidence.

"Being open to criticism requires humility and forbearance and toleration," Rauch explained. "Scientists, journalists, lawyers, and intelligence analysts all accept fallibilism and empiricism in principle,

even when they behave pigheadedly (as happens with humans)."
Scientific findings can be replicated or refuted by new experiments;
laws can be challenged through freshly discovered evidence and re-
fined arguments; journalists ideally keep digging toward a deeper
and more nuanced comprehension of events. That's the nature of
the Constitution of Knowledge. It's a shared endeavor, an evolving
quasi document, its nature an acknowledgment that no one person
holds all the answers or cards, its health and growth dependent on
most people accepting that.

Intellectual humility allows us to revisit our assumptions, and the
necessity of that is proven by how often we've been wrong or wrong-
headed. Scientific racism was a rage in progressive circles in the early
1900s; in the 1990s, the global march of democracy looked inevitable
to much of the political establishment, a thinking emblemized in Francis Fukuyama's premature elegy to history. On both fronts, we know
better now, and we know better because we weren't arrogantly stuck
in our thinking. In his book, Rauch, who is gay, recalled the near una-
nimity with which political leaders once denounced homosexuality (as
did, I should volunteer, major news organizations such as the *New York
Times*) in the 1950s, 1960s, and even into the 1970s; not until 1973 did
the American Psychiatric Association remove homosexuality from its
official compendium of mental disorders. That all seems, well, bonkers to most Americans now. Even given the rightward movement of
most of the Republican Party over the past decade, thirty-nine House
Republicans joined all House Democrats to ensure the December 2022
passage of legislation to safeguard same-sex marriage nationwide, and
twelve Senate Republicans joined their Democratic colleagues to give
that measure a filibuster-proof majority in the Senate. As recently as
1996, bipartisan majorities in both chambers had passed legislation
that did the opposite, denouncing same-sex marriage.

To be grounded in truth is, paradoxically, to remain open to the idea that the understanding of truth may need to shift as we learn more and as some of those lessons lay bare our prejudice and ignorance. "You must assume your own and everyone else's fallibility and you must hunt for your own and others' errors, even if you are confident you are right," Rauch wrote. "Otherwise, you are not reality-based." His "you" is a universal one, a caution and a summons to various stakeholders.

We Need Humility from Our Political Leaders

The *Times* column that I wrote for the weekend of Trump's inauguration in January 2017 took into account the peculiarities of the pitch that he'd made to American voters ("I alone can fix it"), the trademarks of his showman–meets–con man personality, and the actual text of his inauguration remarks, in which I noticed something telling: The word "humbled," which had been present in the first inaugural remarks of both Barack Obama and George W. Bush, was nowhere to be found. Nor were any of its variants. That whole sentiment and politesse were missing, as they had been during a campaign centered around his supposed omniscience. "The President Who Buried Humility" was the headline I affixed to that column, in which I observed that Trump was "a braggart beyond his predecessors in the Oval Office, and that says something sad and scary about the country that elected him and the kind of leader he's likely to be. With Trump we enter a new age of arrogance. He's the cock crowing at its dawn."

With any luck, he'll soon warble meekly at its dusk. But he'll have done his damage regardless, by sending the message to Americans that triumph is an individual act, that winning redeems whatever ruthlessness and cheating it required, and that strength is figuring out how to bend the world to your advantage and not being troubled by anything so prissy as rules and rectitude. There are now mini-Trumps aplenty in American politics, but anti-Trumps will be our salvation, and I make that statement not along partisan or ideological lines. I make it along the lines of character and, even more so, of how a society holds itself together. It does that with concern for the common good, with respect for the institutions and procedures that protect that, and with political leaders who ideally embody those traits or at least promote them.

Earlier I mentioned Charlie Baker, the former Massachusetts governor, citing his durable popularity as a moderate Republican in a Democratic state. Something else about him has always piqued my curiosity and drawn my attention, and perhaps it's entwined with that popularity: he repeatedly stresses the importance of humility in an effective leader. He's fond of quoting Philippians 2:3; he invoked it as a lodestar for his administration. "Do nothing out of selfish ambition or vain conceit," it says. "Rather, in humility value others above yourself."

That's great practical advice for anyone in government, where almost everything is teamwork, almost everything is consensus, and almost nothing of real and lasting consequence is accomplished alone. Governing, as opposed to demagoguery, is about earning others' trust, commitment, and cooperation. Exhibiting an interest and a willingness to listen to and to hear them goes a long way toward that. It's a demonstration of humility.

"Insight and knowledge come from curiosity and humility," Baker wrote in a 2022 book, *Results*, whose coauthor was his chief of staff, Steve Kadish, a Democrat. "Snap judgments—about people or ideas—are fueled by arrogance and conceit. They create blind spots and missed opportunities. Good ideas and interesting ways to accomplish goals in public life exist all over the place if you have the will, the curiosity, and the humility to find them."

Humility was also something that Bill Haslam, the former two-term governor of Tennessee, extolled. He's a Republican who ran a predominantly Republican state, so humility wasn't an attribute that aided a necessary appeal across the partisan divide. But he deemed it essential to making the changes in Tennesseans' lives that he'd pledged to make—to avoiding any prideful attachment to his first-blush ideas and a schedule of glitzy appearances and Fox News interviews that would have stolen time and energy from problem-solving. And he indeed amassed a record of substantive accomplishment that was impressive in its heft and its occasional deviations from conservative orthodoxy. He made community college free for Tennesseans. He cut taxes on food while raising them on gasoline. He vetoed culture-war distractions such as a bill to make the Bible the official state book of Tennessee. A few years after leaving office in early 2019, he wrote a reflection on leadership, "Humble Leadership? Yes, *and* Humility Can Restore Trust," for *The Catalyst*, a journal published by the Bush Institute. "Humble leaders who can admit fault are key to uniting a nation," read an italicized precede to his essay. Haslam's opening line: "It has been said that those who seek the high road of humility in politics will never run into a traffic jam." His closing one: "And think how much better served we are by leaders who have the humility to want to get the best answer, not just their own answer."

Humble politicians don't insist on one-size-fits-all answers when those aren't necessary as a matter of basic rights and fundamental justice, and in a society like ours now, when there's scant trust between partisans and when resentment toward political opponents runs high, both parties should consider devolving power to the state and local levels when possible. Republicans have traditionally supported that in theory and then routinely contradicted themselves, in an unhumble fashion, when that suited them. They should do better at living their stated principles about local control, and Democrats shouldn't be so quick to assume that local control equals a reckless opportunity to wriggle free from federal safeguards. In some of the blue cities within red or purple states, local control would mean more respect and freedom for aggrieved people whose progressive ideals are squashed at the statehouse (just as it would mean more respect and freedom for the aggrieved rural denizens of blue states).

In my home state of North Carolina, where Republicans have maintained a big majority (and sometimes contrived a supermajority) in both chambers of the state legislature through gerrymandered districts, they've prevented local officials in places such as Durham from enacting the sorts of gun safety and environmental measures that an overwhelming majority of the city's hundreds of thousands of citizens want. To what end? The preemption of local laws by broad state edicts has been on the rise in recent years, and it's a trend that intensifies grievances.

We Need Humility from Journalists

In late April 2018, President Trump traveled to Michigan for a rally, where his remarks were a mash of favorite themes. He bragged about what a fabulous job he was doing. He bellyached about all the injustices he endured. And he bashed the news media. Oh, how he loved to bash the news media.

"Very dishonest," he said. "They don't have sources. The sources don't exist."

While he was painting this unflattering portrait of us, what image were we projecting? That night, at the White House Correspondents' Association dinner, journalists swanned into a ballroom as thick with self-regard as any Academy Awards ceremony. They hobnobbed with the Hollywood stars whom they'd invited—and in some cases competed over—to be guests at their tables. And they listened to the comedian Michelle Wolf do what she was hired to do: savage Trump and his aides in vicious and occasionally vulgar terms that predictably caused the media's enemies to trumpet that we journalists are no more dignified than the president whose indecency we lament.

"Every caricature thrust upon the national press—that we are culturally elitist, professionally incestuous, socioeconomically detached and ideologically biased—is confirmed by this train wreck of an event," the journalist Tim Alberta wrote in *Politico*. He got it right. We keep behaving in a manner that hastens the public's erosion of confidence in us. We keep playing into the grievance era's taxonomy of insiders versus outsiders. And we thus keep undermining our credibility when we try to speak truth to grievance, on those occasions when we do try.

We responded to Trump's excessive (and usually dishonest) focus on our vices by focusing excessively on our virtues. The *New York Times* began its "The Truth Is" ad campaign: "The truth is hard," "the truth is hidden," and so on. On the top of the front page of its printed paper and the home page of its website, the *Washington Post* placed the legend "Democracy Dies in Darkness." All that self-congratulation prompted the longtime media critic Jack Shafer to write, in *Politico*, that while he wouldn't "dispute that journalists are crucial to a free society," he nonetheless felt that "the chords that aggrieved journalists strike make them sound as entitled as tenured professors."

That works against us and against a healthy society, because the *Post* is right on the merits: democracy does die in darkness. Trustworthy journalists doing trustworthy work bring a crucial light, providing a check on government and redress for people whose voices are unheard. So how do we make ourselves and our work more trustworthy? We go further in leavening our self-interest with public interest. When we're not writing or speaking in a venue or under a rubric that signals the subjective opinion in our words, we take greater care not to let our political orientations and biases drive our coverage, not to Trojan-horse subjectivity into supposedly objective accounts. We resist the forging of personal brands that are contingent on predetermined and inflexible viewpoints, which make us ripe for dismissal. And as an industry, we try, within the inevitable constraints of profitability, to create more spaces that earnestly welcome and showcase a diversity of perspectives and allow truth to emerge in the manner that Rauch rightly venerates, from a contest of arguments designed to yield something deliberate and dependable.

We Need Humility from Activists

Rauch spotlighted the sea change in American openness to same-sex marriage. The success of the movement that advocated for it is instructive, in terms of not only how to get from point A to point B but also how to do that without activating maximal grievance. The marriage-equality movement showed that progress is often made not by shaming people—not by telling them how awful they are—but by suggesting how much better they can be. Marriage-equality advocates emphasized a brighter future that they wanted to create, not an ugly past that they wanted to litigate. They also wisely assured Americans that gay and lesbian people weren't trying to explode a cherished institution and upend a system of values, but instead wanted in.

"I don't want to disparage shouting and demands—everything has its place," Evan Wolfson, the founder of the pivotal advocacy group Freedom to Marry, told me when we revisited the movement's philosophy and tactics during a conversation in 2022. At times, he acknowledged, champions of a cause "need to break the silence, we need to push, we need to force."

"But I used to say, 'Yes, there's demanding, but there's also asking,'" he recalled. "And one is not the enemy of the other. People don't like being accused, people don't like being condemned, people don't like being alienated. It's a matter of conversation and persuasion."

The writer Andrew Sullivan, another early and profoundly influential proponent of marriage equality, has made similar observations, drawing a contrast between the approaches of gay-rights advocates in decades past and the bearing of transgender-rights advocates today. "Nothing in your life had to change to accept gay equality," he wrote in his Substack newsletter in June 2023. Permitting gay people to marry didn't have any substantive effect on straight people's marriages—and, in fact, flattered those marriages, inasmuch as it saw them as models and aspirations. And while new laws forbade the firing or eviction of someone for being gay, lesbian, or bisexual, those laws didn't compel anyone to adopt a whole new philosophy of humanity. "Compare that with the transqueer movement," Sullivan wrote, detailing an agenda he regards as bullying. "They are as hostile to a free society as the worst fanatics of the far right."

In the spring 2023 issue of the journal *Liberties*, the writer James Kirchick provided examples of what Sullivan had in mind: "Materials published by the San Diego Unified School District, for instance, call for a 'linguistic revolution to move beyond gender binaries,' whereby men are to be called 'people with a penis' and women 'people with a vulva.' A document promulgated by the Portland Public Schools maintains that the gender binary is a vestige of 'white colonizers' and that terms such as 'girls and boys,' 'ladies and gentlemen,' and 'mom and dad' should be replaced with 'people,' 'folx,' and 'guardians.' An education guide for teachers in Grades 3-8 promulgated by the Human Rights Campaign advises replacing the term 'Snowman' with 'Snowperson' so that students be made to 'understand the differences between gender identity, sexual orientation and sex assigned at birth.'" That's an ambitious agenda.

An unhumble one, too. And that may well jeopardize the rights—such as legal protections from employment and housing discrimination and safety from physical assault—that transgender people unequivocally deserve. It does that in part by vilifying Americans who have and express understandable questions or qualms about transgender women competing in women's sports and children below a certain age receiving certain kinds of "gender-affirming" medical care. Yes, there are determined bigots out there, many of them state lawmakers enacting needlessly harsh restrictions and bans. But there are also plenty of well-intentioned people with un-answered questions and thoughtful reservations, and some of them are feeling forced into league with the bigots. There are principled, exemplary medical professionals puzzling in earnest over how to treat children who identify as trans but may still be figuring out who they are, and there are journalists correctly reporting on disagreements among doctors and on clinics and clinicians too quick to affix trans identities to troubled patients. Denouncing those doctors and journalists is unwarranted. It's unwise, as it risks alienating not only them but also confused people watching from the sidelines. It's also irresponsible: it elevates conviction over an honest inquiry with enormous relevance to the long-term welfare of patients making immensely consequential decisions.

Across many causes, many advocates traffic in an absolutism that's born of grievance and spawns yet more of it. The hubristic and wholly unrealistic reach of the Green New Deal did as much to drive apart people on opposite sides of the debate over how aggressively we should fight climate change as it did to guarantee the best and wisest action in the present or near future. If a cause's advocates are interested in durable progress, and if they respect the importance of an entire society's stability, they should be reasonably humble about what's essential, what's utopian, what's doable, and what demonstrates as much respect for others as they're demanding for themselves. They should be clear-eyed about whether and when a righteous bid for dignity becomes a self-righteous magnet for hostility.

They should consider the message delivered by Loretta Ross, a longtime racial justice and human rights advocate, through a class that she taught at Smith College, a popular TED Talk, media interviews, and an essay that she wrote for the *Times* in 2019. Troubled by the frequent targeting and pillorying of people on social media, she urged the practice of calling *in* rather than calling *out* those who've upset you. "Call-outs make people feel fearful of being targeted," she wrote in her *Times* essay. "People avoid meaningful conversations when hypervigilant perfectionists point out apparent mistakes, feeding the cannibalistic maw of the cancel culture." Instead, she advised, engage them. If you believe they need enlightenment, try that route, "without the self-indulgence of drama," she wrote. She was preaching humility.

She was also recognizing other people's right to disagree—to live differently, to talk differently. Pluralism is as much about that as it is about a multiracial, multifaith, multigender splendor. That doesn't mean a surrender or even compromise of principles; a person can hold on to those while practicing tolerance, which has fallen out of fashion, supplanted by grievance. But tolerance shares DNA with respect. It recognizes that other people have rights and worth *even when* we disagree vehemently with them.

We Need Humility from Ourselves

We carry wounds, and some of us carry wounds much more numerous and much graver than others. We confront obstacles, and some are unfairly big, unjustly unyielding, and especially senseless. We must tend to those wounds. We must push hard at those obstacles. But we mustn't treat every wound, every obstacle, as some cosmic outrage or mortal danger. We mustn't lose sight of the struggle, imperfection, and randomness of life. We mustn't overstate our vulnerability and exaggerate our due.

That's part of what Jonathan Haidt and Greg Lukianoff are saying when they lament the "safetyism" of contemporary education: the increasingly absurd demand that students be insulated from unkind words, troubling ideas, and all other manner of unpleasantness. That insulation is more than a roadblock to a robust, real education. It gives excessive power to those words and ideas and that unpleasantness, creates the unreal expectation that they can be kept at bay, and sets up young Americans to feel aggrieved—victimized—when that doesn't happen. "The new protectiveness may be teaching students to think pathologically," they wrote in the article in the *Atlantic* that preceded and grew into their bestseller, *The Coddling of the American Mind*.

Lisa Damour, a prominent clinical psychologist who works with teenagers, has also sounded the alarm about pathologizing normal, everyday hardship. "Much of the time, the presence of distress, the experience of distress, is evidence of mental health," Damour told my *Times* colleague Ezra Klein in a May 2023 interview for his podcast. "What I mean by that is there are lots of circumstances in daily life where we fully expect to see distress." Treating perfectly rational emotions as psychological emergencies and unfair burdens can set a dangerous precedent, and Damour emphasized the importance of not getting carried away with our natural and understandable instinct to protect young people from grief and pain. "There's something kind of extraordinary about how much maturation arrives as a function of them actually grappling with a very painful feeling," she told Klein. "They become more broad-minded. They become more philosophical. And there's actually, for me, almost a universal marker of when this is happening, which is that they become actually very annoyed with their age mates for having concerns that feel, to them, very petty or minor."

While grievance blows our concerns out of proportion, humility puts them in perspective. While grievance reduces the people with whom we disagree to caricature, humility acknowledges what Eboo Patel, the founder and president of Interfaith America, wrote in his 2022 book, *We Need to Build*: "People are endlessly complex and fascinating. You can never tell simply from someone's group identity how they will experience the world, or know from their experience what conclusions they will draw."

I watched only the first season of the Apple TV+ series *Ted*

Lasso; after that, life—and other Apple TV+, Netflix, and HBO Max shows—got in the way. But like many other Americans, I adored it. I adored Ted, a man whose wife has moved on, whose heart is broken, whose new home of Britain is a bit of a mystery to him, whose new job as a soccer coach there is a setup for failure, and whose humble response is to try his hopeful best to turn all of that around. The show's out-of-the-gate conceit is that a protagonist inhabiting the stereotype of the blissful fool is wiser than the rest of us and has more to teach than to learn.

Ted Lasso began streaming in 2020, when, my *Times* colleague Margaret Renkl astutely observed, we were all "mired in an America we no longer recognized, a nation so dangerously polarized that many people would think nothing of cutting off their closest family members if they didn't vote the 'right' way." And the show struck a nerve, Renkl added, because there was "something about Ted Lasso's sunny optimism and faith in silliness as a social lubricant, something about his openness and his unshakable kindness, that lifted Americans' pandemic-worn hearts." Renkl recalled a particular scene in which Ted tells a player who is stewing over a defeat which animal is the happiest in the world: "A goldfish. It's got a ten-second memory."

By all reports, *Ted Lasso* grew darker as it and he aged. Maybe some subconscious premonition turned me away from the show before it could bring me down. Ted himself had a memory much longer than ten seconds, as his pining for his wife proved; the finned paragon that he held up for that player is absurd, even dangerous.

But the idea that we're too often held hostage by our grudges, too frequently fixated on what in our lives isn't exactly as we'd like it to be? There's indeed something there. And an amalgam of kindness, openness, and silliness might be an effective solvent for grievance. We could try a dab of that.

Or we could unhumbly cling to the conviction that we're singularly unappreciated and cruelly situated against hostile forces in a disintegrating world that compels us to wrest what we can while we can, before it disintegrates even further. That's the road we've been on for a perilous while now. It's not too late to turn around.

Acknowledgments

There's no way to mention all the friends, relatives, neighbors, colleagues at the *New York Times*, colleagues at Duke University, and people at Avid Reader Press, Simon & Schuster, and Creative Artists Agency to whom I'm indebted and for whom I'm grateful. To name names is to forget someone inadvertently, so I'm taking the coward's way out and rendering this omnibus thanks. Those of you who've helped me know who you are, and I very much hope I've shown you my appreciation. If I haven't, this is your chit for a cocktail on me. Okay, two cocktails.

I do need and want to acknowledge specifically the Duke students who signed up for my America in the Age of Grievance class in the spring of 2023 and patiently rummaged through some of the ideas in this book with me. Ian Acriche, Rohan Bhambhani, Allie Brice, Katelyn Cai, Lana Gesinsky, Hadrian Gonzalez Castellanos, Isabel Hogshire, Bella Larsen, Katherine LoBue, Effie Mehbod, Mia Meier, Julien Mermelstein, Chase Pellegrini de Paur, and Hana Stepnick—thank you all very much.

And the specific contributions of Eric Johnson and Chris Miraglia—in terms of research, conceptualization, and more—inform every chapter of this book. You both have my deepest gratitude.

Further Reading

Allen, Danielle. *Justice by Means of Democracy*. Chicago, IL: University of Chicago Press, 2023.

Applebaum, Anne. *Twilight of Democracy: The Seductive Lure of Authoritarianism*. New York: Doubleday, 2020.

Bail, Chris. *Breaking the Social Media Prism: How to Make Our Platforms Less Polarizing*. Princeton, NJ: Princeton University Press, 2021.

Bishop, Bill. *The Big Sort: Why the Clustering of Like-Minded America Is Tearing Us Apart*. New York: Houghton Mifflin Harcourt, 2008.

Case, Anne, and Angus Deaton. *Deaths of Despair and the Future of Capitalism*. Princeton, NJ: Princeton University Press, 2020.

Christakis, Nicholas A. *Blueprint: The Evolutionary Origins of a Good Society*. New York: Little, Brown Spark, 2019.

Cramer, Katherine J. *The Politics of Resentment: Rural Consciousness in Wisconsin and the Rise of Scott Walker*. Chicago, IL: University of Chicago Press, 2016.

Fisher, Max. *The Chaos Machine: The Inside Story of How Social Media Rewired Our Minds and Our World*. New York: Little, Brown, 2022.

French, David. *Divided We Fall: America's Secession Threat and How to Restore Our Nation*. New York: St. Martin's Press, 2020.

Gillespie, Andra. *Race and the Obama Administration: Substance, Symbols, and Hope*. Manchester, UK: Manchester University Press, 2019.

Haidt, Jonathan, and Greg Lukianoff. *The Coddling of the American Mind: How Good Intentions and Bad Ideas Are Setting Up a Generation for Failure*. New York: Penguin Press, 2018.

Hughes, Robert. *Culture of Complaint: The Fraying of America*. New York: Oxford University Press, 1993.

Kaminer, Wendy. *I'm Dysfunctional, You're Dysfunctional: The Recovery Movement and Other Self-Help Fashions*. New York: Vintage, 1993.

Klein, Ezra. *Why We're Polarized*. New York: Avid Reader Press, 2020.

Klinenberg, Eric. *Palaces for the People: How Social Infrastructure Can Help Fight Inequality, Polarization, and the Decline of Civic Life*. New York: Crown, 2018.

Leonhardt, David. *Ours Was the Shining Future: The Story of the American Dream*. New York: Random House, 2023.

Levin, Yuval. *A Time to Build: From Family and Community to Congress and the Campus, How Recommitting to Our Institutions Can Revive the American Dream*. New York: Basic Books, 2020.

Levitsky, Steven, and Daniel Ziblatt. *How Democracies Die*. New York: Crown, 2018.

McWhorter, John. *Woke Racism: How a New Religion Has Betrayed Black America*. New York: Portfolio/Penguin, 2021.

Meacham, Jon. *The Soul of America: The Battle for Our Better Angels*. New York: Random House, 2018.

Mounk, Yascha. *The Great Experiment: Why Diverse Democracies Fall Apart and How They Can Endure*. New York: Penguin Press, 2022.

Nichols, Tom. *Our Own Worst Enemy: The Assault from Within on Modern Democracy*. New York: Oxford University Press, 2021.

Packer, George. *Last Best Hope: America in Crisis and Renewal*. New York: Farrar, Straus and Giroux, 2021.

Patel, Eboo. *We Need to Build: Field Notes for Diverse Democracy*. Boston: Beacon Press, 2022.

Phillips, Steve. *How We Win the Civil War: Securing a Multiracial Democracy and Ending White Supremacy for Good*. New York: New Press, 2022.

Pinker, Steven. *The Better Angels of Our Nature: Why Violence Has Declined*. New York: Viking, 2011.

Potter, Andrew. *On Decline: Stagnation, Nostalgia, and Why Every Year Is the Worst One Ever*. Windsor, ON: Biblioasis, 2021.

Rauch, Jonathan. *The Constitution of Knowledge: A Defense of Truth*. Washington, DC: Brookings Institution Press, 2021.

Ripley, Amanda. *High Conflict: Why We Get Trapped and How We Get Out.* New York: Simon & Schuster, 2021.

Rosling, Hans. *Factfulness: Ten Reasons We're Wrong about the World—and Why Things Are Better Than You Think.* New York: Flatiron Books, 2018.

Sykes, Charles J. *A Nation of Victims: The Decay of the American Character.* New York: St. Martin's Press, 1992.

Tippett, Krista. *Becoming Wise: An Inquiry into the Mystery and Art of Living.* New York: Penguin Press, 2016.

Turchin, Peter. *End Times: Elites, Counter-Elites, and the Path of Political Disintegration.* New York: Penguin Press, 2023.

Twenge, Jean. *Generations: The Real Differences Between Gen Z, Millennials, Gen X, Boomers, and Silents—and What They Mean for America's Future.* New York: Atria Books, 2023.

Walter, Barbara F. *How Civil Wars Start: And How to Stop Them.* New York: Crown, 2022.

About the Author

FRANK BRUNI is the author of four *New York Times* bestsellers, including the memoir *The Beauty of Dusk*, and spent more than twenty-five years on the staff of the *New York Times*, in positions as varied as op-ed columnist, White House correspondent, Rome bureau chief, and restaurant critic. In April 2021, he was named Eugene C. Patterson Professor of the Practice of Journalism and Public Policy at Duke University's Sanford School of Public Policy. He continues to work for the *Times* as a contributing opinion writer. He lives in North Carolina.